# KAMEI MIRAKU

## 15 Generations of Fine Art for Tea

亀井味楽

15代にわたる茶陶美術

# KAMEI MIRAKU

15 Generations of Fine Art for Tea

# 亀井味楽

15代にわたる茶陶美術

© Pucker Art Publications, 2025

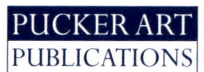

PUCKER ART
PUBLICATIONS

Published by / 発行者:
Pucker Art Publications
Boston, Massachusetts 02116

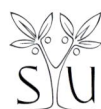

Distributed by / 発行所:
Syracuse University Press
Syracuse, New York 13244

Design by / デザイン: Leslie Anne Feagley
Photography by / 写真: John Davenport and the Kamei Family
Editing by / 編集: Jeanne Koles and Beth Plakidas
Translated by / 訳: Mugi Hanao (花生 麦)

Printed in Canada by / 印刷所: Friesens Corporation

Library of Congress Cataloging-in-Publication Data available from the publisher upon request.

ISBN: 978-1-879985-48-3

| | | | |
|---|---|---|---|
| **FRONT COVER:** | 表紙 | **BACK COVER:** | 裏表紙 |
| MIRAKU KAMEI XV | 15代亀井味楽 | MIRAKU KAMEI XIV | 14代亀井味楽 |
| Rhombus-form | 菱形うるし蓋付水指 | Tea Bowl | 茶碗 |
| Water Container with | 2016年 | 1970s | 昭和50年代 |
| Lacquer Lid | 掛分 | Kakewake glaze | 掛分 |
| 2016 | | XIV3 | |
| Kakewake glaze | | | |
| XV94 | | MIRAKU KAMEI XV | 15代亀井味楽 |
| | | Tea Bowl | 茶碗 |
| | | 2013 | 2013年 |
| | | Kakewake glaze | 掛分 |
| | | XV8 | |
| | | | |
| | | HISAAKI KAMEI | 亀井久彰 |
| | | Tea Bowl | 茶碗 |
| | | 2022 | 2022年 |
| | | Verdigris glaze | 緑青釉 |
| | | HK44 | |

# KAMEI MIRAKU

## 15 Generations of Fine Art for Tea

亀井味楽

15代にわたる茶陶美術

Andrew L. Maske

アンドルー・L・マスキ

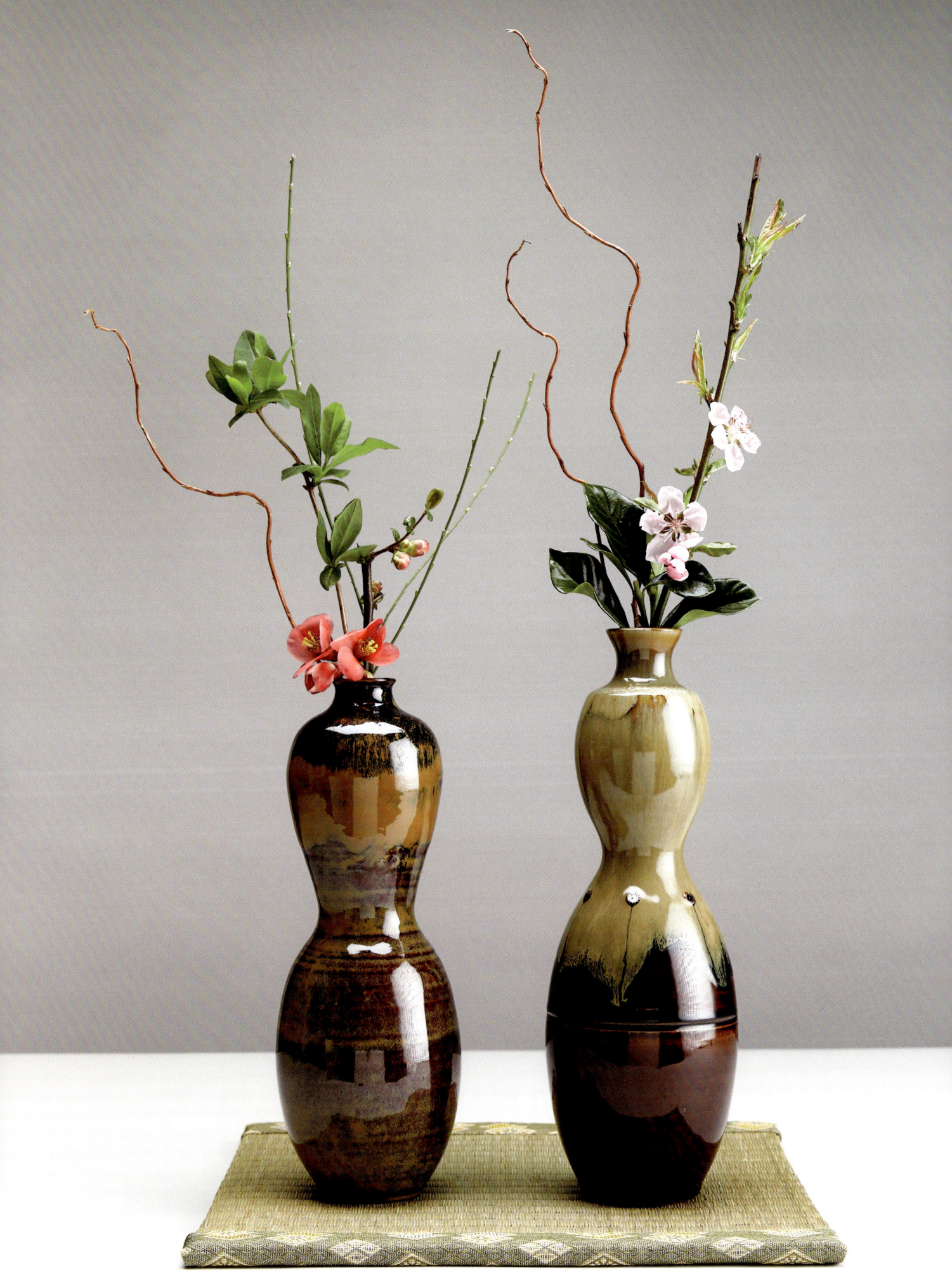

# Contents | 目次

OPPOSITE PAGE:
HISAAKI KAMEI
Gourd-form Flower Vase
2016
Yellow glaze
HK5

反対側のページ
亀井久彰
瓢形花入
2016年
黄釉

MIRAKU KAMEI XV
Gourd-form Flower Vase
2016
Kakewake glaze
XV114

15代亀井味楽
瓢形花入
2016年
掛分

# The History of Takatori Miraku Kiln

## Miraku Kamei XV

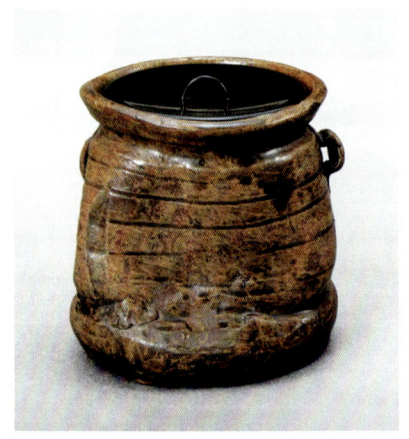

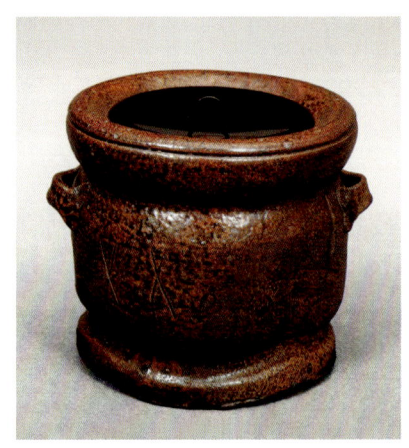

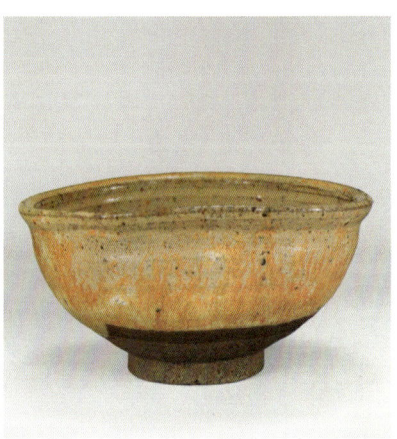

| | |
|---|---|
| **Oribe Takatori**<br>**Water Container**<br>**Early 1600s**<br>**Ame glaze** | 織部高取<br>水指<br>1600年代初頭<br>飴釉 |

| | |
|---|---|
| **Oribe Takatori**<br>**Water Container**<br>**Early 1600s**<br>**Ame glaze** | 織部高取<br>水指<br>1600年代初頭<br>飴釉 |

| | |
|---|---|
| **Oribe Takatori**<br>**Tea Bowl**<br>**Early 1600s**<br>**White glaze** | 織部高取<br>茶盌<br>1600年代初頭<br>白釉 |

TAKATORI WARE WAS FOUNDED IN 1606 after Josui Kuroda (Kanbei Kuroda), first feudal lord of Fukuoka domain, and his son, Nagamasa Kuroda, brought a potter named Hassan back from Korea to Japan with them, and founded the Eimanji Takuma Gama (kiln) at the foot of Mt. Takatori (Nōgata City). Takatori ware was greatly influenced by Furuta Oribe, a feudal lord and great tea master of that era. Work from that time is known as Oribe Takatori and it pursued an unconventional beauty, which can be seen in heavily distorted tea bowls (kutsu chawan) or water containers (mizusashi). Then, influenced by Kobori Enshū (also a feudal lord and great tea master), came Enshū Takatori, which is based on kirei-sabi (combining the purity of beauty and the imperfections of time).

After these transitions, the 4th feudal lord, Tsunamasa, ordered the building of the Higashi Sarayama kiln in Sawara Nishijin Machi and designated it as the official kiln of the Kuroda domain. Miraku-gama has its roots in this Higashi Sarayama kiln.

My great-grandfather, Yatarō Miraku XIII, was born as the first son of Hisasuke Jusen XI. After graduating from Nishijin Higher Elementary School in 1897 (Meiji 30), Yatarō started his pottery training under his father. Around this time, due to the establishment of prefectures in place of feudal domains, Takatori ware lost the protection of the Kuroda domain, which inevitably forced Yatarō to become independent and change his business to a private enterprise. In 1904, he took the name Kamei from Hohmanzan Kameibo

# 高取焼味楽窯の歴史について

## 15代亀井味楽

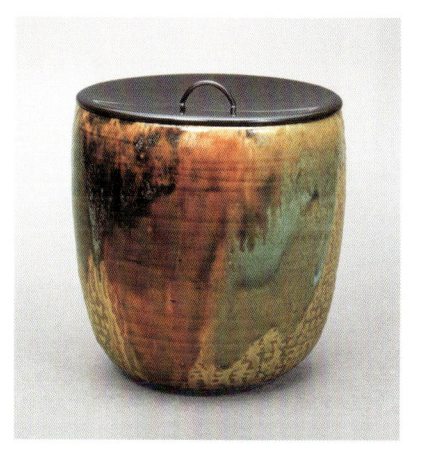

Enshū Takatori
Water Container
1630s
Sansai glaze

遠州高取
水指
1630年代
三彩釉

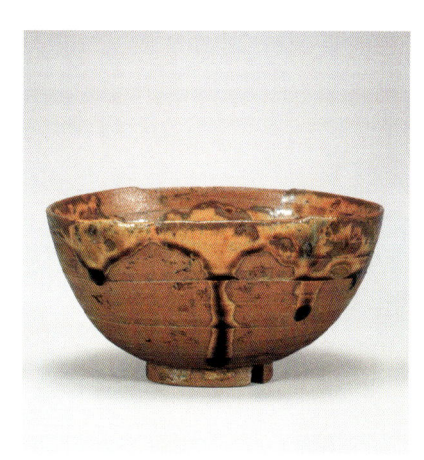

Enshū Takatori
Tea Bowl,
Brush Washer Shape
Early 1630s
Green-brown glaze

遠州高取
筆洗形茶盌
1630年代
高宮釉

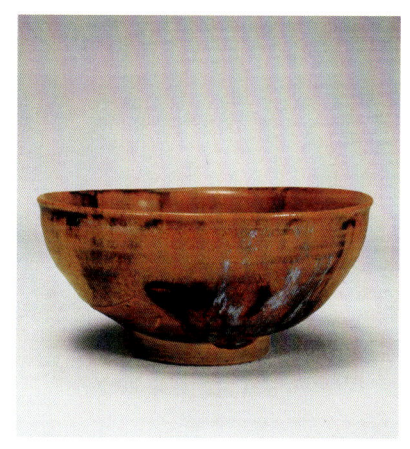

Enshū Takatori
"Needle Frost"
Tea Bowl
Early 1630s
Green-brown glaze

遠州高取
霜柱茶盌
1630年代
高宮釉

高取焼は福岡藩の藩祖、黒田如水・初代藩主の長政親子が朝鮮から八山という陶工を連れ帰り、1606年鷹取山（直方市）の麓に永満寺宅間窯を開かせたのが起源とされる。この時代の大名茶人・古田織部の影響を受け、大きく歪んだ沓茶盌や水指など破調の美を追求した「織部高取」や、織部に続く大名茶人・小堀遠州の「綺麗さび」を基調とした「遠州高取」などの変遷を経て、1708年黒田4代藩主綱政は、早良郡西新町に黒田藩御用窯として東皿山窯を築かせた。味楽窯はこのルーツを持つ窯元である。

高取焼11代久助寿泉の長男として生まれた私の曾祖父である13代弥太郎味楽は、西新高等小学校卒業後、明治30年から父について修業。この頃高取焼窯元は廃藩置県の影響で藩主の庇護がなくなり、必然的に自立自営を余儀なくされ個人企業の形態に移行することとなった。明治37年大宰府天満宮の裏山にある山伏の修験場宝満山亀井坊の名を取って「亀井」と改姓し、土管工場の経営にあたる。しかし本家（中川家）の家督を相続した弟の死により高取焼13代を継承する事となった。

大正7年から7年間もの間、福岡市会議員を務めるなど地方政治にも活躍したが、表千家の茶人である岩井宗麟の忠告により茶陶に専念、号名を「味楽」とした。命名に関しては口伝ではあるが9代未楽の残した作品に感銘を受けた13代弥太郎

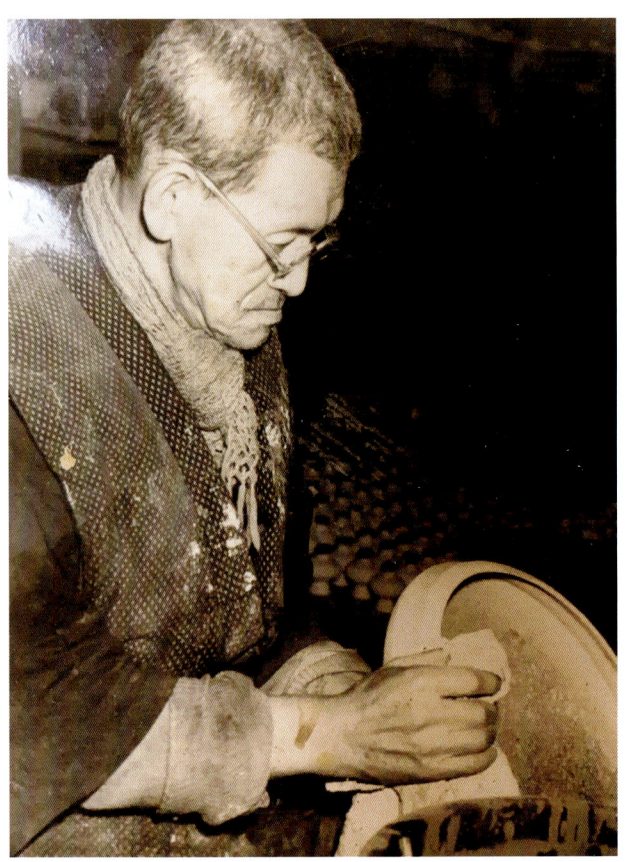

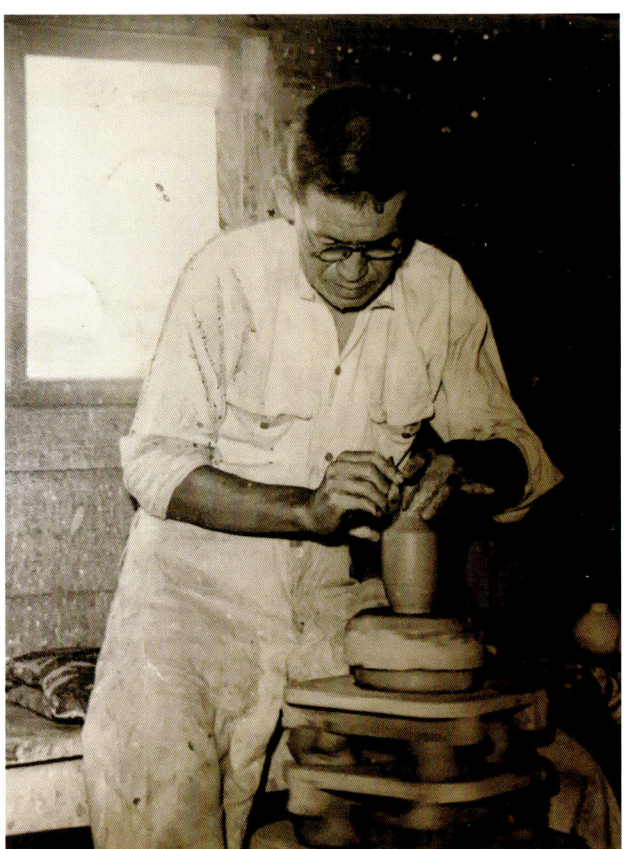

**Miraku Kamei XIII**
**c. 1955**

13代亀井味楽
昭和30年頃

(a training venue for Japanese mountain ascetics located in the back hill of Dazaifu Tenmangū Shrine) and managed an earthenware pipe factory. When his younger brother (who had inherited headship of the main branch, the Nakagawas) passed away, Yatarō became the 13th generation to inherit Takatori ware.

Yatarō became active in local politics and, beginning in 1918, served as a member of the Fukuoka City Council for seven years. However, following advice from Sorin Iwai, a tea master of Omotesenke School of tea ceremony, Yatarō decided to dedicate himself to making *chatō* (tea wares). Regarding his name, legend has it that Yatarō changed his other name to "Miraku" because he was very impressed by the pieces of Miraku IX and hoped to become a potter just like him. Yatarō was certified as a conservation craftsman for cultural properties by the Ministry of Agriculture and Commerce in 1944. He

established a reputation as an outstanding craftsman and contributed greatly to revitalizing Takatori ware.

My father, Miraku XIV, often said that the work reveals the character of the potter. The pieces by XIII show gentleness, at the same time dynamism. I can imagine what kind of person XIII was by observing his pieces. In particular, his tea caddies were especially reputable, so much so that he was called a "master of tea caddies." These tea caddies truly reveal the characteristics of XIII, I believe. Recently, I have been more exposed to the pieces by XIII, and I was unexpectedly impressed to see his careful and faithful application of *usuzukuri* (thin pottery), which is quintessential to Takatori ware, to both small and sensitive pieces like tea caddies and big pieces like decorative plates. Needless to say, XIII had marvelous techniques.

My father, Genhachirō Miraku XIV, was born in 1931 as a grandson of Yatarō Miraku XIII. He studied

味楽が、自分自身9代未楽のような陶工になりたいという願望を込めての命名だったようである。昭和19年には農商務省の技術保持者に認定されるなど名工として名が高く、高取焼の復興に尽力したようである。

作品は人間の現れであると、父14代が日ごろ口にしていたが、13代の作品は柔らかではあるがそこに豪快さを秘めた逸品が多い事に気づく。何となくではあるが13代がどんな感じ人であったか、作品を見ることによってその人物像が分かる気がする。

特に茶入れは「茶入造りの名人」と言われたほどであり、13代の姿そのものと言えるほどにその人間性を現した作品であると私は思う。

最近13代作の作品に出合う機会が多くなったが、茶入のような繊細で小さな作品から、飾り皿のような超大物まで、その意匠には高取焼の真髄ともいうべき薄造りが忠実に再現されていることにも驚きを隠せない。素晴らしい技術であることは言うまでもない。

そして昭和6年、13代弥太郎味楽の孫として生まれた私の父である14代源八郎味楽は13代に師事し、昭和39年14代味楽を襲名する。

昭和52年、福岡市無形文化財工芸技術保持者第一号の認定を受けたことは味楽窯の歴史の中でも特筆されるものであると思う。

戦後焼物ブームとなり、陶芸教室なるものが巷で流行りだし、その先駆者となったのも14代味楽であった。

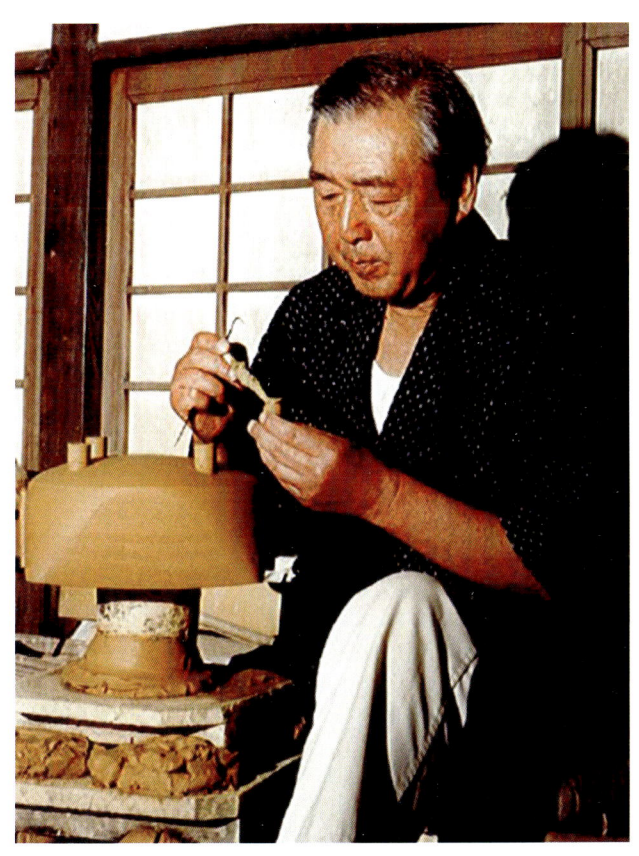

**Miraku Kamei XIV**
c. 2010 ｜ 14代亀井味楽
平成22年頃

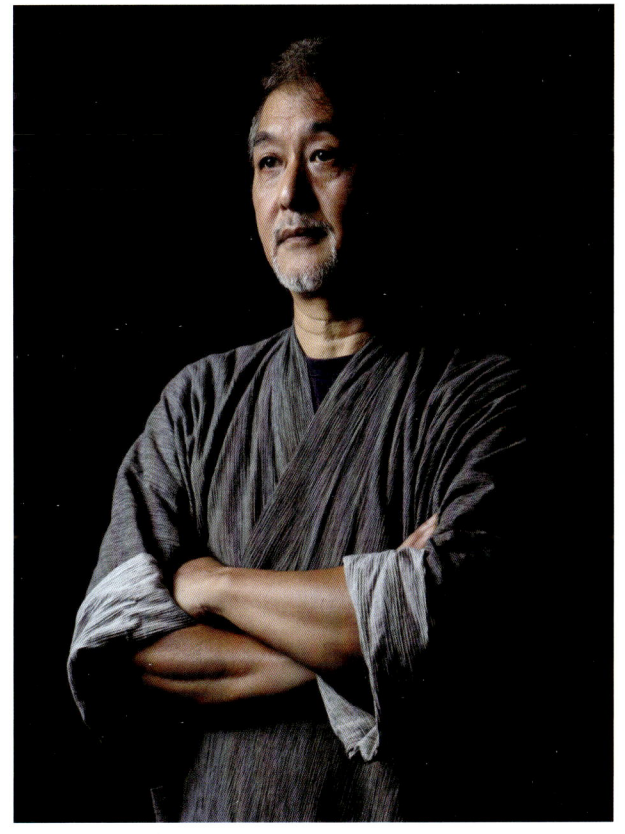

**Miraku Kamei XV**
2021 ｜ 15代亀井味楽
令和3年

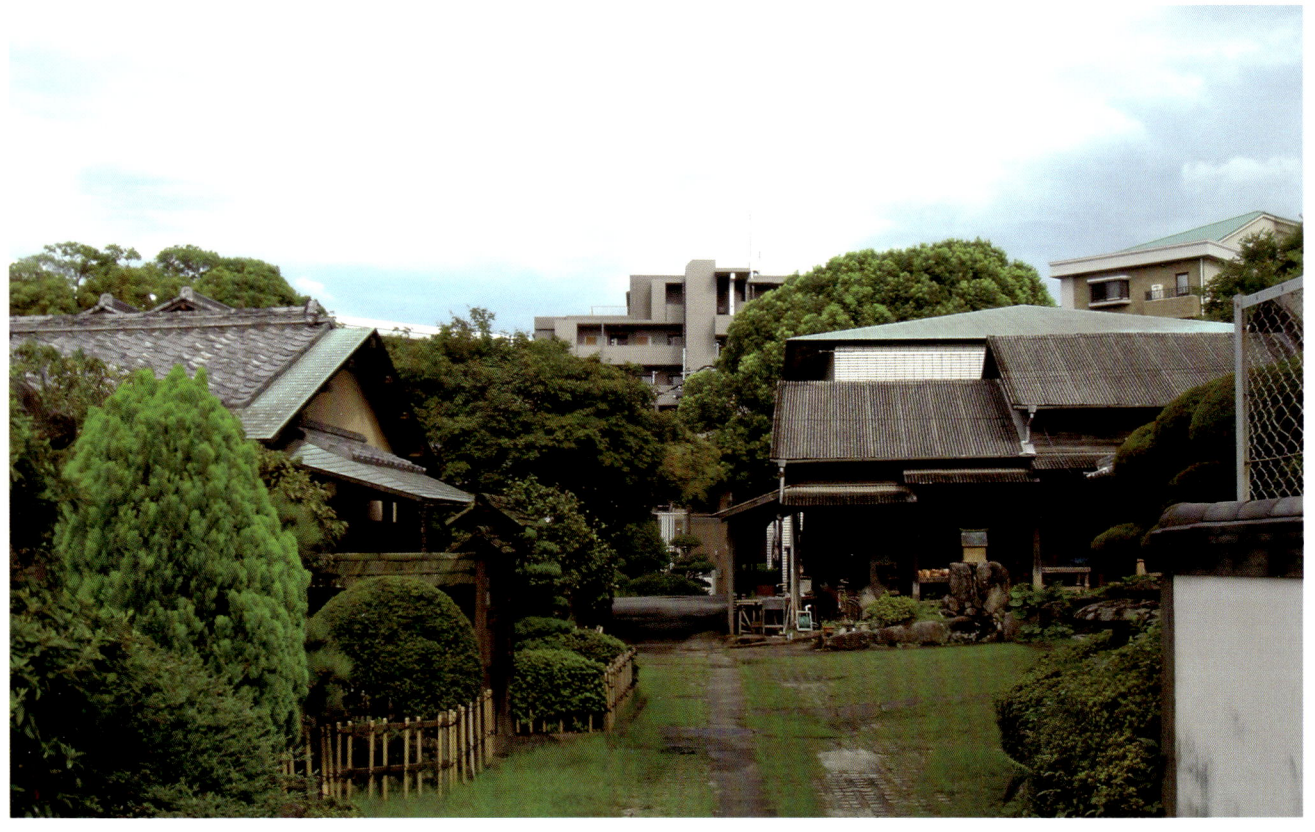

This picture is taken from the entrance of the kiln. On the left side is the main house, on the right side is the working studio, on the far left is the tea room, and on the far right is the climbing kiln and Miraku-gama Museum. (2021)

この写真は窯の入り口から撮ったものである。左側には母屋、右側には作業場、左奥には茶室、右奥には登り窯および味楽窯博物館が見える。(令和3年)

pottery under his own father (my grandfather), then inherited Miraku in 1964 to become XIV. It is a noteworthy event in the history of Miraku ware that my father was certified as the first "Holder of Intangible Cultural Asset in Art and Craft" by the Fukuoka City government.

After World War II, pottery became very popular and, as a result, so did pottery classes. Miraku XIV became a pioneer in offering pottery classes. With post-war economic growth, Takatori tea ware became popular and established a favorable reputation among many tea masters in Japan.

Today, I feel strongly and deeply for the hardships faced by my father, who took over as head of the family when he was in his 30s and passed away at the age of 82. I believe that one's 30s should be a period of challenging oneself to try many things and of accumulating more experiences through trial and error. When I look back on my own life as a potter in my 30s, I remember that I challenged myself to create several different types of pottery, to seek out my own ways of shaping and using glaze. Suddenly taking over the headship of the family in his 30s meant focusing on the family business rather than on what he really wanted to do. It must have been quite a hard life for him.

Now I understand well the reason why my father waited until I was 40 years old, and he was 70 years old, for me to inherit headship of the family. After I inherited the headship, my father XIV enjoyed making pottery daily, and challenged himself to take on unfinished tasks from when he was younger. My

戦後の高度成長期の背景もあり高取焼茶陶は人気も高まり、日本各地のお茶人に好評を得ていたようである。

　30歳代にして家督を受け継ぎ、82歳で逝去した父、14代の苦労をしみじみと痛感する今日この頃である。

　と言うのも、私自身の陶歴を振り返ってみると、30代という年は次代を背負う為に色々な事に挑戦し試行錯誤を繰り返しながら自分の引き出しを増やしていくと言った年回りであると思う。

　私もこの年代には造形法や釉薬等も新しい自分独自の境地を求めて色々な事に挑戦したものである。

　その様な年代に突然家督を譲り受けると言う事

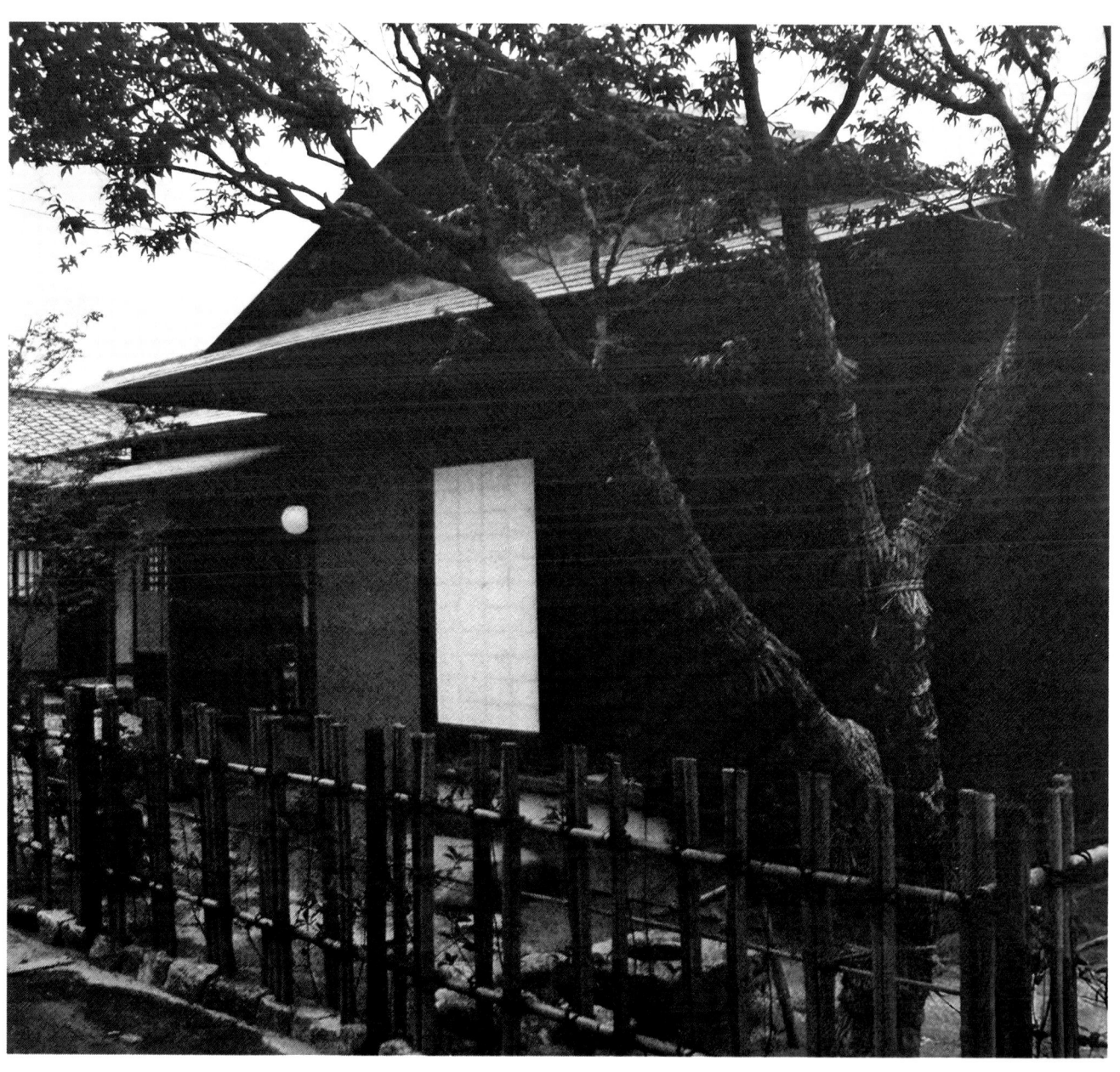

The Miraku-gama Museum consists of a showroom, ceramics classroom, exhibition space of historical works, and a tea room. (1982)

味楽窯博物館は展示室、陶芸教室、過去の作品、および茶室を備えている。(昭和57年)

father even started making raku *chawan*. I was very frustrated with him, wondering why the master of Takatori ware was trying to make raku *chawan*. If the biggest reason, however, for my father to transfer the headship of the family to me was to free himself, then I thought I should close my eyes and ignore him, as a form of filial piety. Overall, for 12 years I let him make whatever he wanted. I believe he enjoyed his life immensely.

I was 40 years old when I inherited the headship from my father. On Christmas Eve of that year, we were sitting at the table eating dinner together, and he suddenly said, "I will transfer the headship to you next year." I said without any hesitation, "I understand," however I did not anticipate how much pressure I would feel after that. Receiving the headship of the family means taking on the responsibilities of both "job" and "family." Looking back now, though, I think I was lucky to inherit the headship while my father was still alive.

It has been almost 20 years since I became the head of Miraku ware. At the time of the succession of Miraku, I was clueless. All I remember now is that without any advice from my father, I worked and worked single-mindedly with my wife, my life partner. I took various roles, even a part-time lecturer at a high school, thinking that I would be extremely busy with my succession anyway so why not? Many people said that I was riding on my father's coattails, or similar things, before my succession to the headship. To overcome that, I started to take completely different approaches from my father to various fields. Luckily, the seeds that I planted started to bloom and I became confident that I was forming my own Miraku ware, different from my father's era.

While my father was in a hospital bed, knowing he did not have much time to live, I visited him with my son and second daughter. My father opened his arms and asked us to hold his hands. I held his right hand, and my son and my daughter held his left hand. He told my son, "You must have a good son," and said once and for all, "My son is great, isn't he?" Then he said to me, "Thank you for inheriting the headship. Now I can entrust you to take it." We were so stunned by what he said out of the blue, and we were totally lost. "My son" meant myself. The relationship between my father and myself had been quite confrontational because of our conceptual differences regarding pottery, so I had never dreamed of hearing those words. Needless to say, my children and I burst into tears in the hospital.

My son, next Miraku XVI, who was with us in the hospital, told me later that he realized that the happiest thing in the life of a potter was "to have someone to inherit the tradition." In that moment, he made a firm decision to inherit Miraku ware. What beautiful words I received!

It has been 8 years since my son graduated from the School for Training Pottery run by Kyoto Prefecture and returned to our kiln. In 2017, we held a milestone event, the "300-year anniversary of Nishi Sarayama Kiln Opening," and I persuaded my son, who had just returned, to participate in the event. We successfully held a grand event (which was my responsibility as Miraku XV), including a gala party with more than 300 invitees and an exhibit at a local department store (of work by me and Hisaaki). It has been 300 years since the Takatori ware established its roots in this area. I expressed my gratitude to my ancestors and others who have been preserving this place, and I made my firm decision to preserve it for the next 100 years.

Takatori of Sawara-ku in Fukuoka City, where Miraku-gama is located, used to be called Nishijinmachi

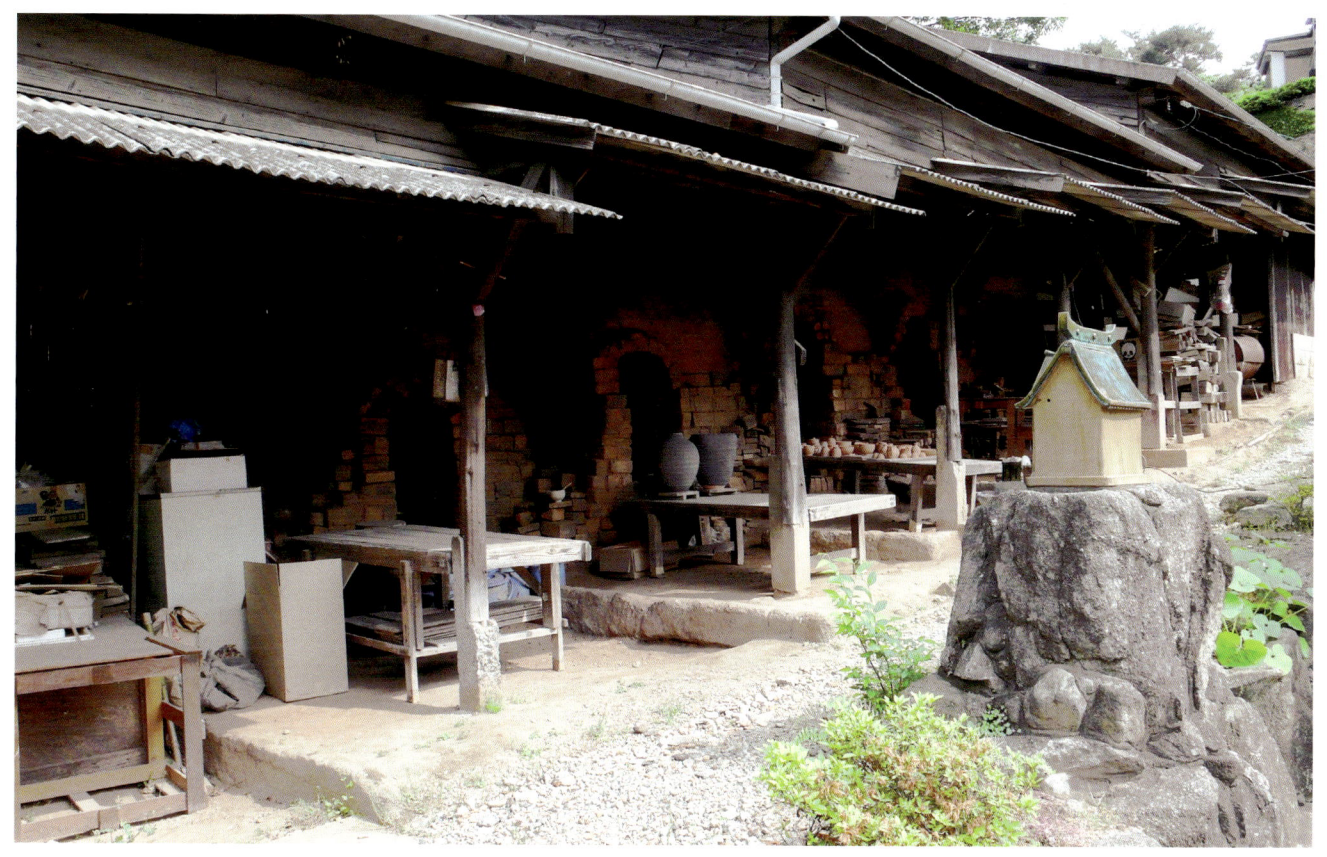

The Miraku wood-fired climbing kiln was active in this location for over 300 years, up until Miraku Kamei XV was in his 20s. Now the Miraku family mainly uses a gas kiln, to which they will occasionally add wood at high temperatures. (2021)

亀井家の薪による登り窯は、15代亀井味楽が20代になるまで、300年以上この場所で使用されてきた。現在、亀井家はガス窯を使用しており、高温で薪を追加することもある。(令和3年)

は自分自身のやりたいことに封印をし、嫌でも家業に専念しなくてはならないと言うかなり過酷な人生であったと思う。

今になって分かる事であるが、私が丁度40歳、父70歳の時に私に家督を譲らせたわけもここにあったのであろうと思う。

私に代を継承させた後、父14代は水を得た魚の如く日々作陶を楽しみ、若かりし頃にやり残した事に再チャレンジする毎日であったように思える。「楽茶盌」にまで手を出していたのであるから。

最少は高取焼の大家が「楽茶盌」を作るとはどうしたものかと、私自身父の仕事に不満を抱いていたのだが、私に代を譲った大きな理由がそこにあるとすればこんな親孝行もありかと目をつぶって

いたものである。結局12年間は父の思い通りに好きな作陶をさせていたので、父にとっては最高の人生であったと思う。

私が父より代を譲り受けたのが丁度40歳。その年のクリスマスイブの日の事、食卓を囲んでの夕食時いきなり父が「来年お前に代を譲るからな」と言うではないか。その時は何のためらいもなく「わかった」と言い返したが、この後とんでもない重責に苦しむ事となった。

何せ、代を引き継ぐと言う事は「仕事」と「家」両方を任されると言う事である。しかしながら今にして思えば、先代が存命のうちに代を引き継がせてもらえたと言う事は一番の幸せであったと思う。

そして味楽窯も我代となり、もうかれこれ20年

Sarayama. When Fukuoka City became a designated city, the name of this place was changed to Takatori, from Takatori ware. As time went by, the subway opened, land was reclaimed, and this area turned into one of the best districts. As a natural consequence, high-rises have been built and the town has become totally urbanized. Our climbing kiln, which sits on our property, cannot be utilized due to a fire prevention ordinance by Fukuoka City. We are now in the era of not even having smoke coming out of the kiln.

I was told that the foundation of this climbing kiln was built in the 1700s, and in the Meiji Era, the chambers were rebuilt without touching the foundation. This is truly a cultural heritage.

During my father's headship, we had a plan to move our studio to somewhere outside the city, but it did not materialize. I received a wonderful letter from an expert in Tokyo, which says, "Even if you move to the countryside, it is inevitable for any place to be urbanized at some point and you will end up

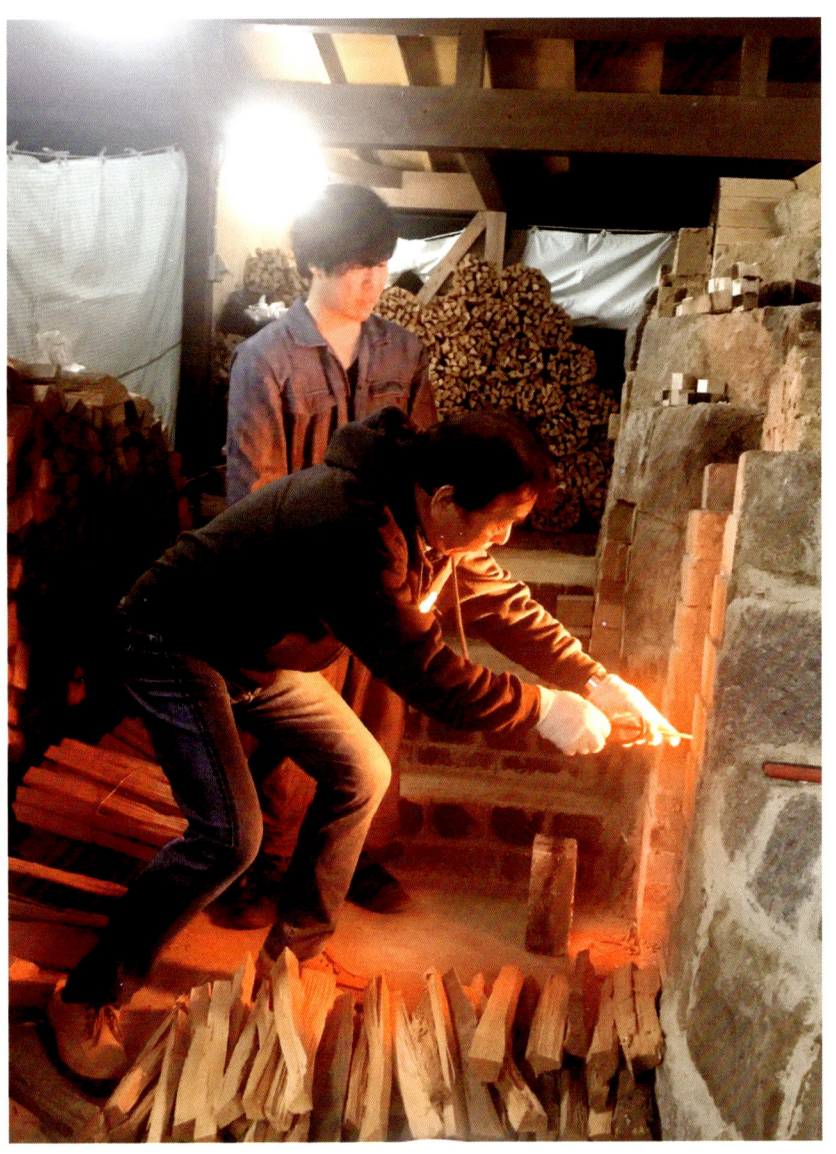

**Hisaaki Kamei (top) and Miraku Kamei XV (bottom) demonstrate how to fire a climbing kiln. (2021)**

登り窯の火入れをしている亀井久彰（上）と15代亀井味楽（下）（令和3年）

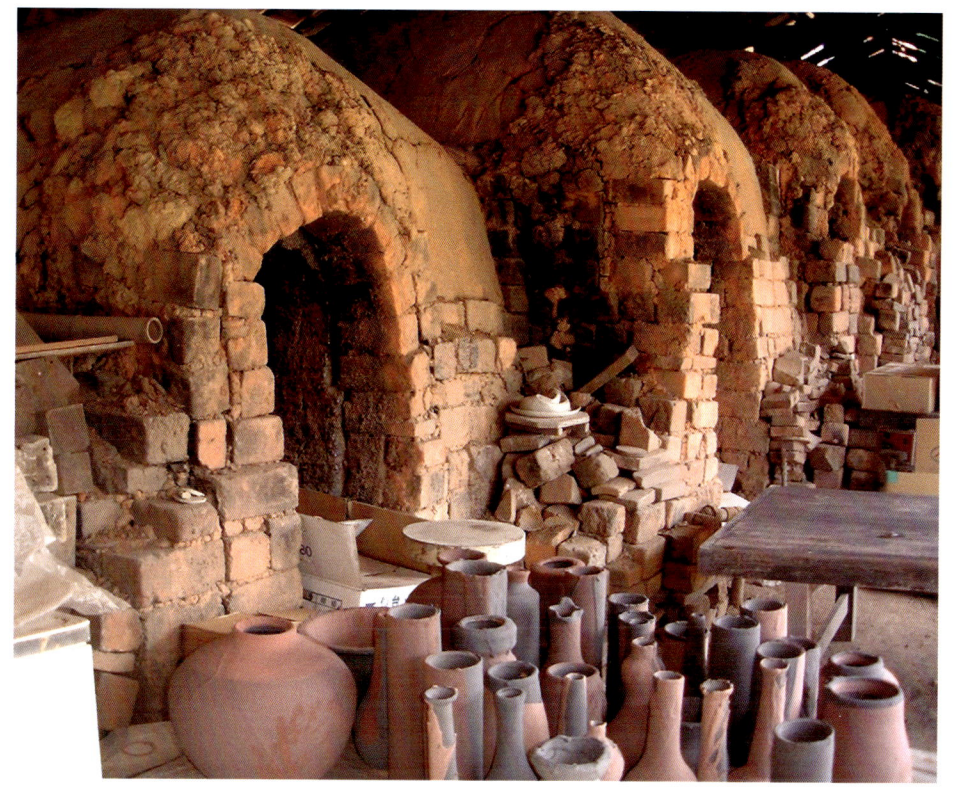

The climbing kiln was built in the 1700s and used until the late Showa period. It is no longer in use due to fire prevention regulations resulting from the urbanization of the surrounding area, but it is lovingly preserved as a cultural legacy and an important element of the history and tradition of Takatori ware. (2021)

登り窯は1700年代に築かれ、昭和の終わりまで使用されていたが、現在では、防災法により使用できなくなっている。しかし文化財としては非常に優れたものであり、高取焼の歴史と伝統の重要な一部である。(令和3年)

が過ぎてしまった。

　襲名当時はまだ右も左もわからない状況の中、父の助言すらない中、人生の伴侶である妻と共に一心不乱に働いたと言う記憶しか残っていない。振り返れば襲名当時どうせ忙しくなるのだからと、色々な役職や高校の非常勤講師を引き受けたりもした。

　「親の七光り」と言う言葉があるが、私も例にもれずその様な事を襲名前にはよく言われたものだ。それを払拭すべく、父とは全く違うスタンスで多方面へのアプローチをしだしたのもこの頃である。

　幸いにしてその芽が今現在になって開いて、父

の時代とはまた違う「味楽窯」を形作っているのは確かであろうと思う。

　父が病床に伏せて余命の宣告を受けていたある日、私と息子そして次女の三人でお見舞いへと病室を訪ねた。

　そこで父が両手を広げ、その手を握るよう求めてきた。右手を私が左手を息子と娘が握りしめた時、父が息子に向かって「良い息子を持て」と。更には「俺の息子は凄いだろう」と言い放った。

　また「代を受け継いでくれて有り難う、これで安心してお前に代を任せられる」とも。

　突然の言葉に最初は何のことやら意味が分からない状況であったが、「俺の息子」は私の事。それま

facing the same issue. I hope you will stay where you are now and become a pioneer in 'urban *Kama moto*.' I am working hard through trial and error to establish an "urban *Kama moto*" in this place.

Takatori ware has lasted over 400 years, and as I mentioned before, each era has its own style. The Takatori kiln moved from its original place in Nōgata City to Iizuka City, then to Higashi Minemura, and finally to Fukuoka City. The reason for these moves was not only to seek better clay, but also because of changes of the Kuroda domain's feudal lords. It is like when changing the top executive means changing the management policy.

The first feudal lord, Nagamasa, lived in the Sengoku Period (The Period of Warring States), and he had to distinguish himself in the battles to gain fame. On the other hand, during the era of the second feudal lord, Tadanobu, the Period of Warring States was over and the world became more peaceful. The historical background of each era is different. It is undeniable that each feudal lord accommodated his policy to go along with the era he lived in.

Today, even though some differences exist among the Takatori kilns, basically Takatori ware is *chatō* (tea ware). *Chatō* means stoneware tools which are used for *sadō* (tea ceremony), an important part of Japanese tradition. A *Kama moto* (pottery producer) that mainly produces tools for the tea ceremony is called *chatō gama*. My Miraku-gama strictly follows these conventions and produces general tea ceremony tools, mainly tea caddies (*chaire*), water containers (*mizusashi*), and tea bowls (*chawan*). Regarding the tea caddies, it is worth mentioning that the thickness of the finished tea caddy must be an extremely thin 1.5 mm. This has been the specification since the Kuroda domain era. It was a very important requirement from the Kuroda domain to keep this thickness.

Three of the most valuable tea caddies with shoulders, which were owned by Nobunaga Oda and Hideyoshi Toyotomi, are thought to have been made in China during the Southern Song or Yuan Dynasty and brought to Japan during the Period of Warring States. It is commonly believed that the famous Yang Guifei used them as oil containers. "Hatsuhana with a shoulder," "Narashiba with a shoulder," and "Nitta with a shoulder" are now regarded as the most precious containers. Even these containers have a thickness of 2.0 mm. It is worthy of special mention that our containers are thinner than these.

Tea caddies of Miraku-gama have been created strictly following these specifications, and we have many masterpieces. I believe that I was able to inherit the headship as XV specifically because I acquired this skill. My son, Hisaaki, started to focus on making tea caddies, however it will require more training before he reaches the required level. It is fair to say that this is an incredibly high-level technique.

Other than tea caddies, *mizusashi* (water containers) are also one of our signature pottery forms. The lightness which we achieve using our technique attracts the admiration of many tea masters. *Mizusashi* do not have as strict specifications as tea caddies, and more modern-shaped *mizusashi*, rather than classical-shaped ones, are often used. As for *chawan* (tea bowls), it is said, "No.1 Raku, No. 2 Hagi, No.3 Karatsu." This means that in the *chanoyu* (tea ceremony) world, raku *chawan* are regarded as the most precious. Early Takatori pieces were similar to Karatsu ware, in fact many pieces that were appraised as Karatsu ware are now re-appraised as Takatori ware. This means that, depending on the shapes of *chawan*, we can at least rival or create better than Karatsu ware.

The current Miraku-gama creates pieces that go with the flow of the era, under the guidance of several

で陶芸に対するお互いの考えの相違から対立しあう親子仲となった父と私であったのだが、そのような父親からまさかの言葉。私と息子達はその場で泣きじゃくってしまったのは言うまでもないことであった。

その場面に立ち会っていた次期16代嗣の息子は、陶芸家人生の中で一番嬉しく思う事は、「伝統を受け継いでくれる人が現れる事」と言う事に他ならないと、この瞬間に16代を継ぐ決心を固くしたと語ってくれた。何とも嬉しい言葉である。

その息子が京都府立の陶工訓練校を卒業し、我が窯元へ戻ってきて8年が過ぎた。2017年には「西皿山窯開窯300年」と言う節目の行事を行うことになり、まだ窯元に戻って来たばかりの息子も担ぎ出しての一大イベントとなった。

300人を超える祝賀会、そして地元デパートでの展示会（15代味楽・久彰父子展）、および15代としての責務である一大行事を無事に開催する事が

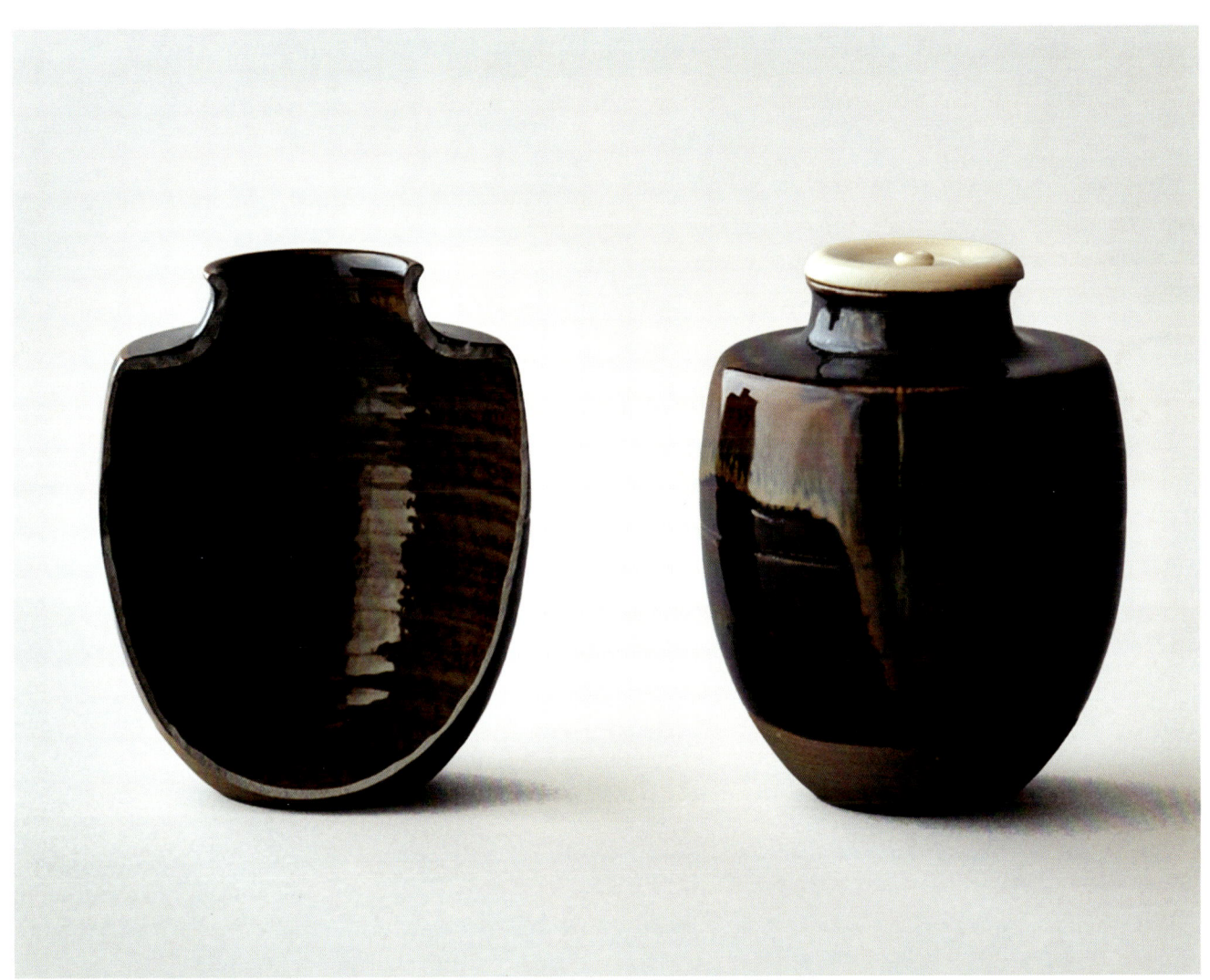

The essence of Takatori ware is its thin structure, achieved through a precise coordination between the artist's tools, their fingertips, and the movement of their feet on the kick wheel. A master of this art, Miraku Kamei XV can throw *katatsuki* (shouldered) tea caddies with a thickness of only 1.5 mm.

高取焼の神髄は、作家が使用する道具、指先の感覚、蹴り轆轤での足の動きにおける精密な調整によって実現されるその薄さにある。15代亀井味楽氏の作る肩衝茶入れの厚さは、驚くべきことに1.5㎜である。

schools of tea ceremony (Omotesenke and Urasenke, etc.) Even though the number of people practicing tea ceremony is declining slightly, there is still much demand for pottery for the tea ceremony.

Some Takatori producers create pottery focusing on *mintō*, which means pottery for daily use. This was probably an agonizing decision made to survive in this industry. At our Miraku-gama, main branch of the Mirakus, when I created coffee mugs for a show, my father XIV scolded me saying, "Don't make anything else but *chawan*." I suppose what he meant was that we, as the *Kama moto*, have been making *chawan*, and

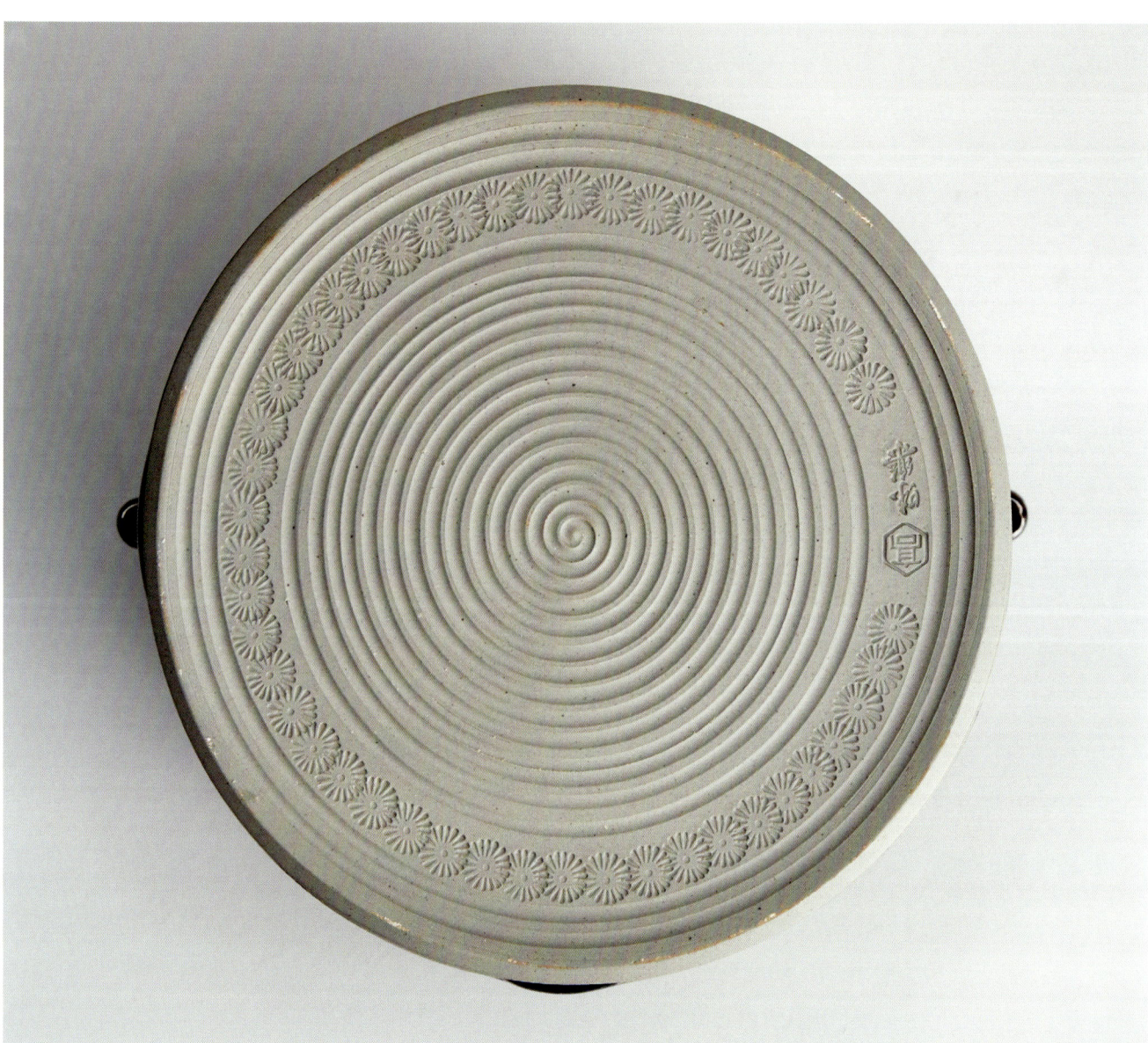

The bottoms of tea bowls are often decorated with signature markings. Appreciation for the clay, the glaze, the shape of the foot, the artist, and their tools (which can be observed by turning over the bowl) is part of the tea ceremony. In this case, Miraku Kamei XV adorned the bottom of a water container with stylized chrysanthemums, the Miraku Kiln stamped mark, and his name. He takes pride in his attention to detail on the bottom of the piece, even if most people never see it.

茶碗の底には通常、作家名が刻まれる。土、釉薬、高台の形、作家、使用された道具(茶碗を反転させることによってみることができる)を愛でるのは、茶道の重要な一部である。15代亀井味楽はこの水差の底に、装飾化された菊、味楽窯の印、作家名を刻み込んだ。15代は、たとえ人が見ることがなくても、誇りを持って作品の底に装飾を施している。

できた。この地に高取焼が根付いて300年。この地を守り続けて来たご先祖様やそれに携わった人々に感謝の意を表しながら、この先また100年と守り続けていく覚悟もしたものであった。

味楽窯の所在地である福岡市早良区高取は、古くは西新町皿山と言う地名であった。福岡市が政令指定都市となったのをきっかけに地名変更があり、高取焼の名を取り「高取」と言う地名になった由来がある。

時代が進むにつれ地下鉄開通や埋め立てが進み、この近辺は一等地となり、当然の如く高層ビルやマンションが建ち都会化が進んだ。

窯元敷地内に鎮座する登り窯も、福岡市火災予防条令により今や煙を出すことも禁じられる時代となっている。

この登り窯の基礎は1700年代の物、明治時代に基礎はそのまま連坊のみ造りかえたと聞いている。まさに文化遺産そのものである。

父の時代、工房を田舎の方へ移築するという計画もあったが断念。

とある東京の有識者の先生よりのお手紙で「田舎へ引っ越してもまた何年か後には都会化が進み同じ状況になるのは必至、ならばこの地で「都会型の窯元」を目指してパイオニア的存在になってください。」と言う素晴らしいお言葉を頂いた。これを機にこの地で「都会型の窯元」を確立させるために日々試行錯誤しながら頑張っている状況である。

さて、400年以上も続く高取焼ではあるが、前にも述べたように時代によってその作風は様々である。開窯の地である直方市から飯塚市そして東峰村、更に福岡市内へと移り変わった理由の中に、良い土を求めてと言う他に黒田藩当主の代替わりも

大きな理由の一つである。現代社会でも同様にトップが変われば経営方針も変わるのと同じような感じである。

初代藩主、長政の時代は当に戦国の世の中。武功を上げて自分の名を世に広めていく時代。2代忠之の時代と言えば戦がなくなり平和な世がおとずれた、と言う具合に時代背景もかなり違ってくる。

その様な中、各代の藩主は次代に沿うような策をとっていることは否めない。では現在はというと、数軒ある高取焼を名乗る窯元個々に違いはあれど、基本的に高取焼は「茶陶」の窯である。

「茶陶」すなわち日本の伝統文化である「茶道」の世界で使われる焼物の道具である。それをメインとして作っている窯元が茶陶窯だ。

味楽窯もこの約束事をきちんと守り、主に茶入、水指、茶碗など基軸とし茶道具全般に渡り製作を手掛けている。

特に茶入に於いては特筆すべきことがある。まずその厚みは1.5mmと言う極薄の仕上げとなっている。これは藩窯時代からの約束事で、藩の命によりこの厚みで作ることが最重視されていた。

織田信長や豊臣秀吉もかつて手にしたことのある天下三大肩衝茶入。

中国の南宋または元時代の作と推定され、戦国時代に日本へと渡来したものとされる。かの楊貴妃が油壷として使用していたという俗説もあり、「初花（はつはな）肩衝」・「楢柴（ならしば）肩衝」・「新田（にった）肩衝」は現在でも大名物とされている。

この肩衝茶入でもその厚みは2.0mm。それをしのぐ厚みで造られていることは本当に特筆すべき重要なことである。

味楽窯の茶入は、この約束事を守って作られた

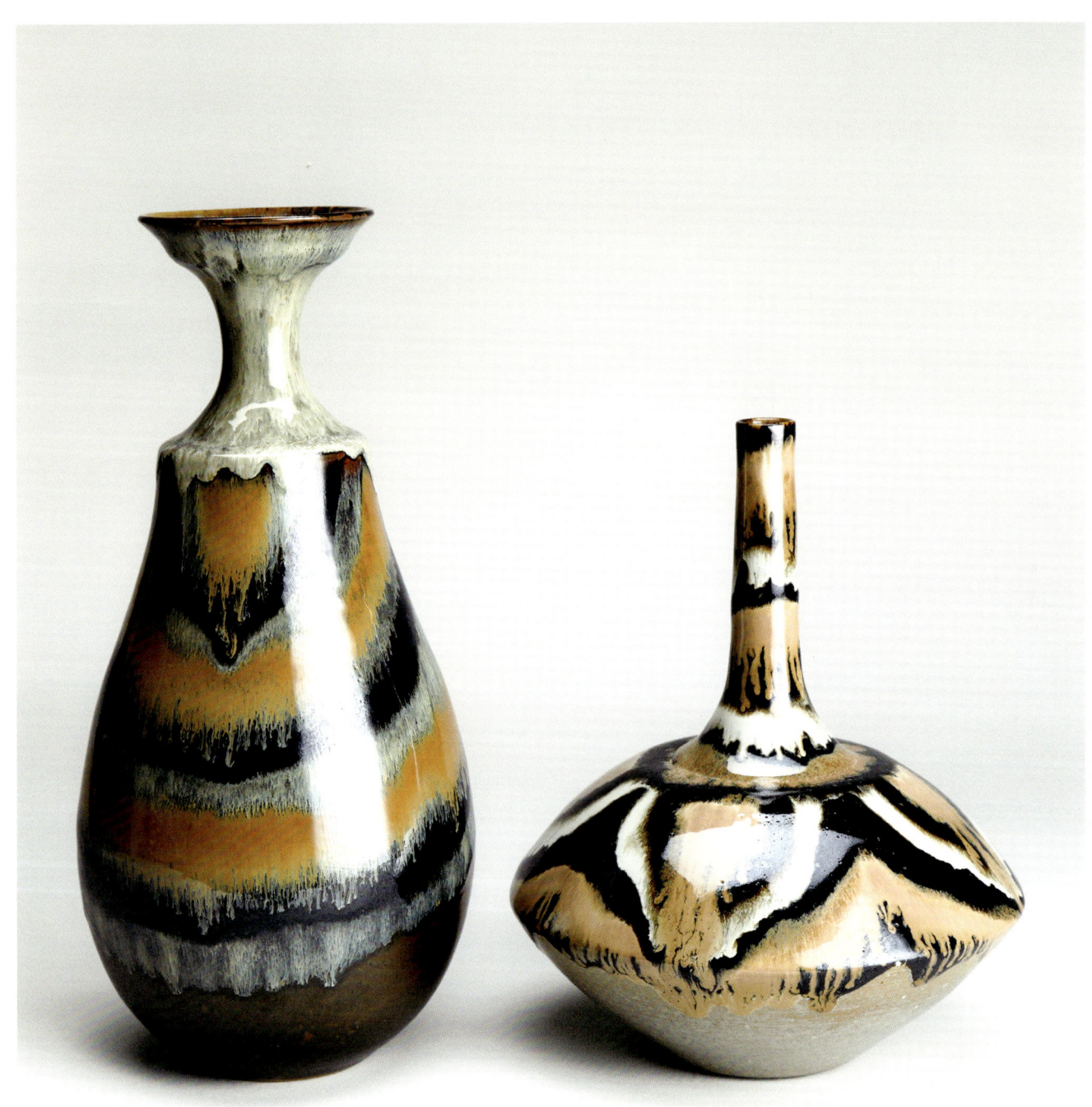

MIRAKU KAMEI XV   15代亀井味楽
Flower Vase   花入
2016   2016年
Dyed glaze   染め釉
XV135

HISAAKI KAMEI   亀井久彰
Flower Vase   花入
2016   2016年
Dyed glaze   染め釉
HK2

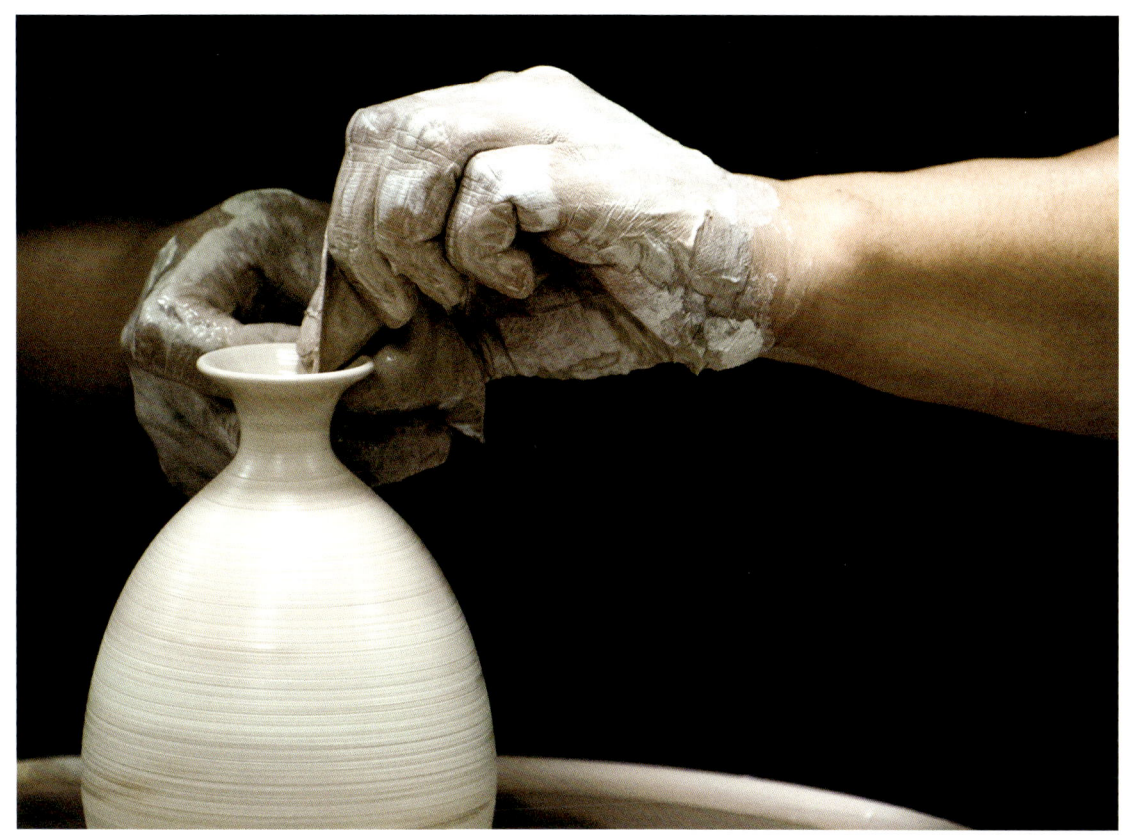

Miraku Kamei XV at a workshop at MIT. (2016) | 15代亀井味楽、MITでのワークショップ（平成28年）

逸品が多いのも確かである。私もこの技術が修得できたからこそ15代を継ぐ事ができたのであろう。息子、久彰は現在この茶入造りにも本腰を入れているようであるが、まだまだその域に達するには相当な修行を要するだろう。それ程難しいハイレベルな技術であることは間違いない。

　茶入の他、茶道で用いられる水指も代表作の一つである。全体的に薄造りからくるその軽さも茶人達には好評を得ている。

　茶入よりもその「しばり」が少なく、現代では古典的なものよりも近代的な造形の水指がしばしば使われることもあるようになった。

　茶盌に関しては「1楽2萩3唐津」とも言われるように、茶の湯の世界では楽茶盌が最高の茶盌となる。しかし開窯当時の高取作品群は唐津焼と似通った作風でもあり、最初は唐津焼と鑑定されていた

作品が最近になり高取焼と再判定された作品も数多くある。

　ということは、高取焼の茶盌も造形次第では唐津に勝るとも劣らないものができると言う事でもある。

　現在の味楽窯は、茶道各流派（表千家・裏千家等）のご指導を賜りながら時代の流れに沿った作品作りを心掛けている。

　茶道人口が減少してきたとは言え、まだまだ茶道具の需要は多い。

　同じ高取焼の窯元の中には民需用の陶器、いわゆる「民陶」に重きを置いて作陶をしているところもあるが、それもこの業界で食べていくための苦渋の選択かもしれない。

　本家である我が窯元に於いても、私が20代の頃、珈琲碗を作って展示場に飾っていたところ、父

coffee mugs were just wrong. However, interestingly, a tea master once requested us to make coffee mugs. He wanted "coffee mugs created by a *chatō* potter." I made a few coffee mugs, and he liked them very much. He is still using them, I heard.

As it is said that "*chatō* is a world of dimensions," it is a challenge to reflect your own technique on pieces that must be made within a very strict framework. In particular, tea caddies with shoulders are very precise. People talk casually about dimensions, since we use tableware daily without thinking much about that. Today, dimensions and shapes are based on ergonomics. In the *chatō* world, ergonomics has for a long time been commonly known as "the world of dimensions." You can see how superb *chatō* is.

Tea ware changes as time goes by, and it is important to produce pottery through observing carefully what the era brings. My father often said, "Creativity is merely originality, not Takatori ware. Learn from the classics." His words have become my personal motto. Every day, I make pottery thinking of two old sayings. One is *Onkochishin* (review the old and know the new) and the other is *Fueki Ryukō* (introduce new based on the tradition). My creative style is to make a piece with both simplicity and breadth. I add things to broaden the possibilities and then deliberately eliminate the unneeded parts to improve perfection. Every day I say to myself, "Once satisfied with the current condition, the rest would only go down," setting an ultimate goal to reduce unnecessary things and produce pottery as naturally as possible.

I have developed my own styles, such as decorations on the clay bodies (deformation, openwork, fluting, etc.) or drawing with glaze. I also make decorative pottery (pots, plates, etc.) in addition to *chatō*.

Looking to the future of Miraku-gama as "urban style *Kama moto*," I think it will be impossible to fire our climbing kiln. From the environmental point of view, I believe it is not permissible to have smoke in the middle of a city. Fortunately, Takatori ware is regarded as *yuyaku mono* (glazed pottery). One of the characteristics of Takatori ware is to use multiple layers of glaze and create various transformations of different types of glazes. Even in the climbing kiln, we would put pottery into containers called saggars to prevent ashes from falling onto the pieces directly. We are currently using a gas kiln. Once the temperature reaches 1200 degrees Celsius, we place small pieces of wood in a secondary opening of the kiln to create some ashes. This method generates less smoke and does not cause our neighbors any trouble. Compared to a climbing kiln, its firing is quite efficient and produces fewer "uneven firing" results. This is perfect for "urban *Kama moto*."

Some pottery lovers say that "pieces fired in a climbing kiln are the best," but this is nonsense in this modern world.

If we absolutely needed a climbing kiln, it could be built in the countryside on land my father XIV purchased. It is not an urgent matter so I will take time to contemplate this issue with my son, Hisaaki. Fukuoka City is a gateway to the Asia-Pacific region and has good access from overseas. Takatori is very conveniently located, close to the airport and train stations. I would like to fully utilize these advantages to create "urban *Kama moto*." Regarding our future development, I would like to gradually increase the variety of the pieces, while taking "*chatō* for overseas" into consideration.

My son, Hisaaki, has established a new technique using the traditional Takatori straw white glaze to achieve a blue color. He named this "aurora glaze" or "Hisaaki glaze" and applies it to his pieces, which attracts younger generations and overseas customers.

Glaze and form work symbiotically here. The cascading glaze is a visual expression of the water contained in the vessel and the orientation of the decoration signals the front of the vessel.

この作品では釉薬と形状の共生が見られる。水指の正面を示す滝状の釉薬は、視覚的な表現を創り出している。

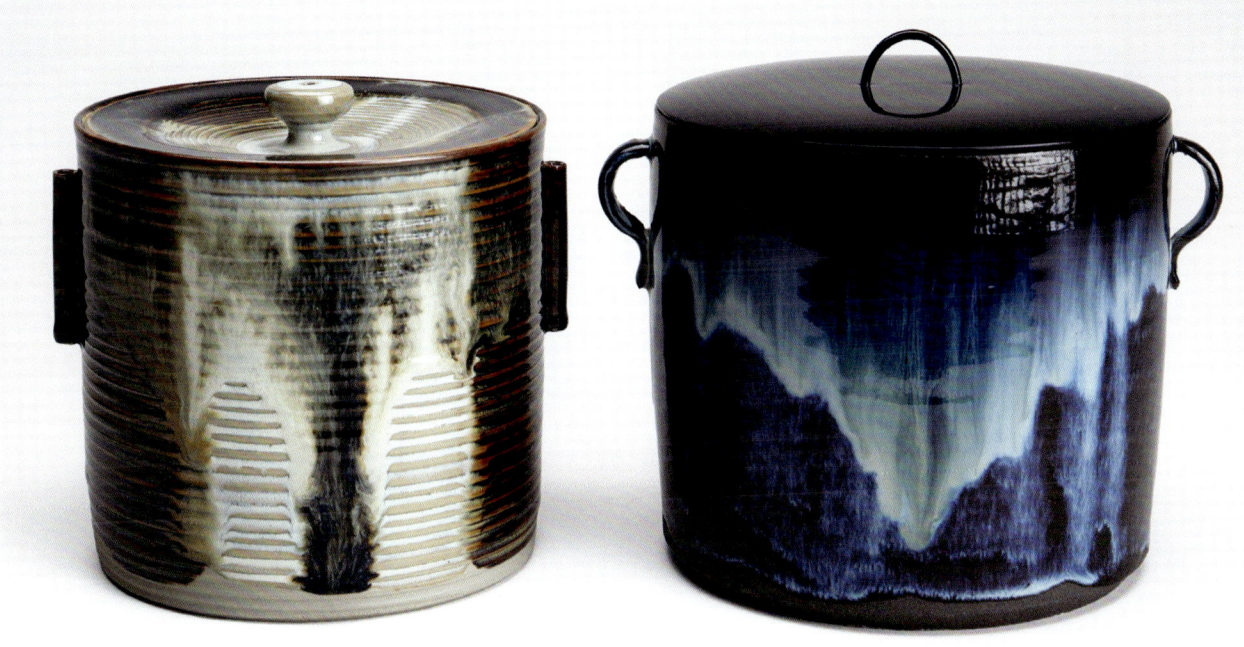

MIRAKU KAMEI XV
Water Container
2024
Kakewake and white glaze
XV210

15代亀井味楽
水指
2024年
掛分に白流し

HISAAKI KAMEI
Water Container with Lacquer Lid
2024
Aurora glaze
HK56

亀井久彰
うるし蓋付水指
2024年
極光釉

A unique facet of Takatori ware is their openness to freedom within tradition. Building upon his father's work, Hisaaki uses a darker clay body to give the white glaze a blueish hue. With the etched design on the lower half of the vase, Hisaaki celebrates the natural clay and creates a tactile experience for the holder.

高取焼の独自性は伝統を踏まえた自由さにある。亀井久彰は15代の作品に基づいて暗色の土を本体に使用し、白釉に青い色合いを表現している。花入の下部に施された割れ目により天然の土が引き立ち、手に取ると心地よい手触りを楽しむことができる。

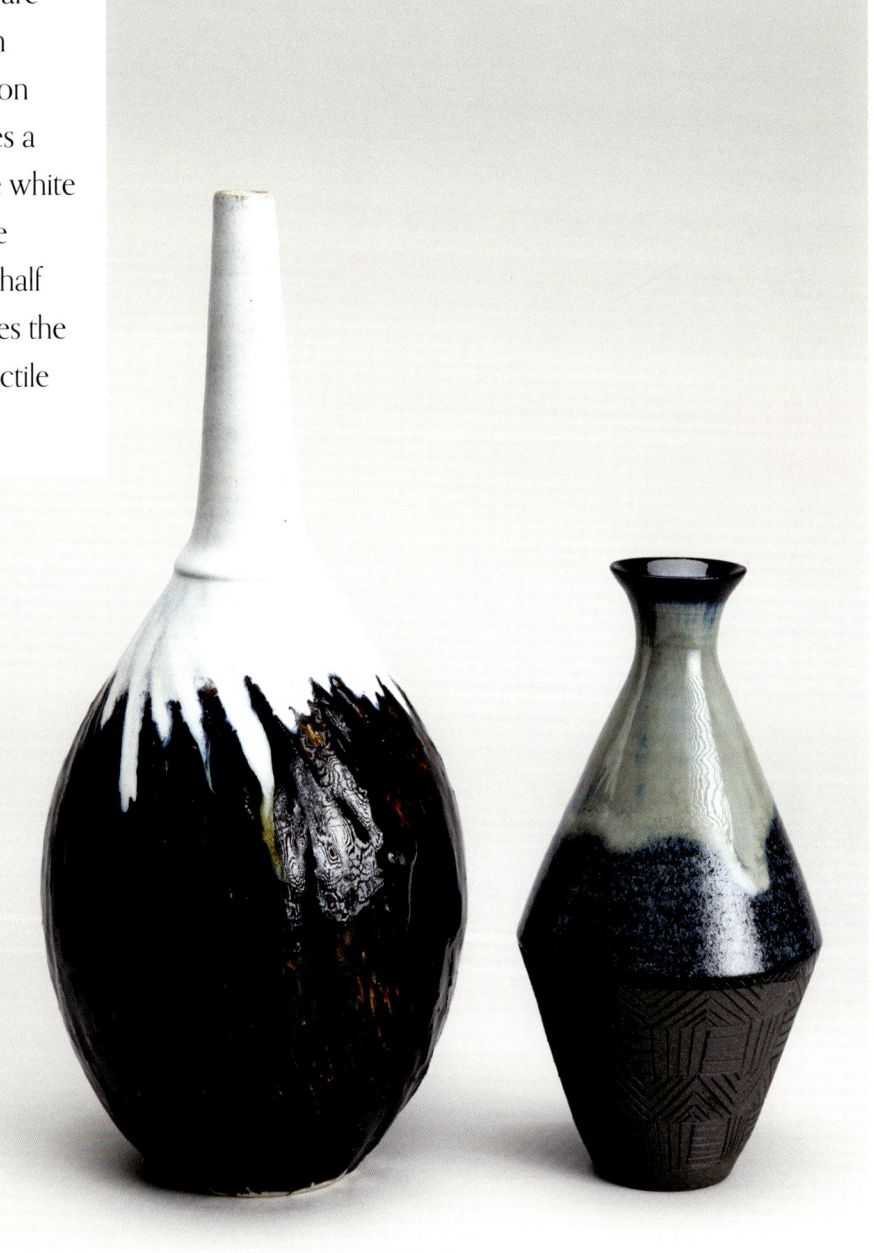

MIRAKU KAMEI XV
Flower Vase with Chatter Marks
2024
Ame glaze
XV218

15代亀井味楽
割目花入
2024年
飴釉

HISAAKI KAMEI
Jar
2024
Aurora glaze
HK60

亀井久彰
壺
2024年
極光釉

14代から「茶陶以外の物は作るな」とどやされたことがあった。茶陶の窯に珈琲碗は邪道と言う事だったのであろう。しかし世の中面白いもので、とある茶人から珈琲碗の製作依頼を受け「茶陶作家が作る珈琲碗が欲しい」との依頼があった。

それで数碗作ったが、とても気に入られて現在でもまだお使いになられているようである。「茶陶は寸法の世界」とも言われ、その枠の中でどれだけの技量が反映できるかが難しいところでもある。

特に肩衝茶入は当にその確たるもの。一口に寸法と言うが私達が日頃何気なく使っている食器も現在では人口科学に基づいた寸法や形状であったりする事を考えれば、それが自然に「寸法の世界」として常識とされていた茶陶の素晴らしさを垣間見ることができると思う。

この辺りは時代の進行とともに変化はあるが、やはり時代を見据えながら作陶をしていく事は今後も大切な事であろう。

「独創は単なるオリジナルでしかなく高取焼とは呼べない。古典から学べ」と言う父14代の言葉。まさにその言葉とおりに、私の座右の銘でもある「温故知新」と「不易流行」の2つを掲げ、現在も作陶に励んでいる。私の作陶スタイルとしては、初めから無駄なく縮こまった作品を目指すのではなく、加飾によって可能性を広げそこから無駄をそぎ落としていき完成度を高めると言ったものである。

「現状に満足すれば下降するのみ」といつも自分に言い聞かせながら作為をそぎ落とし、自然のままに作れるようになることを最高の到達点とし日々作陶に励んでいるといったところである。

素地への装飾（変形・透かし彫り・鎬手など）や、釉薬で絵を描くと言った釉彩技法も私オリジナルの作陶スタイルである。

作品も茶陶を中心に鑑賞陶器(壺・皿・陶板)なども手掛けている。

さて話を「都会型の窯元」に戻してこれからの味楽窯を考えてみると、やはり登り窯を焚くことはまず100%無理であろう。

環境問題の点からみてもこの都心部で煙を上げることは許されぬことだと思う。幸いにして高取焼は釉薬物と呼ばれるように多重掛けされた釉薬の変化が特徴である。登り窯でも直接薪の灰が掛からぬように「さや」と呼ばれる専用のケースに納めて焼いていたものだ。

現在窯元で使用しているのはガス窯ではあるが、1200度を超えてから小割の薪を補助口から投げ入れて若干量の灰を回す工夫をしている。これだと煙の量も少なく近隣の迷惑になることも皆無である。また登り窯に比べても非常に効率よく作品が焼きあがるし、いわゆる「焼きムラ」も少ない。まさに「都会型の窯元」に最適である。

焼き物愛好家の中には「登り窯で焼いた作品が一番」との声もあるが、近代的な今の時代では逆にナンセンスであるともいえる。

どうしても登り窯が必要な時は、父14代が手に入れた田舎の土地に登り窯を築きそこで焼成することも考えてはいるが、急を要する事ではないので息子久彰と今後じっくり考えていくつもりだ。福岡はアジア太平洋の玄関口と言う事で、外国からのアクセスも非常に良い。とにかくこの高取の地は交通の便が良く、空港および駅からも近いと言う地の利を生かして「都会型の窯元」を構築していきたいと思う。

今後の作品展開に於いても「海外向けの茶陶」

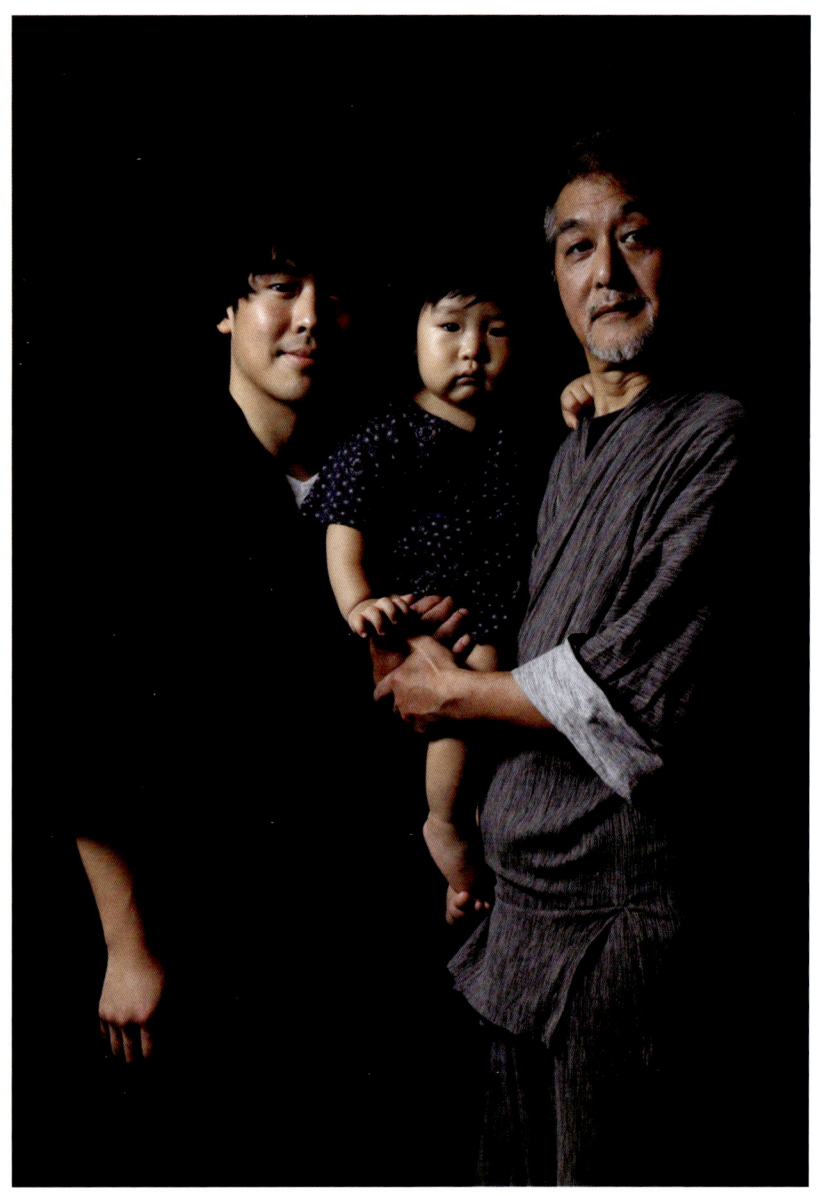

**Miraku Kamei XV, Hisaaki Kamei, Akihito Kamei. (2021)**　|　15代亀井味楽、亀井久彰、亀井彰人(令和3年)

It seems that he will stay on this technique and improve the quality for a while.

We are a father and a son; however, we are eternal competitors. I like to see my son as a rival to improve our skills synergistically.

Lastly, Hisaaki and his wife have a son. I am not sure if my grandson is going to inherit the future XVII, or not. He is simply adorable. He is three years old now. When he comes back from day care, he comes straight into my studio. He sits next to me, creates something out of clay, and dusts my wheels.

His training has already begun. It is so reassuring. Of course, there is no certainty what the future holds for this young child. I cannot help but imagine that he will look at my back and my son's back and become a wonderful potter.

People say that half of the existing jobs will be replaced by AI or robots in the future. Our family will continue to do our best to keep learning, improving, and boosting Takatori Miraku-gama. We will preserve our "handwork" and convey its magnificence to future generations.

も視野に入れながら作品のバリエーションも徐々に増やしていきたいところである。

息子16代嗣久彰は、高取の伝統釉薬である「藁白釉」を独自の方法でブルーに発色させるという新たな手法を生み出している。

これに「極光釉」・「久彰ブルー」と言う呼び名を付けて作品展開をしているが、若い方や外国の方にも評価が高く、当分の間はこの手法での更なる品質向上を目指しているようである。

親子でありながらも永遠のライバル。息子とは常にそう言ったスタンスでお互いのスキルアップを図っていきたいと思う。

最後になるが、息子夫婦に男児が授けられた。将来の17代として窯元の仕事を継ぐ、継がないは別として、やはり孫は可愛いものである。

3歳になるが保育園から帰ってくると真っ先に私の工房に入ってくる。傍らで粘土を巧みに使い何か作ったり、轆轤周りに削り土が溜まっていると掃除してくれたりもする。もう修行は始まっている。

とても頼もしい光景である。この幼い子が将来どのような道を目指すかはまだまだ分からないが、私の背中そして息子の背中を見ながら一人前の陶工に育ってくれることを夢見てやまない。

現在ある仕事の内の約半分がAIやロボットに取って代わる時代が来るとよく言われるが、今の「手仕事」の素晴らしさを窯元家族皆で後世に残すべく、これからもより一層の精進を続け、「高取焼味楽窯」を盛り立てていきたい。

# Tested By Fire:
# The 400 Year Takatori Tradition

## Andrew L. Maske

WHAT DOES IT MEAN TO BE BORN THE heir to a traditional artistic family in Japan?

It means inheriting a name, an occupation, and an artistic style, of course, but it also includes inheriting the family property, workshop, tools, art collections, as well as a trove of documents handed down from past generations, some of which may be secret. One also inherits social standing, relationships with the community, and even clientele. In one way, these assets are a huge boon in comparison to the assets available to the typical budding artist, but they can also be a tremendous burden for a craftsperson/artist whose primary desire is to be independent and creative. The lineage carried on by the Takatori potter Kamei Miraku XV and his son Hisaaki is one that has seen many twists and turns, and many challenges and triumphs over the past four hundred years.

The founder of Takatori ware was brought from Korea by Kuroda Nagamasa (1568-1623), one of Japan's formidable warlords. The potter and his family were among thousands of Koreans who came to Japan during and after the tragic and horrific invasions of Korea ordered by Toyotomi Hideyoshi between 1592 and 1598. Hideyoshi's objective was to conquer Ming China, but he made his attack through the Korean peninsula, with his troops slaughtering multitudes and taking huge numbers of captives as they went.

The first Takatori potter's journey to Japan seems to have been a rare case in which a Korean was not a captive, but instead agreed to go to Japan to work. Not only was he allowed to take his wife and son with him, but family records indicate that he was offered a generous stipend and other support. After arriving in Japan, the promises made were fulfilled: he was provided with a stipend and given assistants to help him establish ceramic production. He was also given samurai status and with it the Japanese name Hachizō. From that time on, Hachizō and his descendants made ceramics as official craftsmen of the Kuroda domain for over 250 years.

As an official potter that was now part of the samurai class, Hachizō also had the right to a family name. Since the first workshop and kiln was located at the base of Mount Takatori, records state that Lord Nagamasa ordered the family be given the name "Takatori" with one character changed to commemorate its roots in Korea. The Takatori potters worked at the lord's pleasure, and on rare occasions received orders directly from the lord himself. However, most of the details of production, such as gathering and processing raw materials as well as the distribution of finished products, was executed by the *han*, the domain administration made up of fellow members of the warrior class who served and supported the Kuroda family. As members of the warrior class themselves (albeit probably without military training) the Takatori potters, like most other samurai, had an assured income stipend. At the same time, they also had to follow the *han* administration's

# ４００年の窯火を絶やすことなく引き継がれる高取焼の伝統

## アンドルー・L・マスキ

高取焼は、16世紀末、太閤豊臣秀吉による壬申の倭乱（文禄・慶長の役）の際、武将黒田長政が日本に連れてきた朝鮮陶工「八山」（読み方不詳）によって始められた。諸々の古文書によると、八山は他の朝鮮陶工とは異なり、強制的に連行されたのではなく、妻と息子の同伴も許され、黒田領内に地行および士族の身分まで拝領することとなった。

秀吉軍の撤退時、黒田の城はまだ豊前中津にあった。古文書には豊前領内の陶器生産に関する記載はないが、少なくとも八山は陶土薬石を探したと思われる。

慶長5年（1600）、黒田長政は徳川家康より筑前国に52万3千石（523,000石）拝領し、福岡に城を築いた。その後まもなく八山は筑前の最東端に窯を築いたと思われる。窯は前の豊前領に最も近い地点であったから豊前でやきものにふさわしい粘土を見つけた裏付けになると考えられる。

この最初の窯は現在の福岡県直方市に近い鷹取山の麓にあった。古文書によると長政公は八山に苗字帯刀を許し、陶工は「高取八蔵」と名乗るようになった。鷹取の「鷹」を「高」に変えた理由は、「高麗」（朝鮮）出身であることを示すためであった。

高取八蔵とその息子である八郎右衛門は鷹取山に築いた小規模の窯で日常陶器と少量の茶陶の製作を続けたが、慶長19年（1614）からは、近くにある内ヶ磯窯で多くの弟子とともに陶器の大量生産に転換した。この窯の茶盌や水指は、江戸時代初期に京都の三条通に並んでいた茶道具店の遺跡から発掘されており、17世紀前半、内ヶ磯窯の高取焼は文化人の眼を引いたと考えられる。

黒田家二代当主である忠之候は、高取焼を大量生産のための窯から御用窯へと転換させた。特に茶道具の中でも最も格の高い茶入の製作を命じ、このために窯場を白旗山に移動させたのである。忠之候は、大名茶人であった小堀遠州から最も流行していた茶入の色、形状、装飾など、茶入の詳細を学ばせるため、八蔵と八郎右衛門を京都に派遣した。遠州の推薦によって、この時期から高取焼の茶入が茶人たちの間で有名になったのである。今でも高取焼は主に茶道具、特に茶入で名が知られている。

1716年、今回は、福岡の黒田城から西2、3キロの場所に新しい窯と工房が建てられた。このころまでには、高取家は4軒の分家に分かれていた。藩では再開された生産を監督、促進する正式な陶芸監視官を配置した。さらに2年後の1718年、500メートルほど離れた丘に、一般販売用の陶器を作る窯が設置された。これらの陶工たちは士族の身分はなかったが、黒田藩から俸給を受け取り、原料供給は藩に依存していた。さらに彼らは、最終製品のほとんどを藩の役人に提出し、商人や卸売りへの販売を任せていた。これらの窯は高取焼の工房/窯の西側に位置していたので、この窯が設置された丘

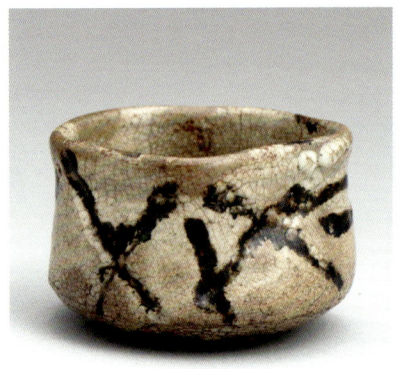
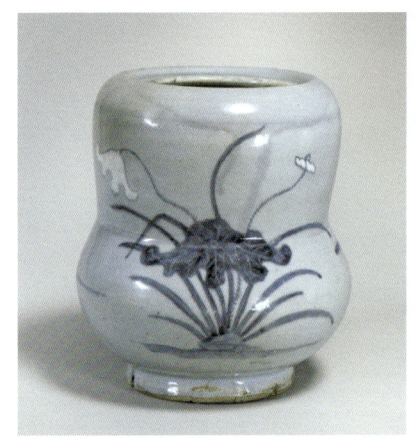
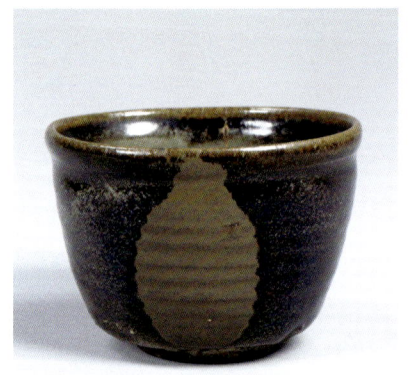
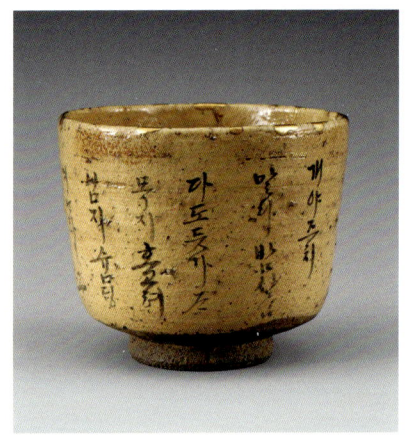
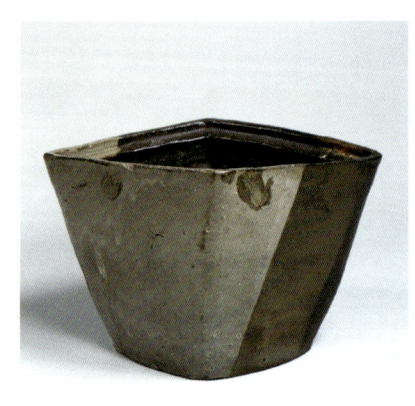

Examples of 17th century ceramics: Karatsu (Kyushu National Museum), Arita (Tokyo National Museum), Satsuma (Tokyo National Museum), Hagi (National Museum of Korea), Agano (Tokyo National Museum).

17世紀の陶器: 唐津焼（九州国立博物館）、有田焼（東京国立博物館）、薩摩焼（東京国立博物館）、萩焼（国立中央博物館、韓国）、上野焼（東京国立博物館）

directions about what types of ceramics and how many to make.

In early 17th century Japan, the most valuable ceramics were those made for use in *chanoyu*, also known as Japanese tea ceremony. Daimyo warlords in western Japan saw the importation of Korean potters as a chance to have tea ceramics made in their own provinces. Korean potters founded numerous ceramic types, including Karatsu, Arita, Hagi, Satsuma, Agano, and other varieties, and their expertise revolutionized ceramics-making at existing production areas throughout the rest of Japan.

The earliest ceramics made by Hachizō and his assistants for the Kuroda domain appear to have been made mostly for sale, since numerous examples have been recovered from the sites of 17th century tea ceramic shops in Kyoto and Osaka. From the 1620s, however, the Kuroda lord himself began to spur the potters to make outstanding unique pieces such as tea caddies according to the aesthetic standards of the most prominent tea master of the time. What an honor it must have been for Hachizō to be chosen to make ceramics specifically for his lord. The Kuroda domain in northern Kyushu was the seventh richest in Japan, making Lord Nagamasa a powerful and influential person indeed.

When Kuroda Nagamasa died in 1623, Hachizō apparently saw an opportunity to extract himself from the obligation to work for the Kuroda and petitioned the new lord, Kuroda Tadayuki, to be allowed return

は西皿山、高取の陶工たちがいる場所は東山と呼ばれるようになった。

西皿山と東山は隣接しており、同じ作陶ということから、両地域では婚姻関係が結ばれ、必要な場合にはお互いに男子を後継ぎとして養子に迎えるという関係になった。高取の陶工は、窯再構築の際に西皿山の窯を借りたり、東山の窯の余分な空間を埋めるために、西皿山の職人が作った実用的な陶器を焼いたりした。19世紀の半ばごろまでには、両地域間での技術や方法はかなり重複する部分が多くなっていた。

1854年、徳川将軍は鎖国を解き、1868年には明治維新、1871年には明治政府の行政改革「廃藩置県」で黒田藩が廃止された。藩の支援を失って、東山の陶工たちは徐々に仕事をあきらめ、1910年までにはすべての分家でも作陶は中止された。

それとは逆に、西皿山の陶工たちは1世紀も続いた旧い黒田藩の制約から自由になり、高取様式を含む生産を拡張していった。以前にも藩に求められなかった残りの陶器を販売することが許されていたため、西皿山の陶工たちは商売という仕組みを知っていた。これによりやきもの生産は財政的に持続可能となったのである。

西皿山には、1718年に小石原からやってきた集団の一員である、中川という姓を持つ家族が居住していた。この家族は明治時代まで西皿山で作陶を続けたが、途中系統の断絶を防ぐために中川家が東山の高取家の高取市朗有貞の息子、和平周規を養子として迎えた。これで中川家と高取家との血縁関係が築かれた。

今日存在する味楽の家系は、13代亀井味楽(1883-1956)(中川弥太郎として生まれる)から始まる。1903年、姓を亀井に変更し、曾祖父から未楽という名前を取り、一字を変更して味楽とした。表千家の茶人から促され、13代味楽は作陶技術を磨き、さまざまな茶陶、特に茶入れの制作に熟練していった。13代には1871年の廃藩置県によって藩の支援を失った高取の混乱状態から道を切り開いた功績があるといってよいだろう。この期間、高取の陶工たちは茶盌から排水管まですべてを作らざるを得なかったのであった。彼は2つの世界大戦を生き延びただけでなく、茶道の流派の家元達が作陶の様式や陶工の評判に多大な影響を及ぼすという新しい環境に対し対応できるよう、息子や孫にやきものの技術を教えた。

14代亀井味楽(1931-2014)にも、戦わなくてはならない挑戦があった。第二次世界大戦後、祖父である13代味楽から工房を受け継いだ14代は、戦後の荒廃したインフラストラクチャや蔓延する貧困などを生き抜く必要があった。やっと経済が回り始めたころ、彼は日本に戻ってきた繁栄にうまく乗ろうとした他の高取様式の陶芸家たちの台頭という形の障害と向き合わなくてはならなくなった。これらの障害にもかかわらず、14代味楽は、自分の技能を磨きつつ、有名な陶芸コンペティションでの賞の獲得や、茶道の家元だけでなく地元の文化人や政治家との関係を築き上げることにより、自身の評判を築き上げていった。14代は1980年代を通じて経済的バブルに乗り、1990年代には、はじけたバブルとその後を体験した。主要な陶芸コンペティションに参加することで、茶陶を超えるものや展示のみを目的としたより大きな作品の制作も手掛けていたが、14代味楽の茶陶の中でも特に美しい水指を作る技術は素晴らしいものであった。引退

with his family to Korea. Lord Tadayuki, however, regarded the request as insubordination and not only refused, but exiled Hachizō and his son Hachirōemon to a backwater of the province. With their stipend suspended, the family was left to support themselves with whatever they could make and sell for a period of several years.

Unlike his father, Lord Kuroda Tadayuki seems to have had a rather mercurial character, reacting emotionally to challenges in ways that were sometimes not in his best interest. He was also, however, an enthusiastic practitioner of *chanoyu*. Because of this, he eventually reinstated his valuable craftsmen and set them to work making tea caddies that he hoped would catch the eye of Kobori Enshū, the most respected tea master of the seventeenth century. Enshū designed some of Japan's most famous gardens and architectural structures of the early Edo period as well.

The work of Hachizō and Hachirōemon so impressed Lord Tadayuki that he sent the two potters to Kyoto to receive instruction directly from Kobori Enshū about the finer points of tea caddy aesthetics. In most tea gatherings, the tea caddy *(chaire)*, a tiny vessel with its own ivory lid and silk brocade pouch, was the most valuable utensil on display. Hachizō's tea caddy skills attained a level of mastery that compelled Tadayuki to commission pieces to offer to the shogun in Edo. From this point on, tea caddies became Takatori ware's claim to fame, and remain so in the tea world today. Takatori Hachizō and Kuroda Tadayuki both passed away in the same year, 1654.

Lord Tadayuki's son, Kuroda Mitsuyuki, was also an ardent patron of the arts and had Hachizō's second son, Sadaaki, set up a workshop on the castle grounds in Fukuoka. There, he and his son Hachiro demonstrated various pottery techniques for the entertainment of the lord, who could make his own instructions directly to the potters. After adopting a son from a collateral domain, Mitsuyuki retired but continued to participate in his various artistic activities, often joined by his adopted son, Kuroda Tsunamasa.

In fact, Kuroda Tsunamasa, who became lord in 1688, was an even more enthusiastic amateur artist than his father, taking lessons from the prominent painter Kano Yasunobu. Furthermore, according to records, he personally painted designs on Takatori ceramics. Even more surprising is that Lord Tsunamasa regularly invited Takatori Hachiro, who was around the same age, to go hunting with him and singled him out for special gifts, including a painting in his own hand on rare paper, a musket, and financial bonuses.

This good fortune came to a crashing end in 1704, when the domain suddenly ordered the potters to cease production immediately and dismantle their kiln and workshop. Apparently, the potters had, with their lord's encouragement, accepted an order to make pieces for the shogun's administrator for the port of Nagasaki. To receive an order from such a powerful person was an honor for the domain as well as for the Takatori potters, but the craftsmen failed to satisfy the administrator's demand, shaming the domain. Just as had happened eighty years before, the potters angered their lord and were disgraced as a result. This time, a full thirteen years passed before they could resume ceramics-making. When production finally resumed, Lord Tsunamasa was no longer living and Takatori Hachiro had retired.

In 1716, a new kiln and workshop were built, this time in a location a mile or two west of the Kuroda castle at Fukuoka. By this time the Takatori family had expanded to four branches. The domain established a

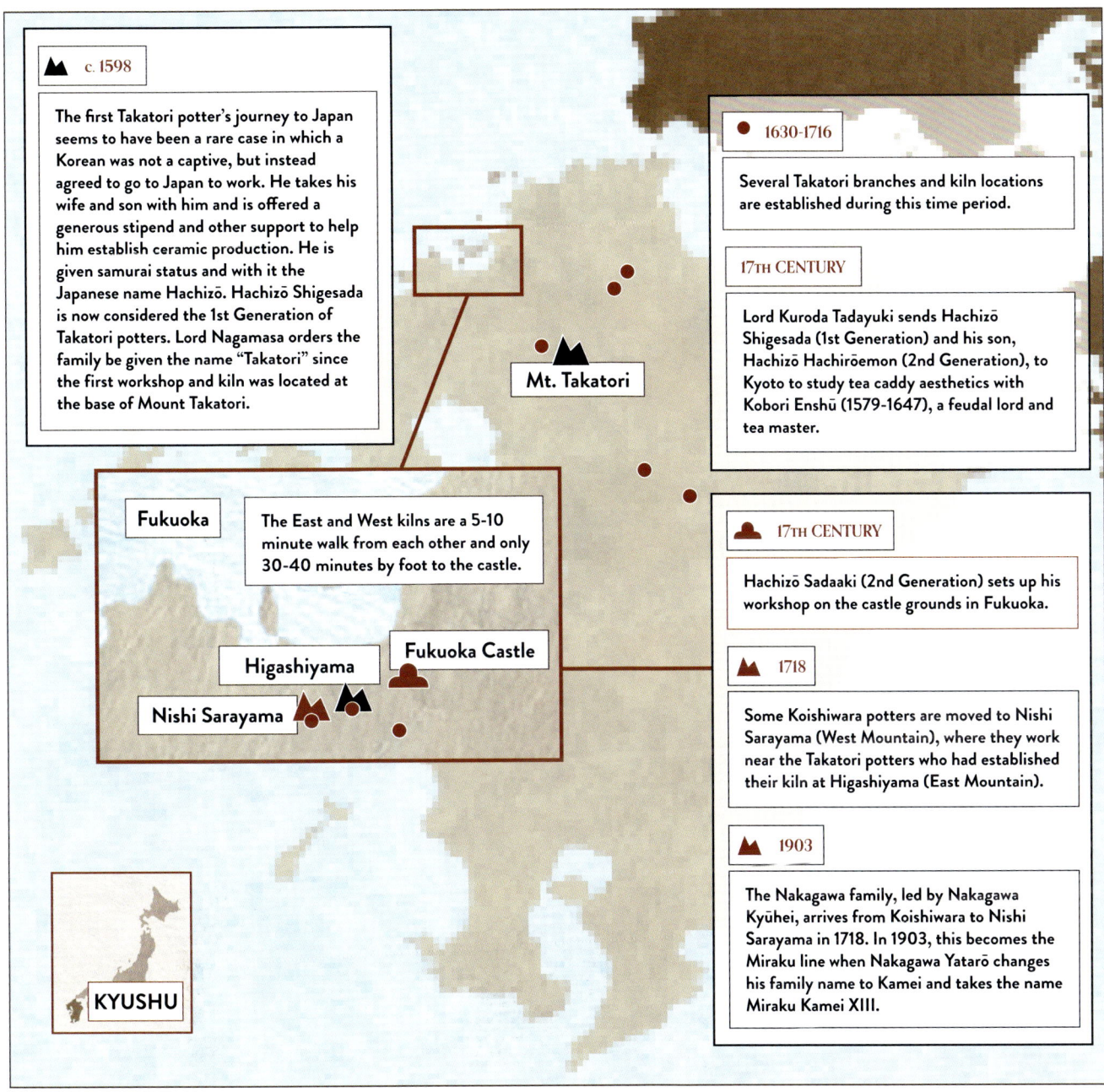

**c. 1598**

The first Takatori potter's journey to Japan seems to have been a rare case in which a Korean was not a captive, but instead agreed to go to Japan to work. He takes his wife and son with him and is offered a generous stipend and other support to help him establish ceramic production. He is given samurai status and with it the Japanese name Hachizō. Hachizō Shigesada is now considered the 1st Generation of Takatori potters. Lord Nagamasa orders the family be given the name "Takatori" since the first workshop and kiln was located at the base of Mount Takatori.

**1630-1716**

Several Takatori branches and kiln locations are established during this time period.

**17TH CENTURY**

Lord Kuroda Tadayuki sends Hachizō Shigesada (1st Generation) and his son, Hachizō Hachirōemon (2nd Generation), to Kyoto to study tea caddy aesthetics with Kobori Enshū (1579-1647), a feudal lord and tea master.

Mt. Takatori

Fukuoka

The East and West kilns are a 5-10 minute walk from each other and only 30-40 minutes by foot to the castle.

**17TH CENTURY**

Hachizō Sadaaki (2nd Generation) sets up his workshop on the castle grounds in Fukuoka.

**1718**

Some Koishiwara potters are moved to Nishi Sarayama (West Mountain), where they work near the Takatori potters who had established their kiln at Higashiyama (East Mountain).

Higashiyama

Fukuoka Castle

Nishi Sarayama

**1903**

The Nakagawa family, led by Nakagawa Kyūhei, arrives from Koishiwara to Nishi Sarayama in 1718. In 1903, this becomes the Miraku line when Nakagawa Yatarō changes his family name to Kamei and takes the name Miraku Kamei XIII.

KYUSHU

Annotated map of region | 地図（注釈付き）

後、14代は「又生庵」という佛名を使用した。

　現在の15代味楽は先祖の恩恵を受けたが、自身の課題にも取り組んでいる。ここ数十年で茶の湯に対する興味が減り、それに伴って茶入、茶盌、水指などの美しいけれども高価な茶道具の需要も減っている。そして不景気により、芸術品を購入するための日本人一般の自由に使える収入の水準にも影響がでている。

　15代亀井味楽は、これらの課題を様々な方法で乗り越えようとしている。15代は茶道界の人脈を広げ、技術および形状を多様化させている。彼は14代が開発してきた地元の人脈を継続させ、イベントを開催したり、一般向けの陶芸教室も開催している。また自分の息子である16代となる亀井久彰にも独自の釉薬の開発を促している。これは極光釉（オーロラ釉）と呼ばれるもので、鷹取山のふもとにあった

full-time ceramics overseer to supervise and facilitate the revived production. In addition, two years later, in 1718, kilns producing wares for sale to the general public were set up on a hill only a quarter mile away. These potters lacked samurai status but still worked for the Kuroda since they received salaries and relied on the domain to supply their raw materials. Moreover, these potters submitted most of their finished pieces to the *han* administrators for sale to merchants and wholesalers. Since these kilns were located west of the Takatori workshop/kiln, the hill where they were located became known as West Mountain, while the Takatori potters' area was referred to as East Mountain.

Because of their close proximity and their shared profession, families from East and West intermarried and provided adoptive male heirs to each other when necessary. The Takatori potters borrowed one of the West Mountain kilns at times that their own kiln was being rebuilt, and used utilitarian items made by West Mountain craftsmen to fill extra space in their kiln in the East. By the middle of the nineteenth century, there was considerable overlap in the skills and methods of the two areas.

In 1854, the shogun's government reluctantly gave in to foreign demands that Japan open itself more widely to the outside world, and in 1871 the domains were abolished, including that of the Kuroda. With the loss of domain support, the East Mountain potters gradually abandoned the ceramics profession, and all branches had ceased to make ceramics by 1910.

In contrast, the West Mountain potters found themselves freed from the old Kuroda restrictions that had existed for more than a century and expanded their production to include more Takatori-style wares. Since they previously had been allowed to

sell any remaining wares not claimed by the domain, the West Mountain potters were also somewhat familiar with commercial enterprise, and this helped to make their production financially sustainable.

One West Mountain family by the name of Nakagawa was interested in focusing on decorative ceramics such as vases. This family was one of the original group that had come from Koishiwara in 1718. Moreover, it had a forebear who had been adopted from a branch of the Takatori family headed by Takatori Ichirō Arisada. Ichirō Arisada's son Wahei was adopted into the Nakagawa family, creating a blood connection to the Takatori family that inspired later generations to passionately pursue the production of Takatori tea ceramics.

The Miraku line of potters as it exists today was established by Kamei Miraku XIII (1883-1956), born Nakagawa Yatarō. In 1903, he changed his family name to Kamei, taking the name Miraku from his great-grandfather but changing one character. Encouraged by a master of the Omotesenke tea school, Miraku XIII honed his fine potting skills, becoming adept at a wide range of tea ceramics, but particularly skillful at tea caddies. He can be credited with negotiating a path forward from the rather chaotic situation of Takatori production following the loss of domain support in 1871 during which Takatori potters made everything from rice bowls to drainpipes. He not only overcame the challenges of two world wars but prepared his son to succeed in a new environment in which the leaders of tea schools would come to have tremendous influence on the reputation of ceramic styles and makers.

Kamei Miraku XIV (1931-2014) had his own challenges to confront. After taking over the workshop from his grandfather Miraku XIII following the end of World War II, he had to struggle to

**Circa 1598**

The Korean potter Palsan, his wife, and their infant son are brought to Japan by the warlord, Kuroda Nagamasa. Once in Japan, the family is made official craftsmen and receive the name Takatori.

**Early 1600s**

After a period of making commercial wares (1600-1630), the Takatori potters transition to making ceramics only for the Kuroda lord and his administration.

**1630-1716**

The Takatori kiln location changes several times and several Takatori branch families are established, continuing to work together.

**1718**

Utilitarian pottery production had also begun in Koishiwara in the 1660s. In 1718, some Koishiwara potters move to Nishi Sarayama (West Mountain), where they worked near the Takatori potters who had established their kiln at Higashiyama (East Mountain) in 1716. The Nakagawa family, led by **Nakagawa Kyūhei**, was among those who arrived from Koishiwara to Nishi Sarayama.

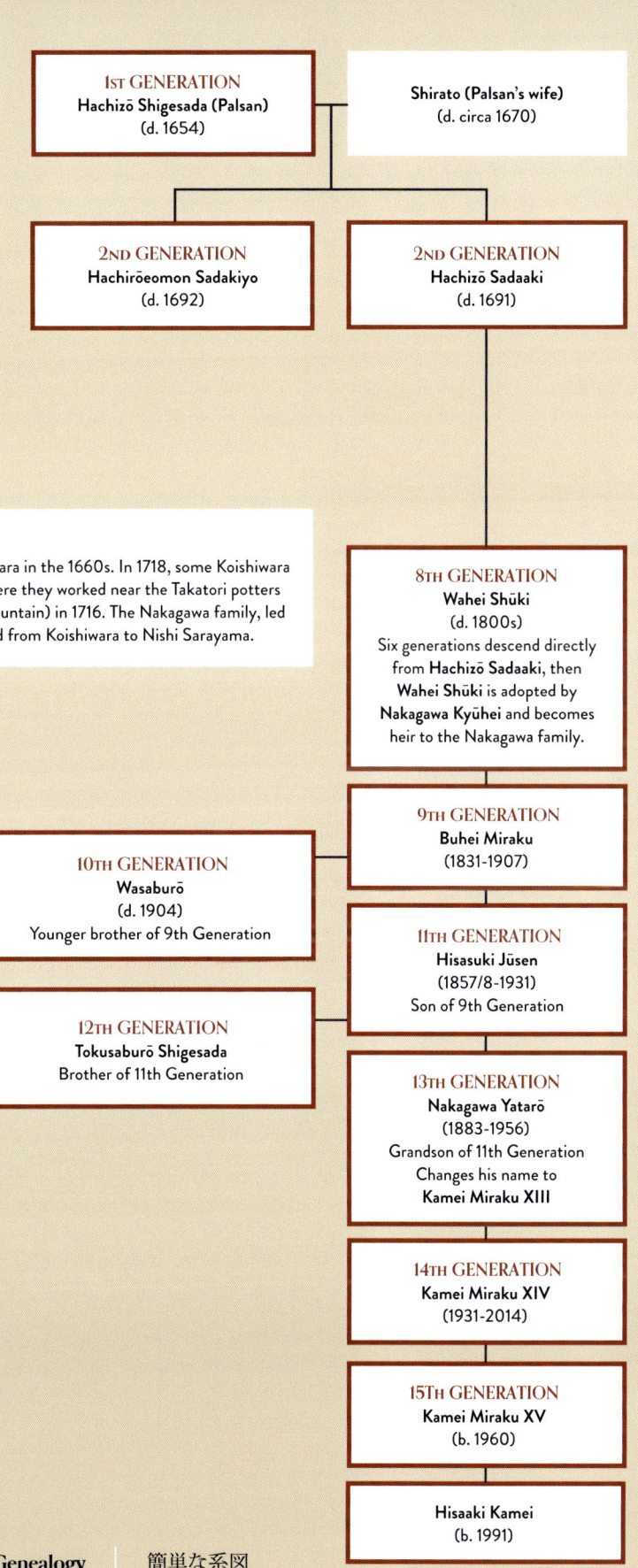

**1st GENERATION**
**Hachizō Shigesada (Palsan)**
(d. 1654)

**Shirato (Palsan's wife)**
(d. circa 1670)

**2nd GENERATION**
**Hachirōeomon Sadakiyo**
(d. 1692)

**2nd GENERATION**
**Hachizō Sadaaki**
(d. 1691)

**8th GENERATION**
**Wahei Shūki**
(d. 1800s)
Six generations descend directly from **Hachizō Sadaaki**, then **Wahei Shūki** is adopted by **Nakagawa Kyūhei** and becomes heir to the Nakagawa family.

**9th GENERATION**
**Buhei Miraku**
(1831-1907)

**10th GENERATION**
**Wasaburō**
(d. 1904)
Younger brother of 9th Generation

**11th GENERATION**
**Hisasuki Jūsen**
(1857/8-1931)
Son of 9th Generation

**12th GENERATION**
**Tokusaburō Shigesada**
Brother of 11th Generation

**13th GENERATION**
**Nakagawa Yatarō**
(1883-1956)
Grandson of 11th Generation
Changes his name to
**Kamei Miraku XIII**

**14th GENERATION**
**Kamei Miraku XIV**
(1931-2014)

**15th GENERATION**
**Kamei Miraku XV**
(b. 1960)

**Hisaaki Kamei**
(b. 1991)

**A Brief Genealogy**　　簡単な系図

survive in the climate of Japan's post-war rebuilding of devastated infrastructure and widespread poverty. Then, just as the economy began to gather steam, new hurdles presented themselves as other Takatori-style potters emerged to take advantage of the country's returning prosperity. Despite these obstacles, Miraku XIV worked hard to not only refine his craft, but to strengthen his reputation by entering and winning prizes at prominent ceramics competitions and cultivating relationships with the leaders of tea schools, as well as local cultural and political figures. He rode the economic bubble through the 1980s and experienced the crash and its aftermath in the 1990s. While his participation in major ceramics competitions required him to expand beyond tea ceramics to also create large

vessels intended only for display, Miraku XIV was particularly skillful at creating beautiful tea ceremony water containers (*mizusashi*). After his retirement, he took the Buddhist name Yūshōan.

The current generation, Miraku XV, has reaped the benefits of those who went before him, but has to confront his own set of challenges. Interest in the practice of *chanoyu* has been declining in recent decades, and with it the demand for the beautiful yet expensive ceramic utensils such as tea caddies, tea bowls, and *mizusashi* (water containers). The economic downturn has also impacted Japanese people's level of disposable income available for purchasing art in general.

Miraku XV has responded to these challenges in various ways. He has worked to broaden his family's contacts in the world of Tea, and has diversified

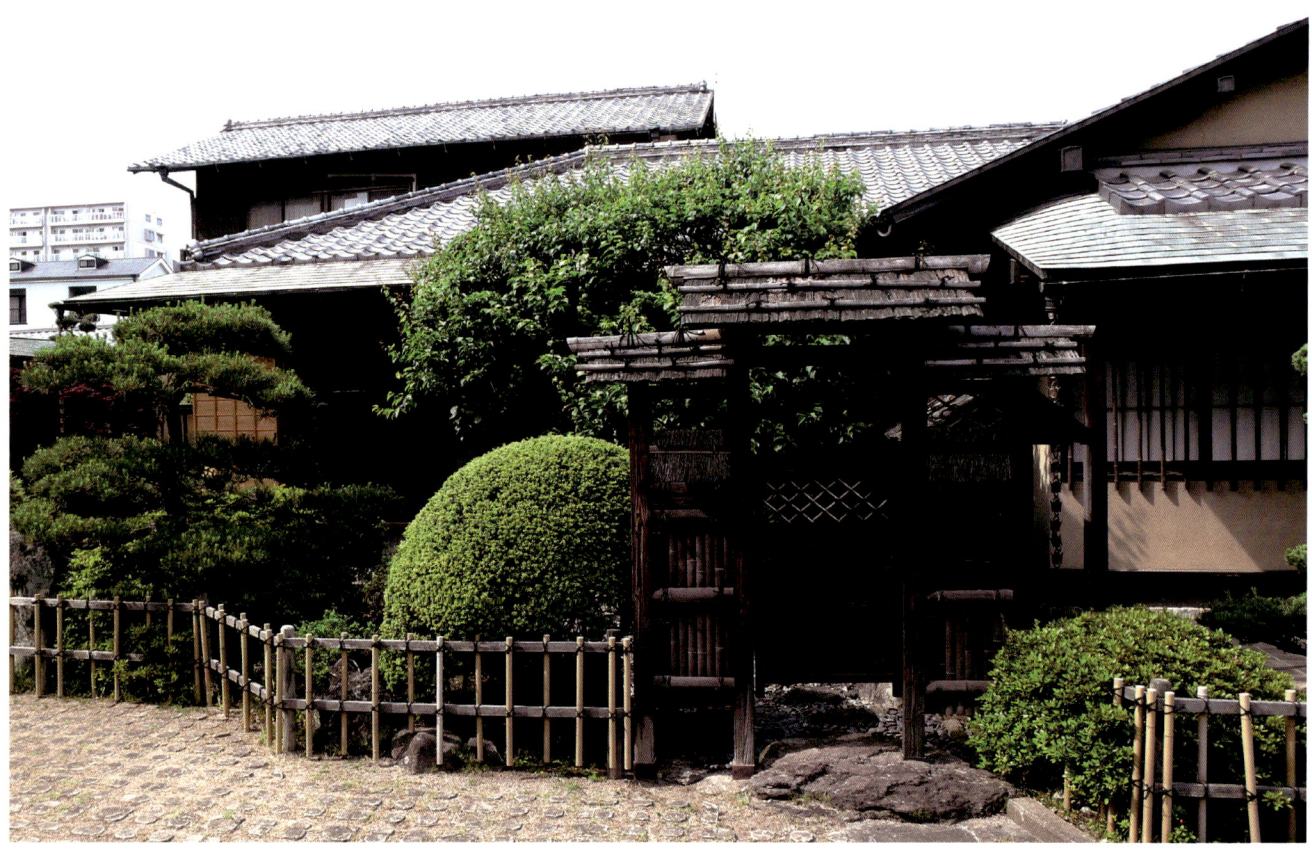

**The Kamei home, kiln, and museum are nestled in what is now a busy urban area of Fukuoka, Japan.**

現在、亀井味楽の自宅、窯、博物館は、福岡市内のにぎやかな都市部に位置している。

最初の高取窯からの作品の釉薬に似ている。

　15代味楽は作品に向き合う上で、陶器の形状への焦点を失うことなく、高取の土を用いた彫刻の可能性を拡大しようとしている。15代は装飾的な持ち手、突起、その他の熟練を要する細工などの彫刻のような細部を作り上げ、それを磨き上げることでこの可能性を広げてきた。また、どの先祖より多くの透彫を取り入れ、その役割を拡大してきた。彼は多分、透彫を茶碗の高台に使用した最初の陶工であろう。

　先人とは異なり、15代は自身の作品を包括的に見つめ、さまざまな釉薬と陶器の形状の物理的な構成との間に生まれるニュアンスの流れを見極めることに集中してきた。陶芸家はすべて釉薬が形状にどのような影響を与えるかを考えるが、味楽は組み合わされた釉薬がどのように相互に関連するか、そして彫られ、刻まれた彫刻のような形状の壺にどのように流れるかに着目している。その結果、絶妙な美しさが生まれるのである。

　現在の味楽は2014年以来、日本を超え2年に1度ボストンでの展覧会を行っている。また、アメリカでの講演や実演も実施している。亀井久彰は、アメリカで父親との展覧会のほかにも、フランスおよびカメルーンで講演および展覧を行っている。

　国際的な評判にも関わらず、亀井家の陶芸家たちは、先祖が1718年にやってきた場所に住み、仕事をしている。1970年代の区画制の変更により高層アパートなどが建てられ、市は伝統的な登り窯の使用禁止を決定した。それにもかかわらず、亀井家は移転を拒否し、現代の高取焼の特徴である顕著な釉薬効果および繊細な形状を実現するために必要な強固な制御を実現できるガス窯を使用している。15代味楽がそのエッセイの中で述べているように、亀井家は、「市中の作陶工房」の運営に専念している。結局のところ、日本における陶芸の伝統とは、ただ特定の様式での作陶だけではない。それは、歴史であり、アイデンティティであり、家族を次世代に繋げることによって先祖が実現したことを称える遺産なのである。

　アンドルー・L・マスキ教授は40年以上も高取焼についての研究を続けている。2011年に英語で出版された"Potters and Patrons in Edo Period Japan: Takatori Ware and the Kuroda Domain (高取焼: 福岡の御用やきもの)の日本語版は現在準備中である。

both his techniques and his range of vessel shapes. He continued the community contacts developed by the 14th generation, holding events and leading ceramics classes for members of the public. He encouraged his son, the emerging XVI generation Kamei Hisaaki, to develop his own signature glaze, which he has named *kyokkoyū* (Aurora glaze). This glaze exhibits similarities with the glaze on pieces from the very first Takatori kiln, located at the foot of its namesake mountain, Takatori-yama.

In the development of his craft, Miraku XV has focused on expanding the sculptural possibilities of the fine Takatori clay while still maintaining a focus on vessel shapes. He has done this by developing and refining the modeled details of his vessels such as decorative handles, bosses, and other crafted additions. He has also expanded the role of openwork far beyond any of his predecessors, and is possibly the first to use openwork as decoration on the feet of teabowls.

In a way that differs from his forebears, Miraku XV looks at his works holistically, particularly in assessing the nuances of interaction between various glazes and the physical structures of his ceramic shapes. All ceramic artists think about how glazes will affect their forms, but Miraku pays special attention to how combined glazes interact with each other and how their fluxing and flowing manifest on the incised, carved and molded features on his pots. The results are often exquisite.

The current Miraku has also expanded his connections beyond Japan, holding exhibitions in Boston on a biannual basis since 2014. He has also given lectures and demonstrations in the United States. Hisaaki has lectured and presented his work in both France and Cameroon, and has shown alongside his father in the U.S.

Despite their growing international reputation, the Kamei family potters continue to live and work in the same little neighborhood their forebears came to in 1718. Zoning changes in the 1970s led to the development of high-rise apartment buildings, and the city government eventually decided that the traditional wood-burning climbing kiln could no longer be fired. Nevertheless, the family has resisted relocating, and now fire in a gas kiln which facilitates the close control required to achieve the striking glaze effects and delicate forms that are the hallmarks of contemporary Takatori ware. As Miraku XV states in his essay, for now, the family has dedicated themselves to operating an "urban pottery studio." After all, a Japanese ceramic tradition is much more than simply making ceramics in a particular style. It is a history, an identity, and a heritage that honors the accomplishments of past generations by ensuring the continuity of the family into the future.

*A full history of Takatori ware's Edo period history can be found in Andrew Maske's book,* Potters and Patrons in Edo Period Japan: Takatori Ware and the Kuroda Domain *(Ashgate/Routledge, 2011).*

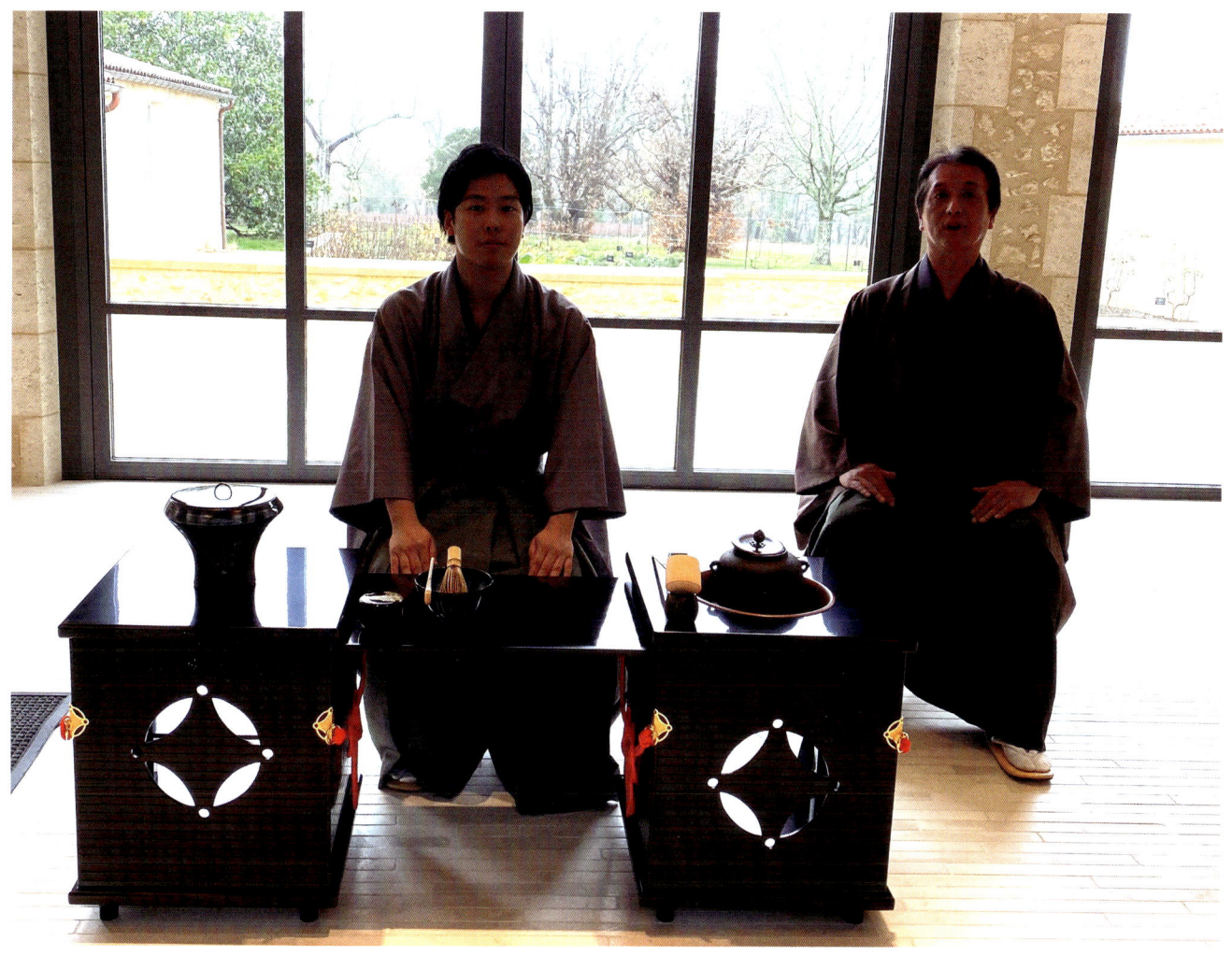

Hisaaki Kamei (left) and Miraku Kamei XV (right) at a chateau in Bordeaux, France. (2021)

亀井久彰(左)および15代亀井味楽(右)、フランス、ボルドーの城にて(令和3年)

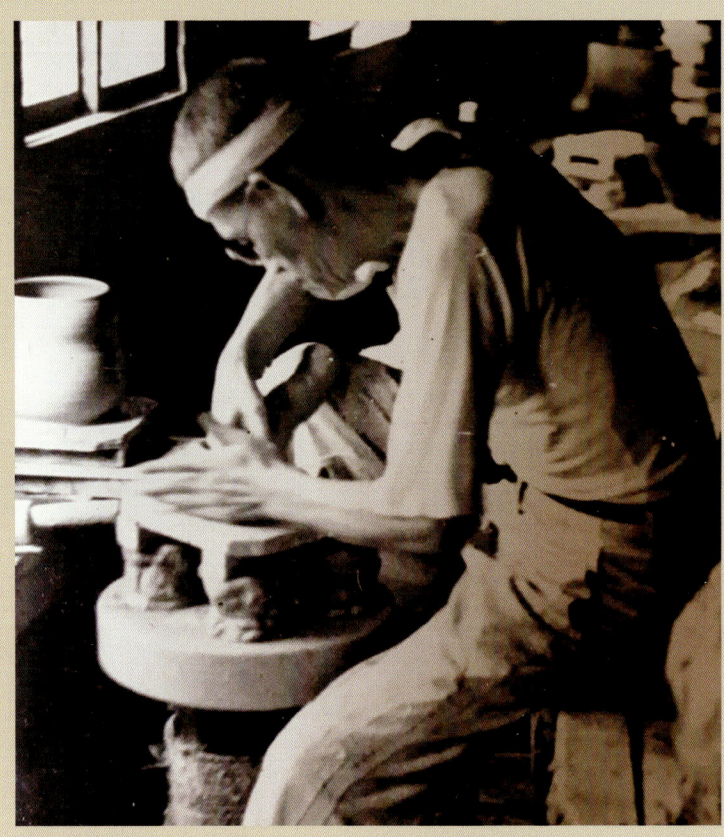

Miraku Kamei XIII
c. 1955

13代亀井味楽
昭和30年頃

# Miraku Kamei XIII
## (1883-1956)

# 13代亀井味楽

In 1903, Miraku Kamei XIII assumed the leadership of the Miraku Kamei kiln. For many years, he had worked as a member of the Fukuoka City Assembly and in other non-pottery related positions. With the encouragement of Iwai Sorin of Omotesenke (tea ceremony school), he decided to devote himself to tea ceramics. He was a highly regarded craftsman who worked exhaustively to revitalize the Takatori ware tradition and was affectionately known as "the Miraku of tea caddies." In 1944, he was recognized by the Ministry of Agriculture and Commerce as a Conservator of the Arts.

1903年、亀井味楽は亀井味楽窯の当主となる。福岡市議会議員を含む陶芸とは無関係の職務に長く従事したが、表千家の岩井宗麟の勧めにより茶陶に専念することとなる。名工として高く評価され、高取焼の伝統の復興に尽力し、「茶入の味楽」と呼ばれる。1944年、農商務省より技術保存者に認定される。

The tea caddy is considered the most prestigious of all of the tea utensils as it stores the *koicha* (thick tea) served in the *goza* (second session) of the tea ceremony.

茶入は茶事における後半部分にあたる後座でふるまわれる濃茶を入れるもので、すべての茶道具の中で最も格の高いものであるとされている。

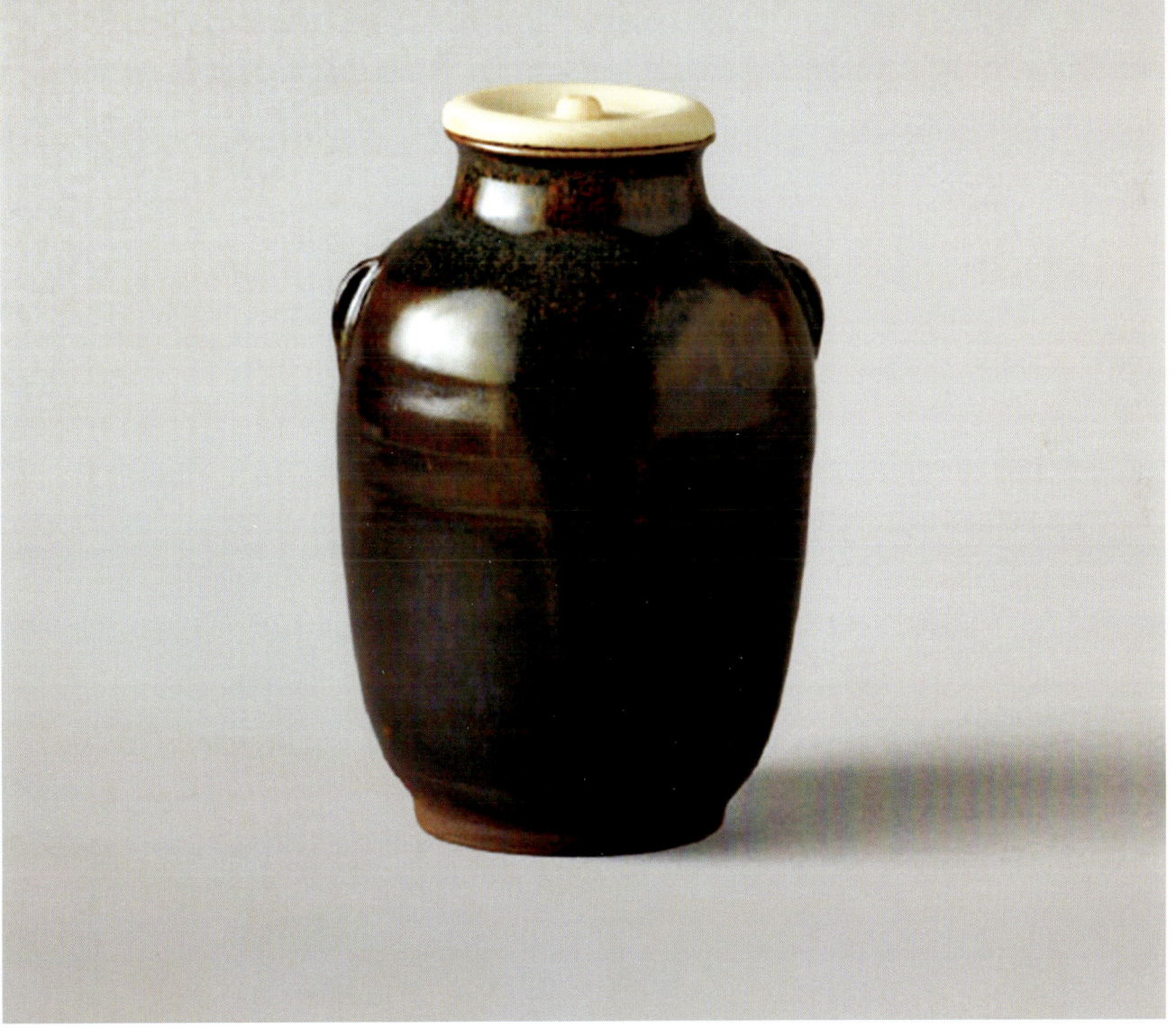

MIRAKU KAMEI XIII
Tea Caddy with Ears
1950s
Thinly applied yellow glaze

13代亀井味楽
耳付撫肩茶入
昭和30年代
黄釉（薄掛け）

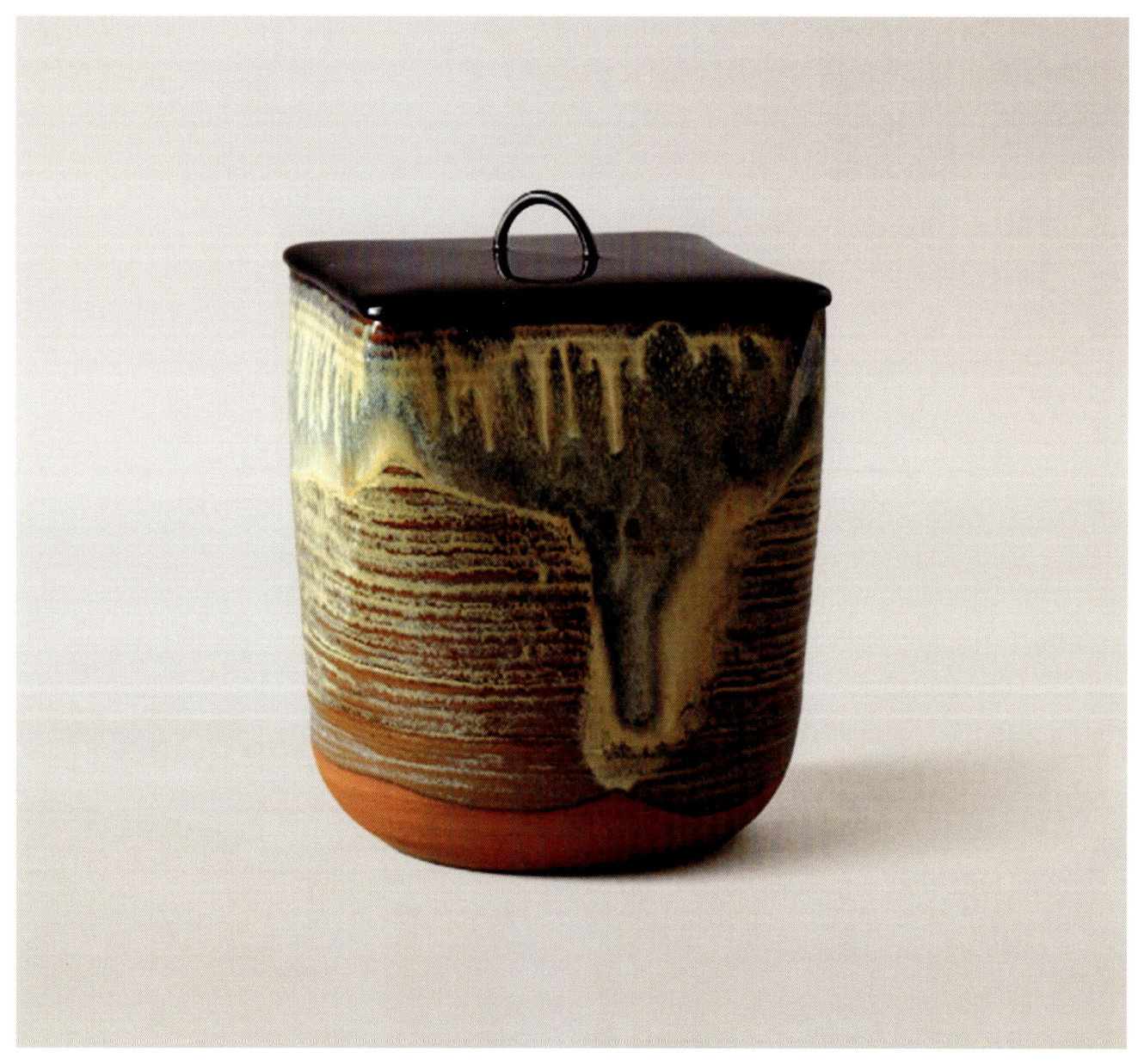

MIRAKU KAMEI XIII　　13代亀井味楽
Water Container with Lacquer Lid　　うるし蓋付水指
1950s　　昭和30年代
White and black glaze　　白釉に黒流し

Miraku Kiln uses the high-quality clay brought to Fukuoka by Lord Kuroda in 1686. It came into their possession at the end of the feudal system and has been used by them exclusively for over 300 years.

味楽窯は、1686年黒田藩主によって福岡に持ち込まれた質の高い土を使用している。この土は江戸時代末期に味楽窯の所有となり、それ以後300年にわたり独占的に使用されている。

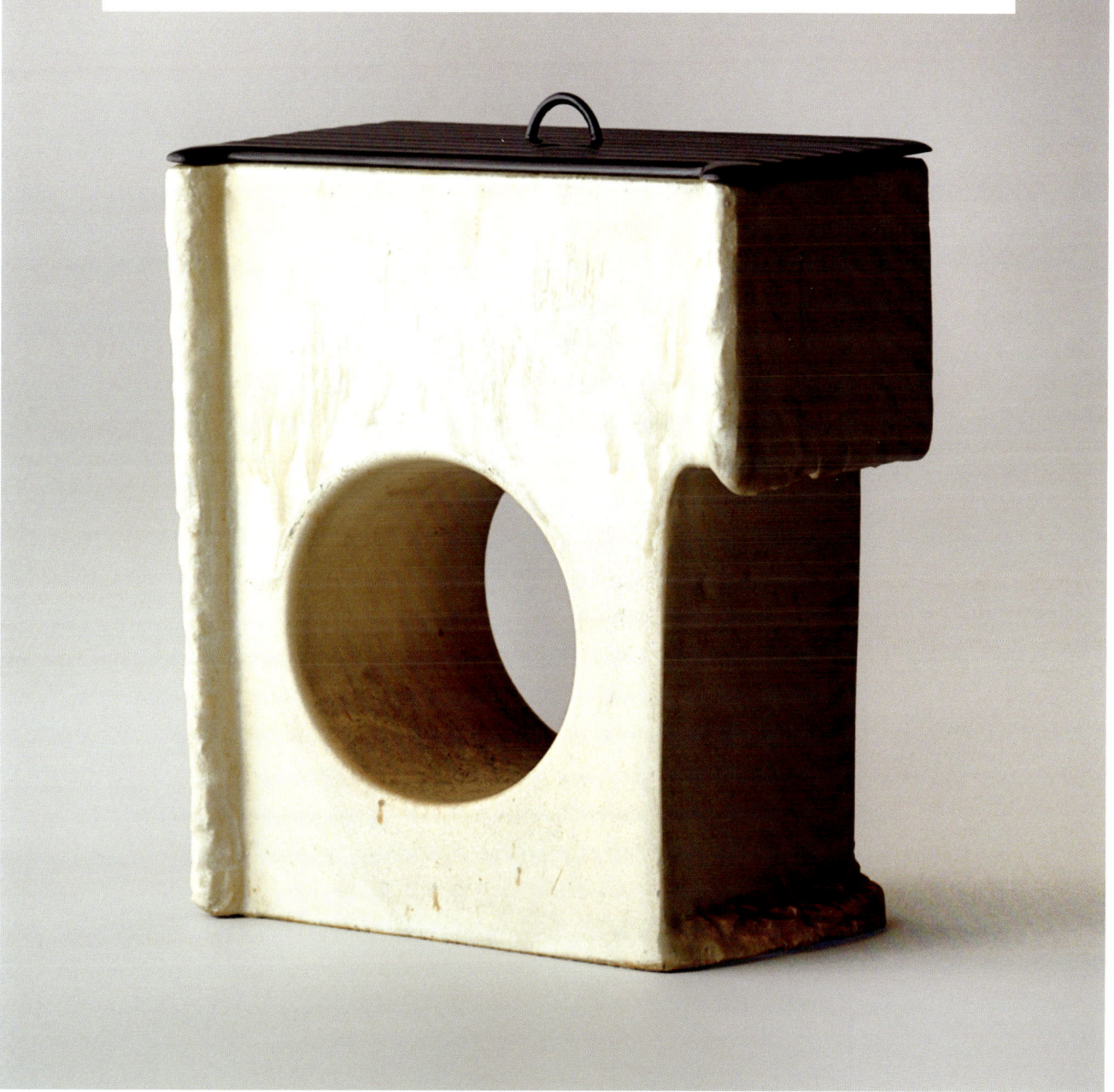

**MIRAKU KAMEI XIII**
**Water Container with Lacquer Lid**
**1950s**
**White glaze**

13代亀井味楽
うるし蓋付水指
昭和30年代
白釉

The seven different glazes of Takatori ware used in the Miraku Kiln are made entirely of natural materials: *kokoyu* (black); *rokushoyu* (green-blue); *furashiyu* (transparent); *oyu* (yellow); *takamiyayu* (green-brown); *dokayu* (copper); and *hakuyu* (white).

高取焼味楽窯で使用される7つの釉薬とは、黒釉(黒色)、緑青釉(緑青色)、布羅志釉(透明)、黄釉(黄色)、高宮釉(緑および茶色)、銅化釉(銅)、白釉(白色)で、天然鉱物のみで作られている。

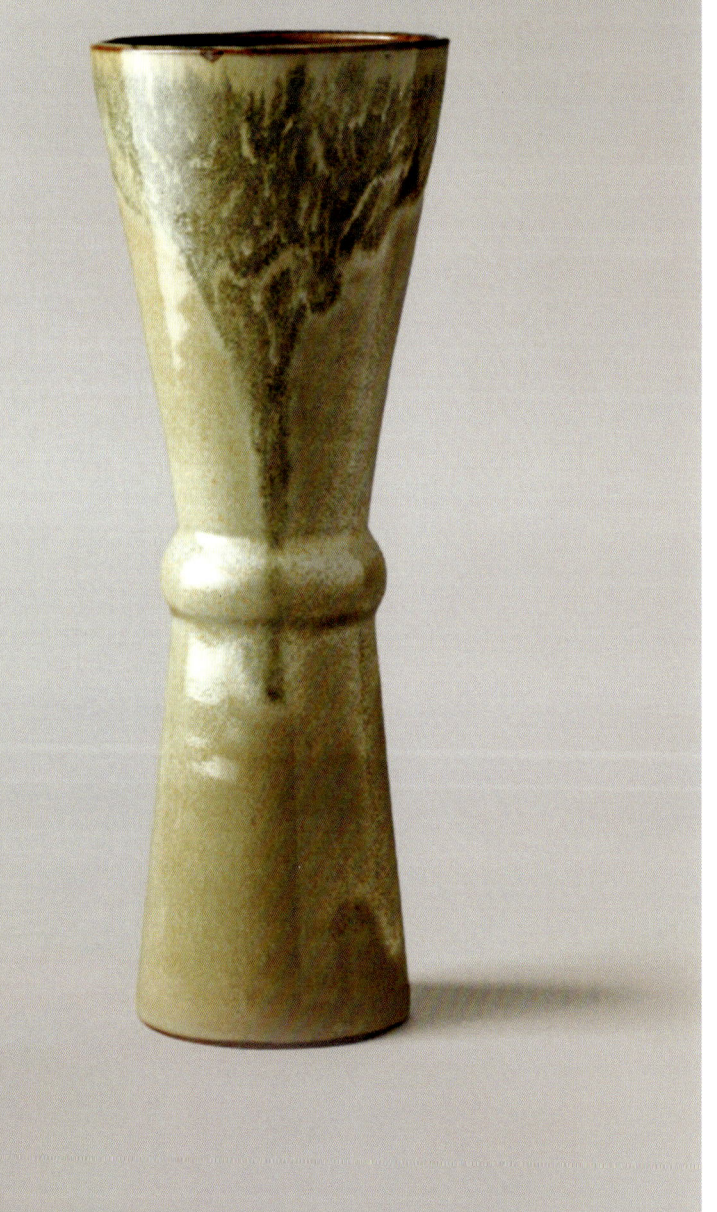

MIRAKU KAMEI XIII
**Pestle-form Flower Vase**
**1950s**
**White and black glaze**

13代亀井味楽
杵型花入
昭和30年代
白釉に黒流し

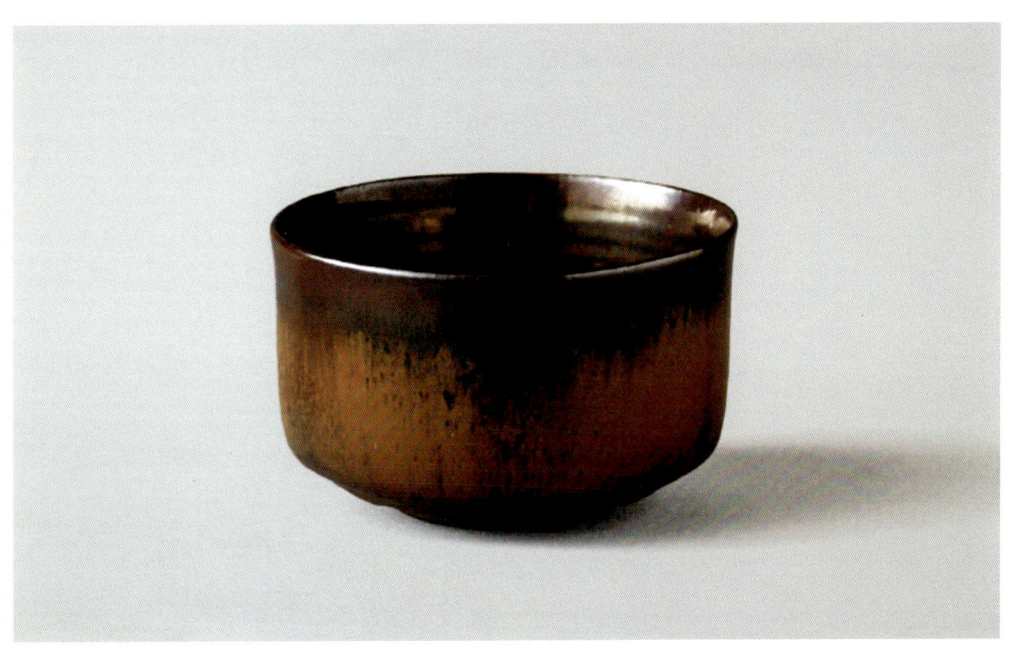

MIRAKU KAMEI XIII | 13代亀井味楽
Tea Bowl | 茶碗
1950s | 昭和30年代
Yellow glaze | 黄釉

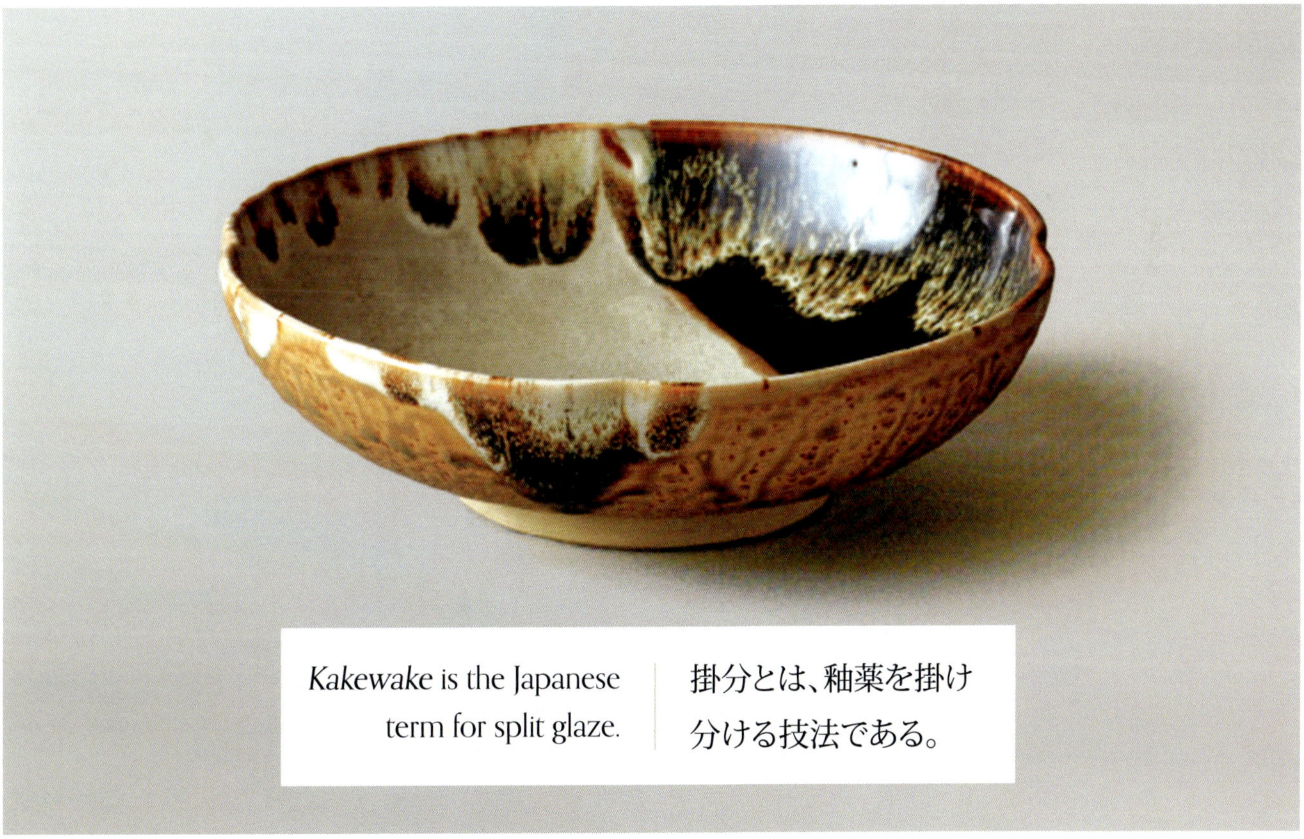

*Kakewake* is the Japanese term for split glaze. | 掛分とは、釉薬を掛け分ける技法である。

MIRAKU KAMEI XIII | 13代亀井味楽
Sweets Tray | 菓子器
1950s | 昭和30年代
Kakewake glaze | 掛分

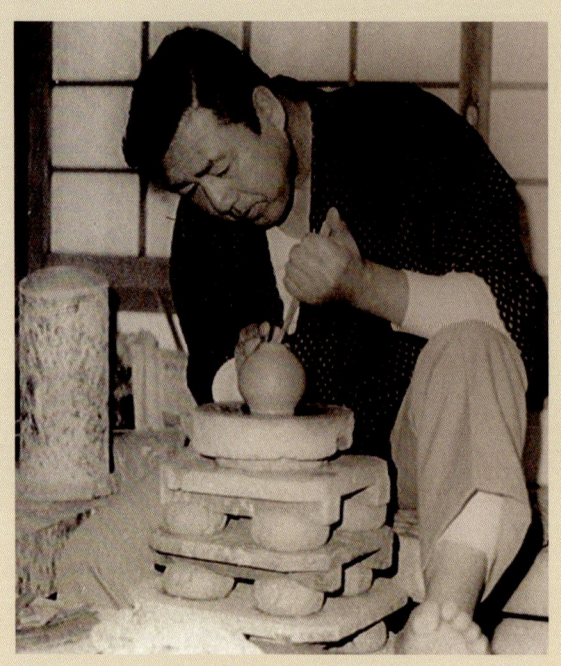

Miraku Kamei XIV
c. 2010

14代亀井味楽
平成22年頃

# Miraku Kamei XIV | 14代亀井味楽
## (1931-2014)

Miraku Kamei XIV excelled in all aspects of tea pottery making. He showcased his work both in Japan and internationally, raising the status of Takatori ware to the level of the most prestigious ceramic traditions in Japan. In 1977, he was designated the first Holder of Intangible Cultural Assets in Art and Craft by the Fukuoka City government. In 1982, one of his apple-shaped tea caddies was purchased by Fukuoka Prefecture and gifted to the Emperor. In 1988, he was awarded an International Art and Culture Prize from the Japan Culture Promoting Association; in 1991, he won a Fukuoka Prefecture Skilled Person of Merit Prize; and in 2001, he was awarded a Yellow Ribbon Medal by the Japanese government.

茶陶制作のあらゆる技術に長け、国内外で作品を発表し、高取焼を日本で最も格の高い陶芸伝統の水準まで押し上げる。1977年、福岡市により第一号の無形文化財工芸技術保持者に認定される。1988年、日本文化振興会により国際芸術文化賞、1991年、福岡県技能功労賞を受賞する。2001年には、日本政府により黄綬褒章を受賞する。

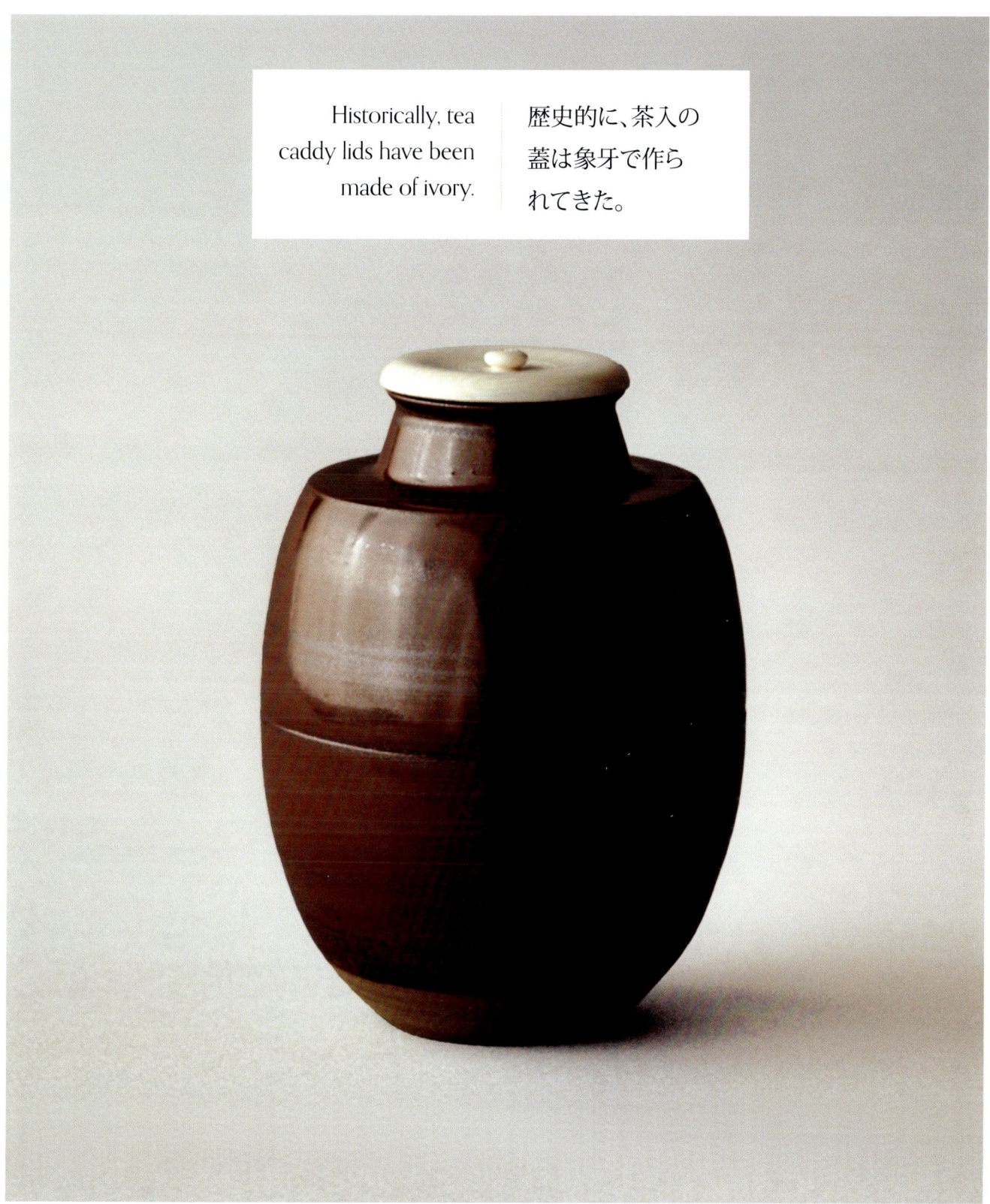

Historically, tea caddy lids have been made of ivory.

歴史的に、茶入の蓋は象牙で作られてきた。

MIRAKU KAMEI XIV
Tea Caddy with Shoulder
1970s
Yellow glaze

14代亀井味楽
肩衝茶入
昭和50年代
黄釉

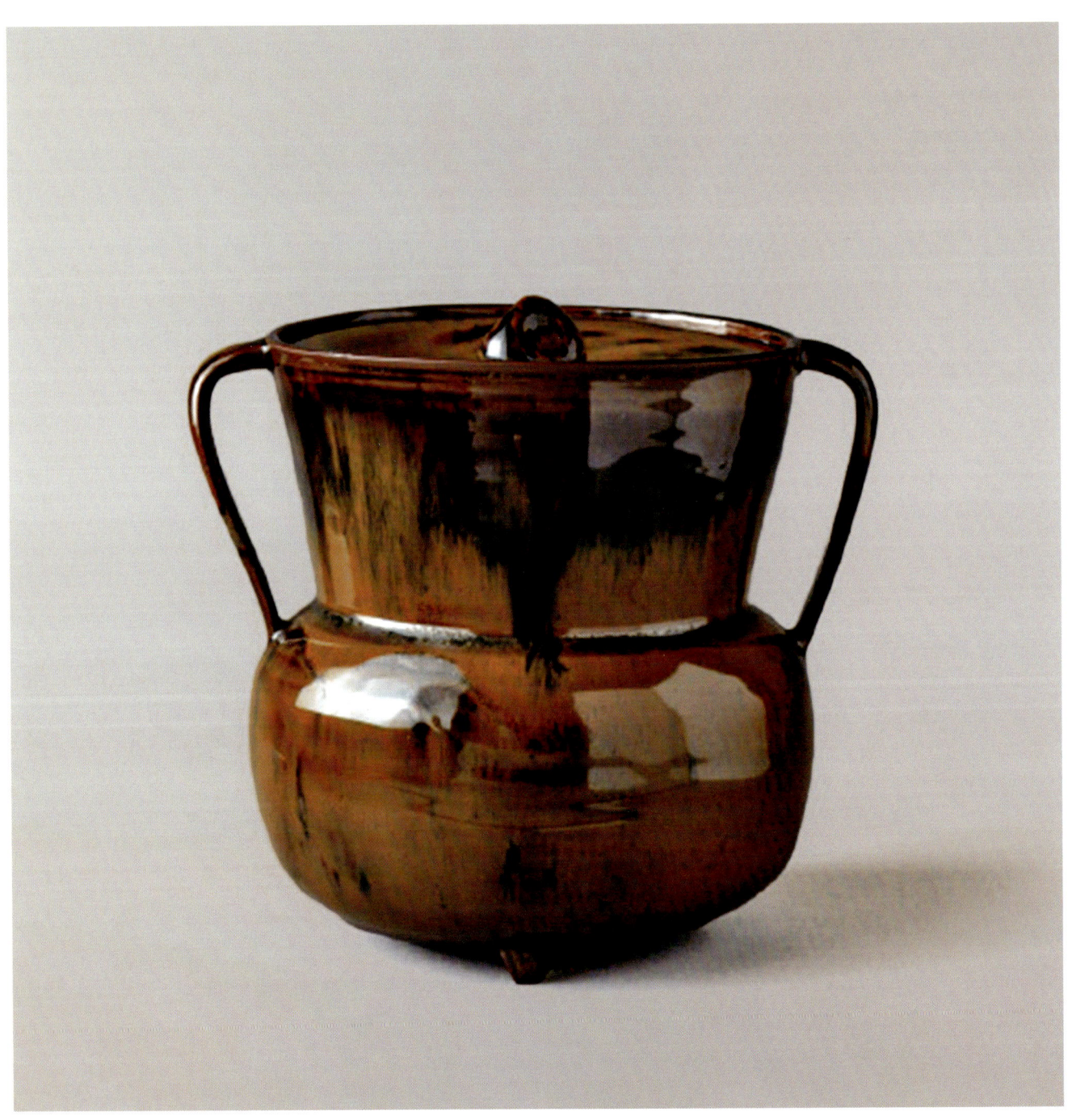

MIRAKU KAMEI XIV
Water Container with Ear-shaped Handles
1970s
Copper glaze

14代亀井味楽
耳付水指
昭和50年代
銅化釉

Archaeological excavations show that *Shippō* (openwork) began in Takatori ware in the 1610s. The superimposed circle designs of *Shippō* form petals or stars that represent the seven treasures of Buddhism and are symbols of harmony.

発掘により、1610年代にはすでに七宝透彫が作られていたことが明らかになっている。多重円の模様は、仏教における7種類の宝物および調和の象徴でもある花びらや星を形作っている。

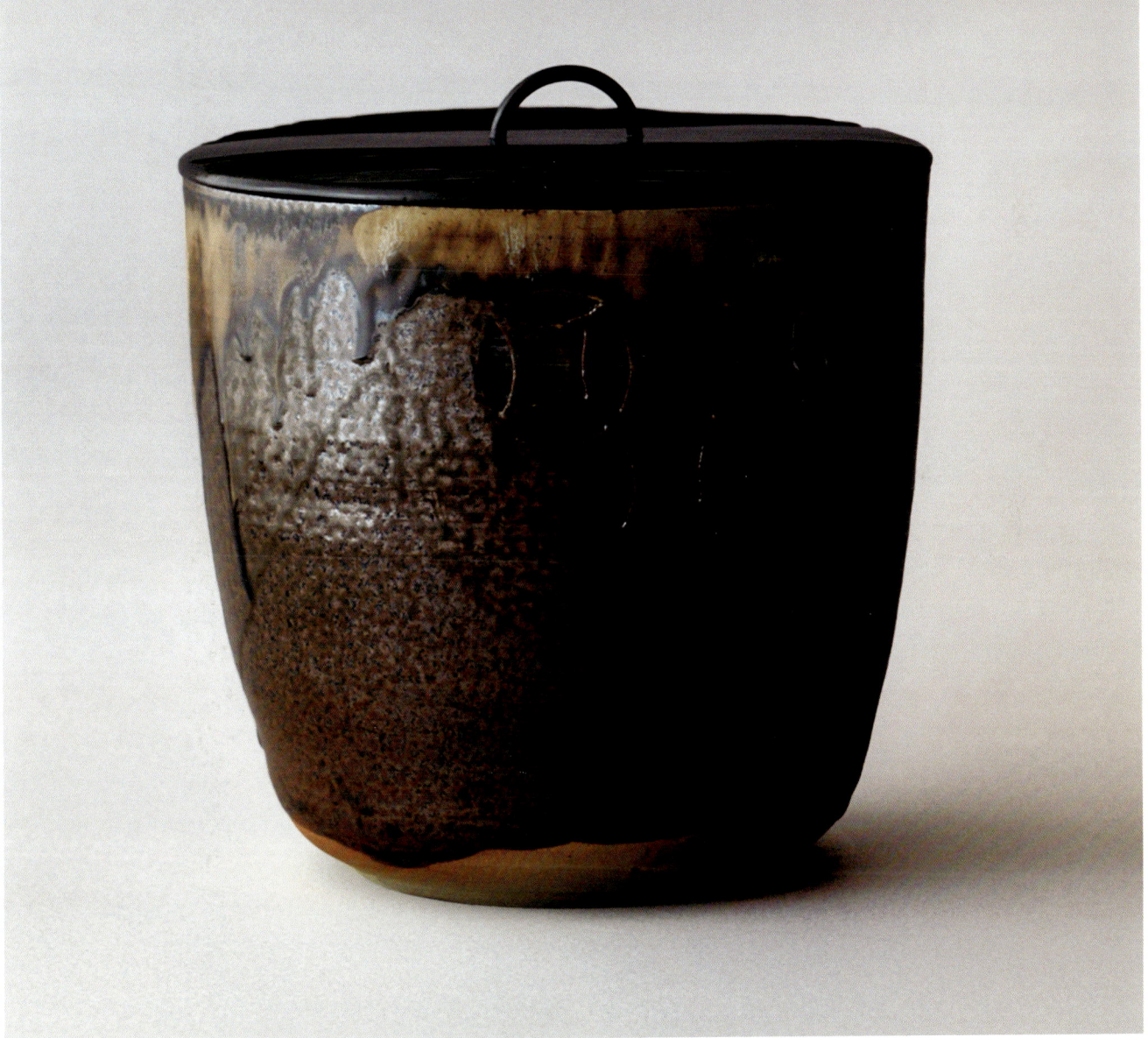

MIRAKU KAMEI XIV
Water Container with Shippō (openwork)
1970s
Yellow and white glaze

14代亀井味楽
七宝透水指
昭和50年代
黄釉に白流し

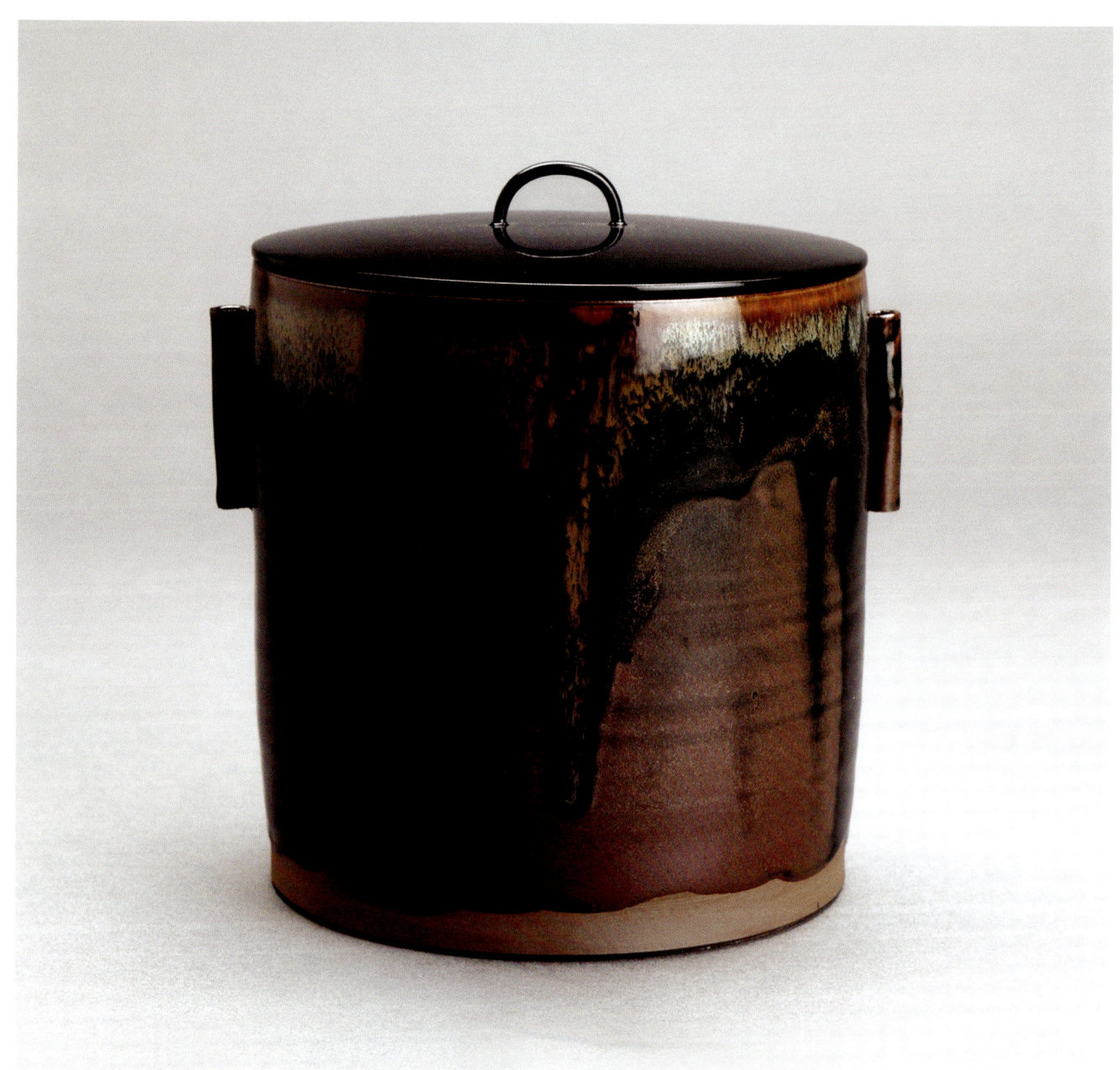

Kudamimi, or "Pipe Ear" handles, were favored by artist and tea master Kobori Enshū (1579-1647).

「管耳」とは作家でもあった大名茶人である小堀遠州(1579–1647)が好んだ把手である。

MIRAKU KAMEI XIV
Water Container with Pipe Ear Handles
1970s
Rust glaze
XIV2

14代亀井味楽
管耳付水指
昭和50年代
錆釉

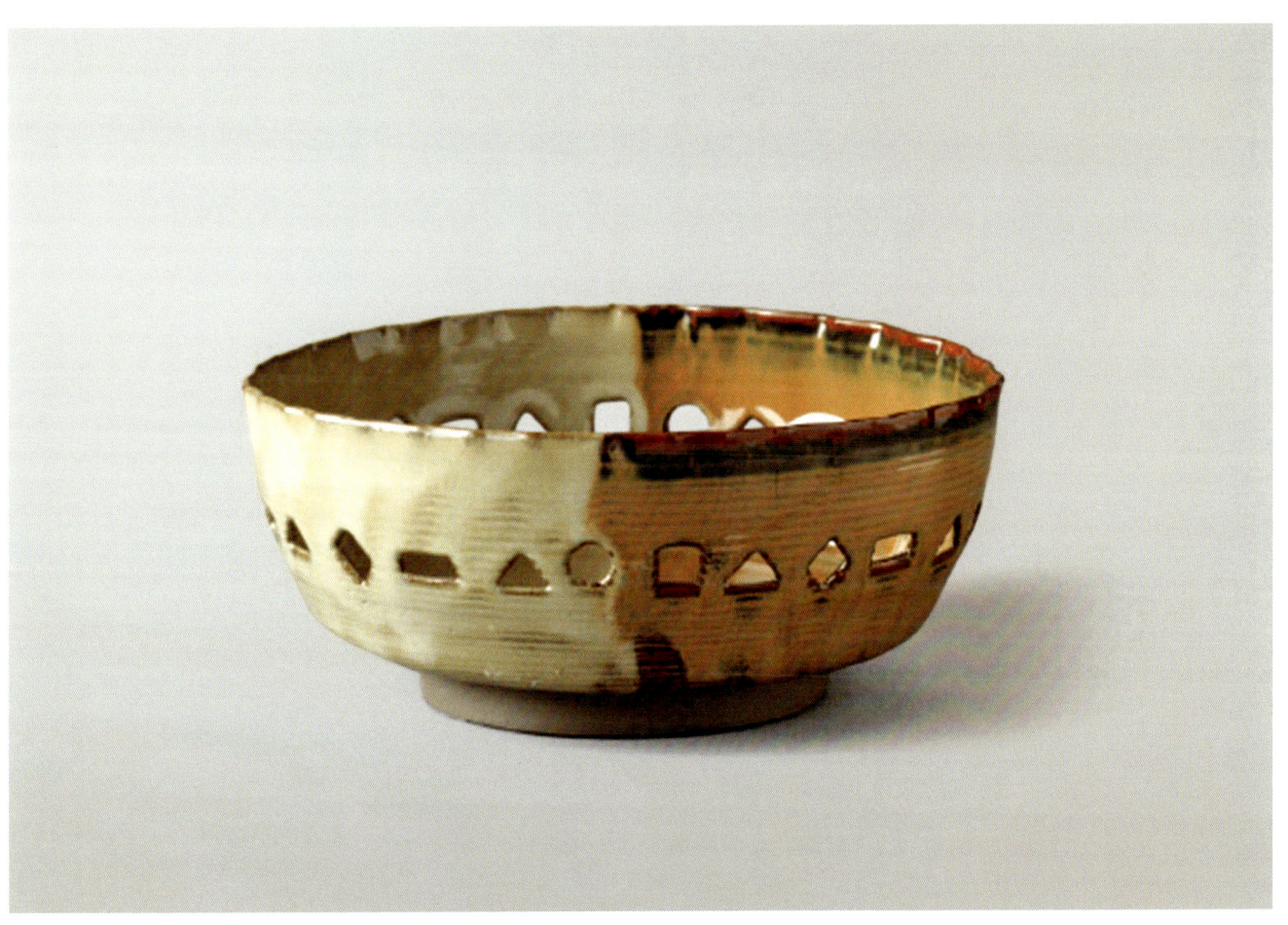

MIRAKU KAMEI XIV
Sweets Tray with Shippō (openwork)
1970s
Kakewake glaze

14代亀井味楽
透菓子器
昭和50年代
掛分

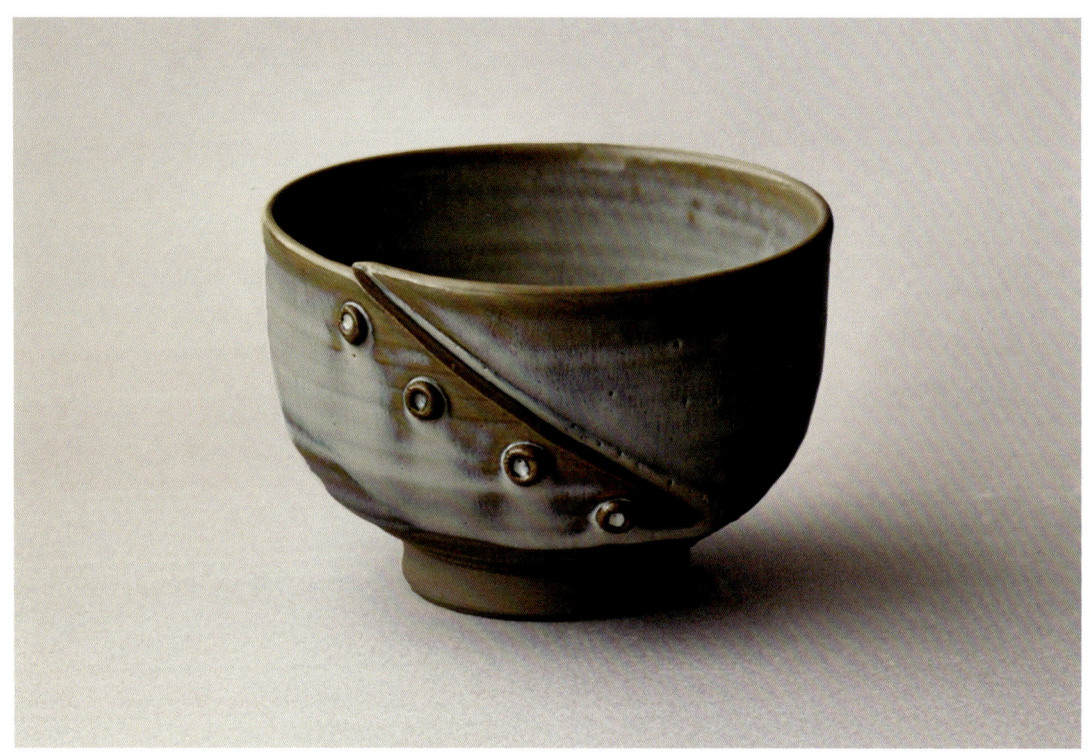

MIRAKU KAMEI XIV     14代亀井味楽
Tea Bowl with Seam     とじめ茶盌
1970s     昭和50年代
White glaze     白釉

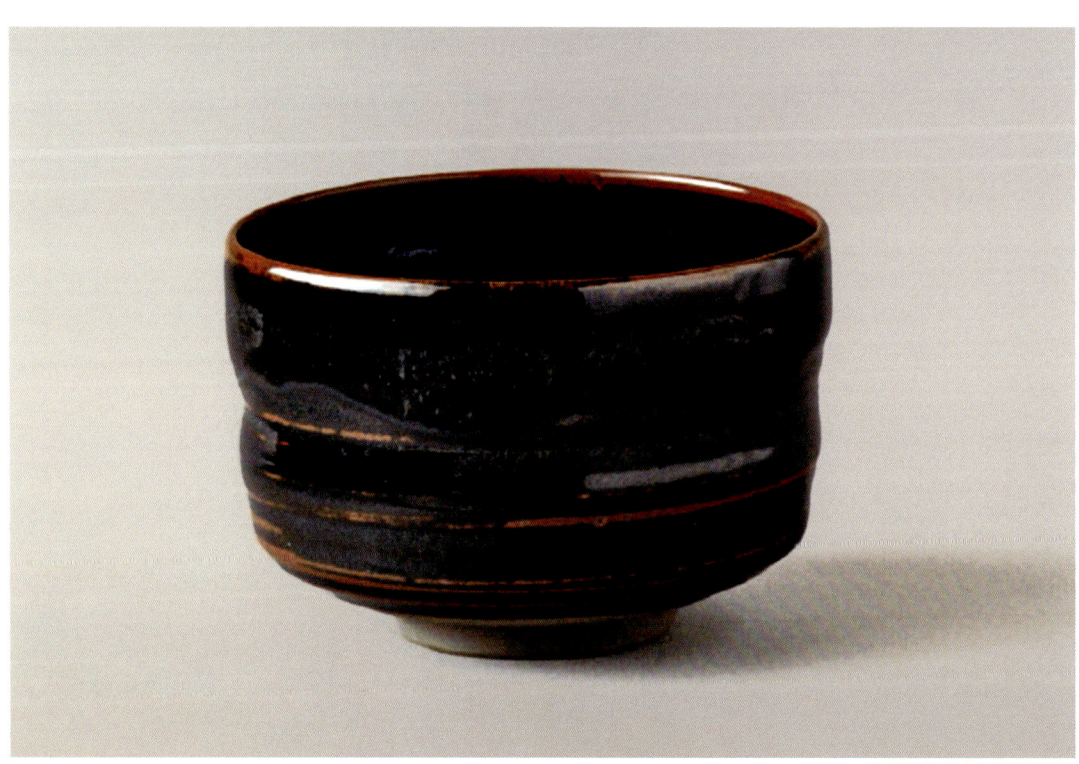

MIRAKU KAMEI XIV     14代亀井味楽
Tea Bowl, Dojime Form     胴締茶盌
1970s     昭和50年代
Black glaze     黒釉

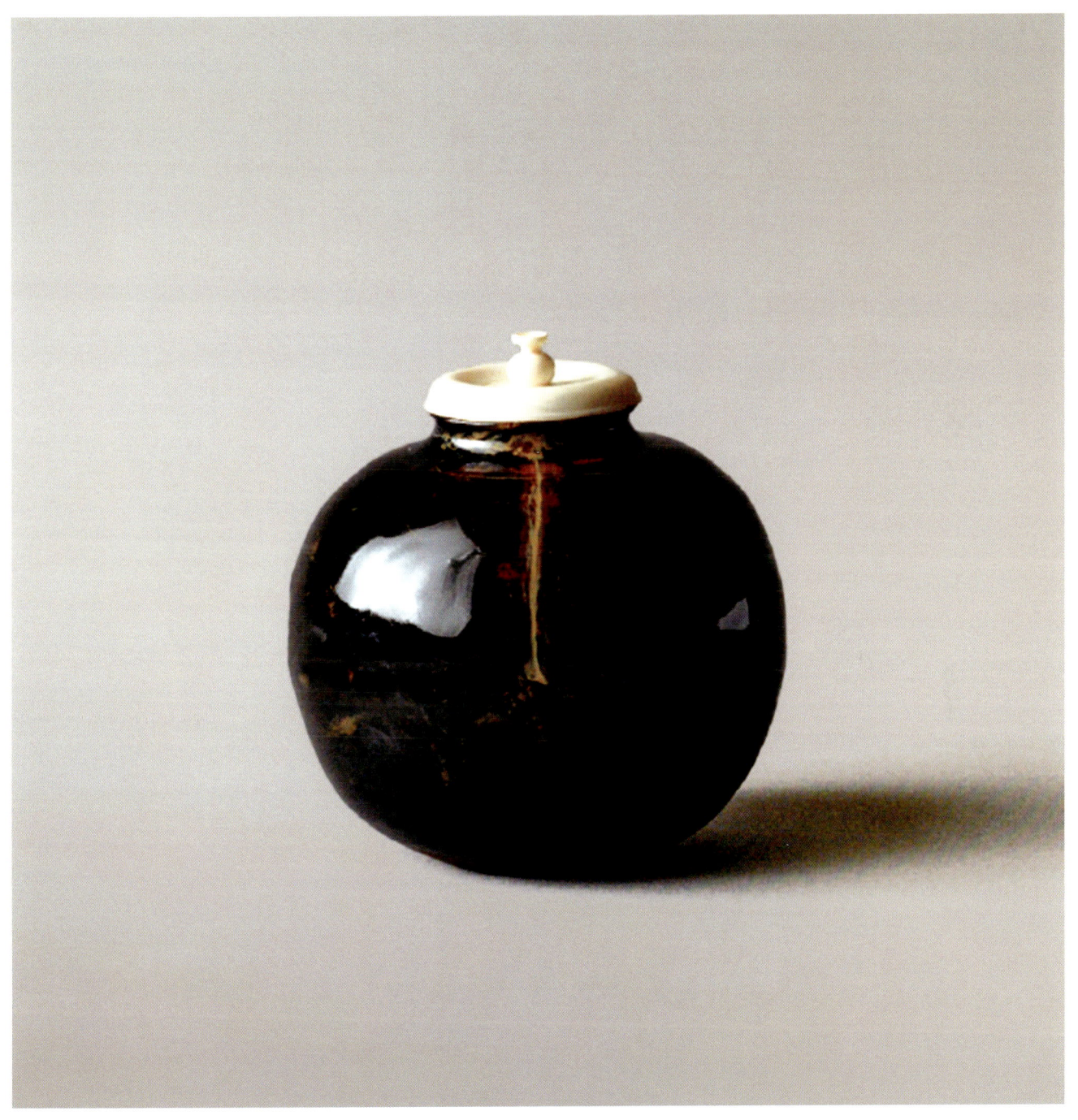

MIRAKU KAMEI XIV　　14代亀井味楽
Tea Caddy　　　　　　文琳茶入
1970s　　　　　　　　昭和50年代
Thinly applied yellow glaze　黄釉（薄掛け）

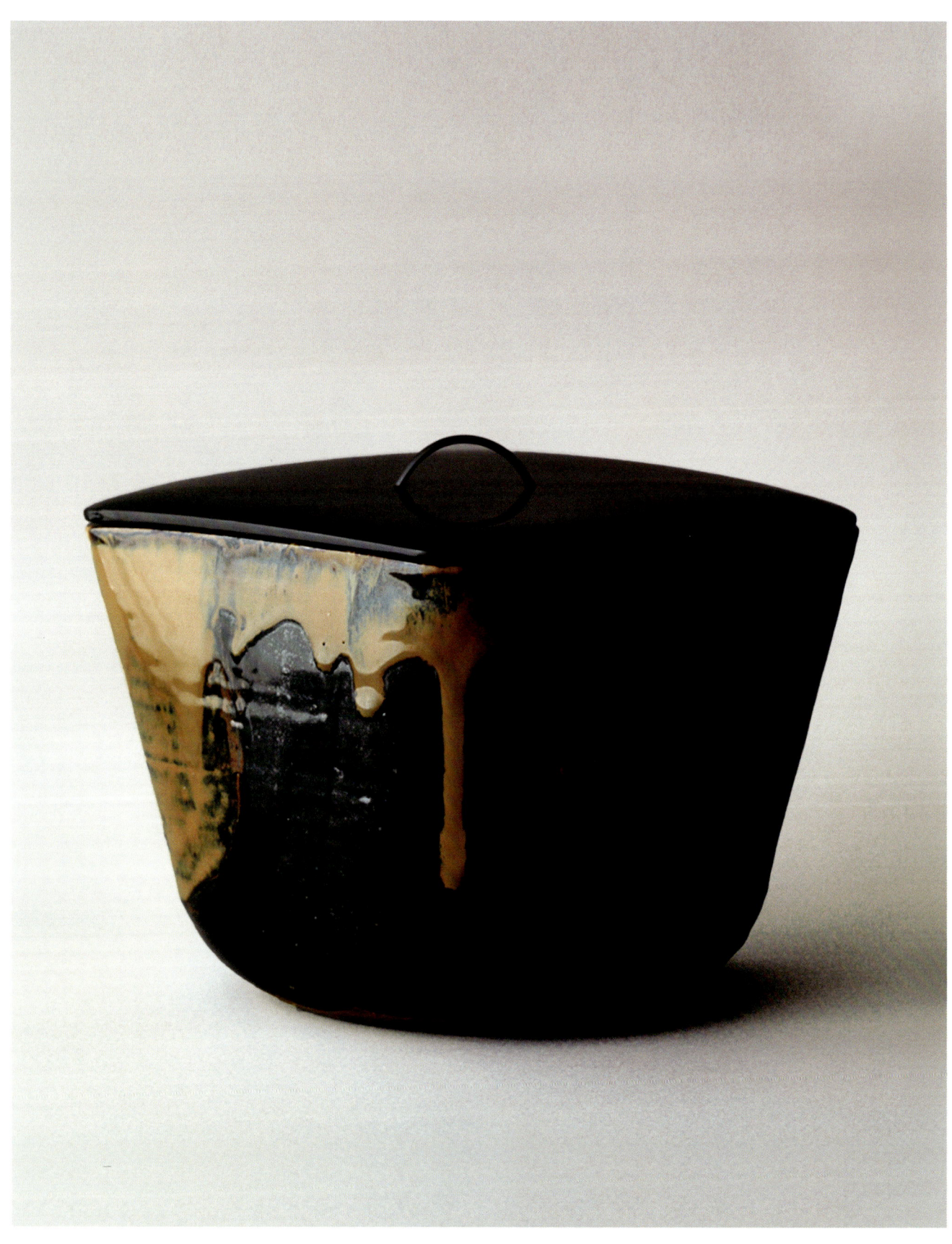

MIRAKU KAMEI XIV
Rhombus-form Water Container with Lacquer Lid
1970s
Yellow and white glaze

14代亀井味楽
うるし蓋付菱形水差
昭和50年代
黄釉に白流し

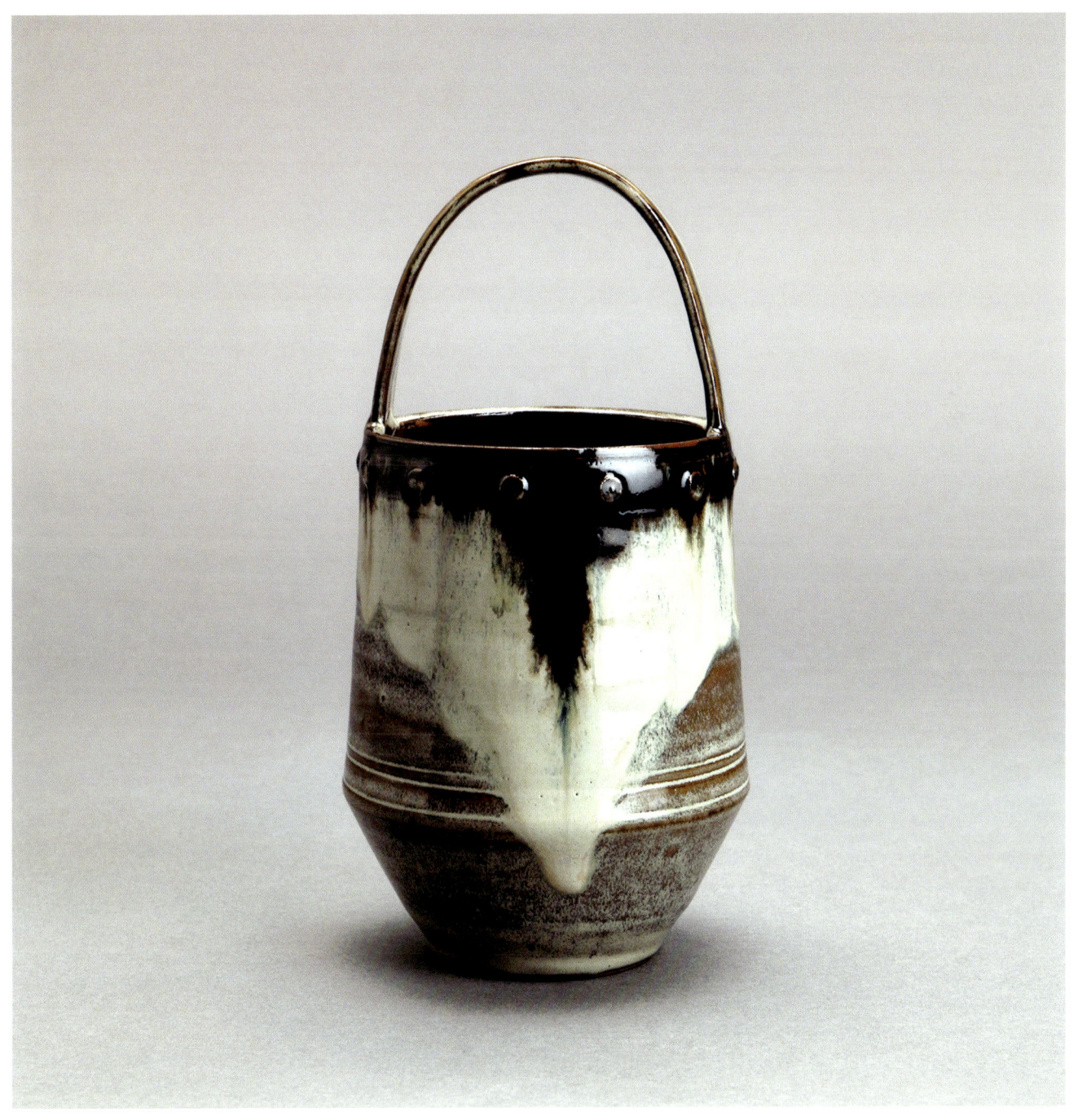

MIRAKU KAMEI XIV
Flower Vase with Bridge Handle
2013
White and black glaze
XIV1

14代亀井味楽
手付花入
2013年
白釉に黒流し

55

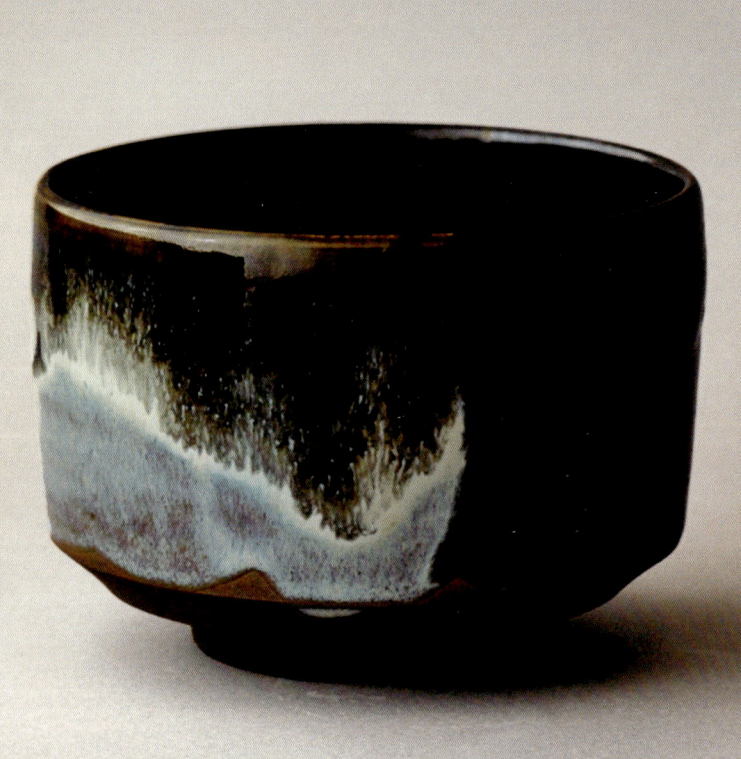

"When we consider how small after all the cup of human enjoyment is, how soon overflowed with tears, how easily drained to the dregs in our quenchless thirst for infinity, we shall not blame ourselves for making so much of the tea-cup."

*The Book of Tea* (1906)
by Okakura Kakuzō

「考えてみれば、煎ずるところ人間享楽の茶碗は、いかにも狭いものではないか、いかにも早く涙であふれるではないか、無辺を求むる渇のとまらぬあまり、一息に飲みほされるではないか。してみれば、茶碗をいくらもてはやしたとてとがめだてには及ぶまい。」岡倉覚三著「茶の本」（1906年）村上博訳

|  |  |
|---|---|
| **MIRAKU KAMEI XIV** | 14代亀井味楽 |
| **Tea Bowl** | 茶盌 |
| **1970s** | 昭和50年代 |
| **Curtain glaze** | 幕薬 |

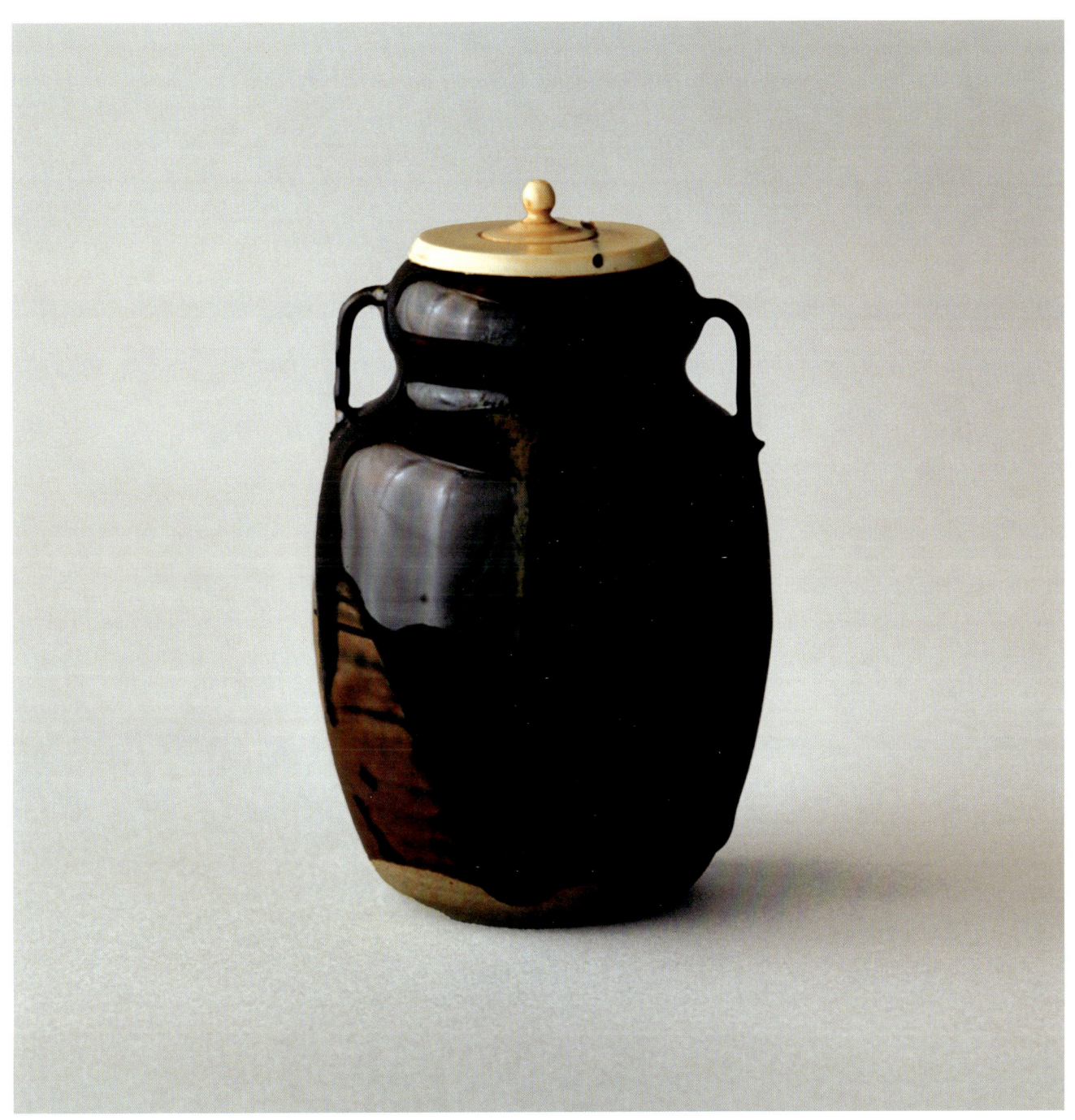

MIRAKU KAMEI XIV
Tea Caddy with Ears
1970s
Yellow glaze

14代亀井味楽
耳付茶入
昭和50年代
黄釉

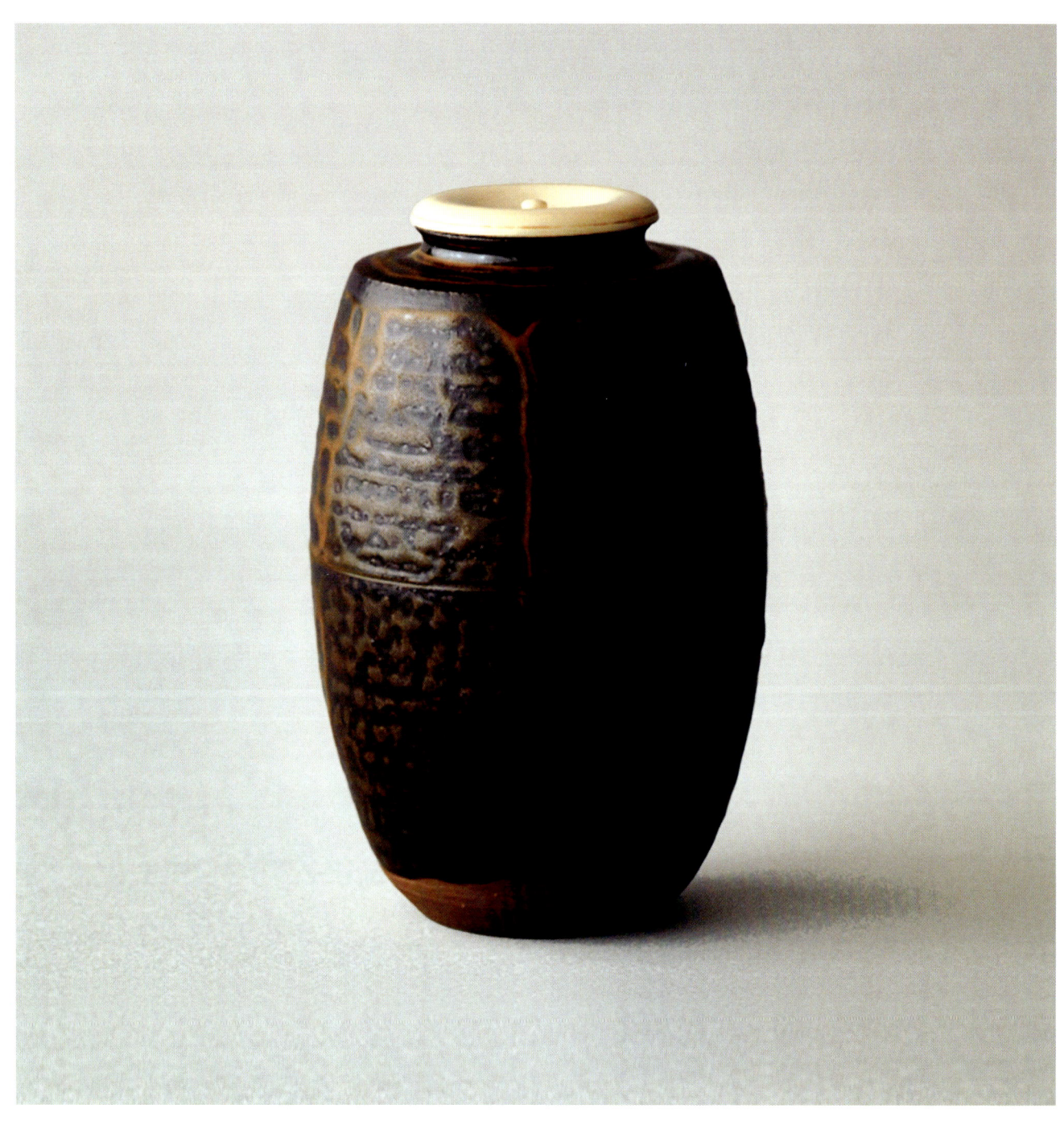

MIRAKU KAMEI XIV              14代亀井味楽
Tall Tea Caddy with Shoulder   肩衝茶入
1970s                         昭和50年代
Yellow glaze                  黄釉

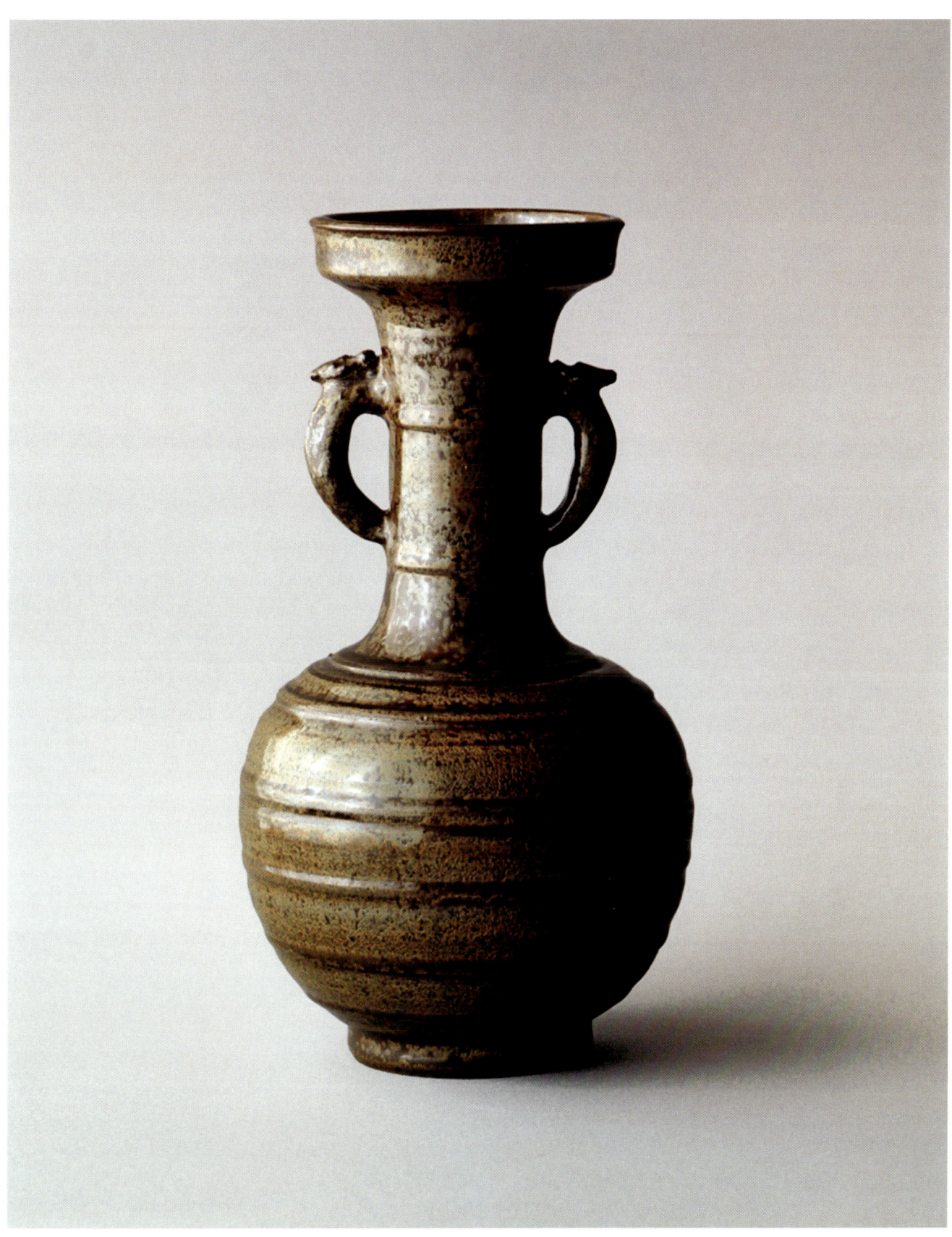

MIRAKU KAMEI XIV      14代亀井味楽
Phoenix Vase with Ear-shaped Handles      耳付花入
2013      2013年
Ginsai glaze      銀彩釉

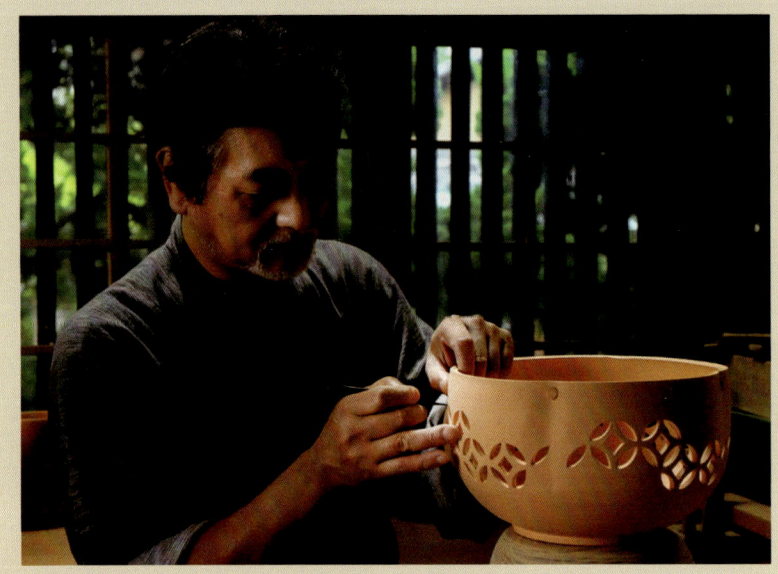

**Miraku Kamei XV**
**2021**

15代亀井味楽
令和3年

# Miraku Kamei XV
### (Born 1960)

# 15代亀井味楽

The eldest son of Miraku Kamei XIV, Miraku Kamei XV completed his university degree in Ceramics at Kyoto Saga University of Arts, earned a doctorate in Fine Art at American Century University, and took the title of the fifteenth generation in 2001. He has carried on the tradition of Takatori ware for more than thirty years. In addition to exhibiting and promoting Takatori ware around Japan, he is an active teacher, training students in ceramics at many institutions around his home city of Fukuoka. He is also president of the Fukuoka/Hakata branch of the Japan Ceramics Association and a member of numerous arts organizations. In 2015, Kamei received the award of Contemporary Master Craftsman, designated to a craftsman with excellent skills from Fukuoka, Japan.

14代亀井味楽の長男として生まれ、京都市立嵯峨美術短期大学の陶芸学科を卒業。米国センチュリー大学芸術博士号を取得後、2001年に15代亀井味楽を襲名する。30年にわたり高取焼の伝統を引き継ぎ、作品の発表および高取焼の振興に貢献している。その他にも、師として自宅のある福岡市の様々な陶芸教室で生徒達の指導に当たる。またさまざまな美術関連団体の会員であり、日本陶磁器協会博多支部の理事を務めている。2015年、福岡県から技能優秀者として表彰される。

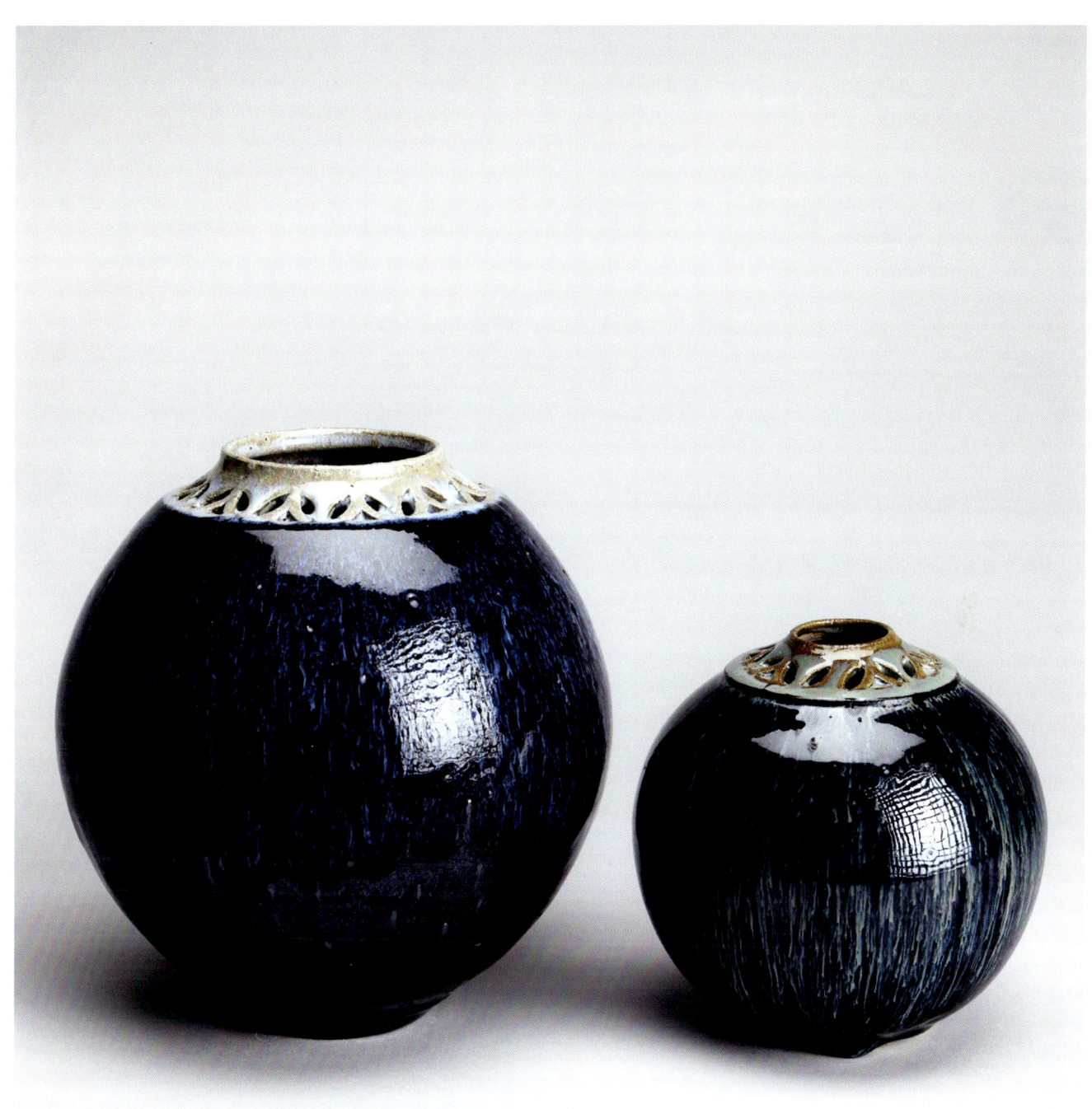

|  |  |
|---|---|
| **MIRAKU KAMEI XV** | 15代亀井味楽 |
| **Jar with Shippō (openwork)** | 七宝透彫壺 |
| 2024 | 2024年 |
| **Black glaze** | 黒釉 |
| XV220 | |
| | |
| **Jar with Shippō (openwork)** | 七宝透彫壺 |
| 2024 | 2024年 |
| **Black glaze** | 黒釉 |
| XV221 | |

Vessels are made at the Miraku Kiln in Fukuoka and lids are made by a lacquer master in another city, but the two work expertly together.

器は福岡市の味楽窯で作られ、蓋は別の街に住む塗師によって作られているが、両者は緊密に協力して作品を完成させる。

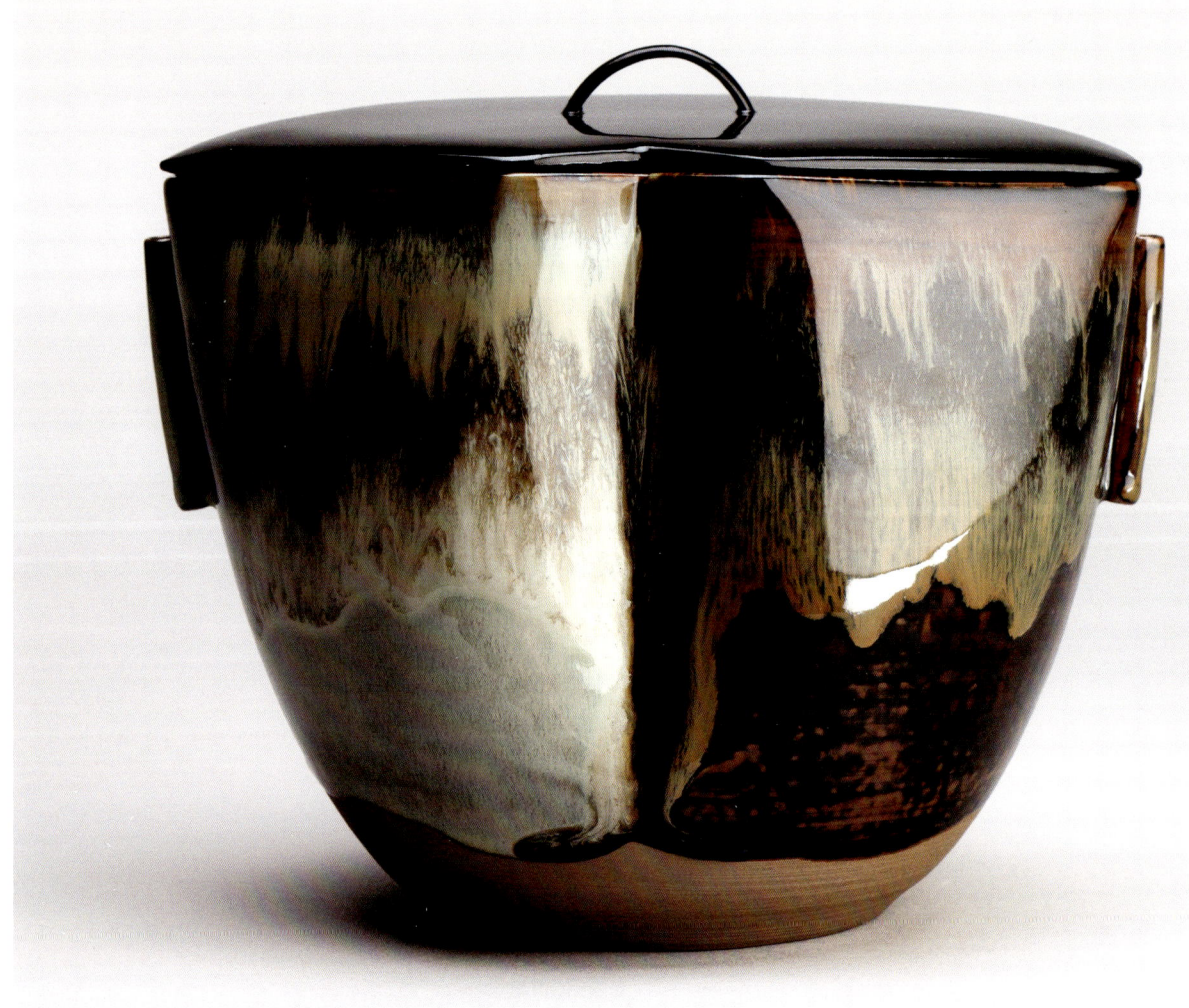

**MIRAKU KAMEI XV**
**Fan-form Water Container with Lacquer Lid**
2018
Kakewake glaze
XV167

15代亀井味楽
扇形うるし蓋付水指
2018年
掛分

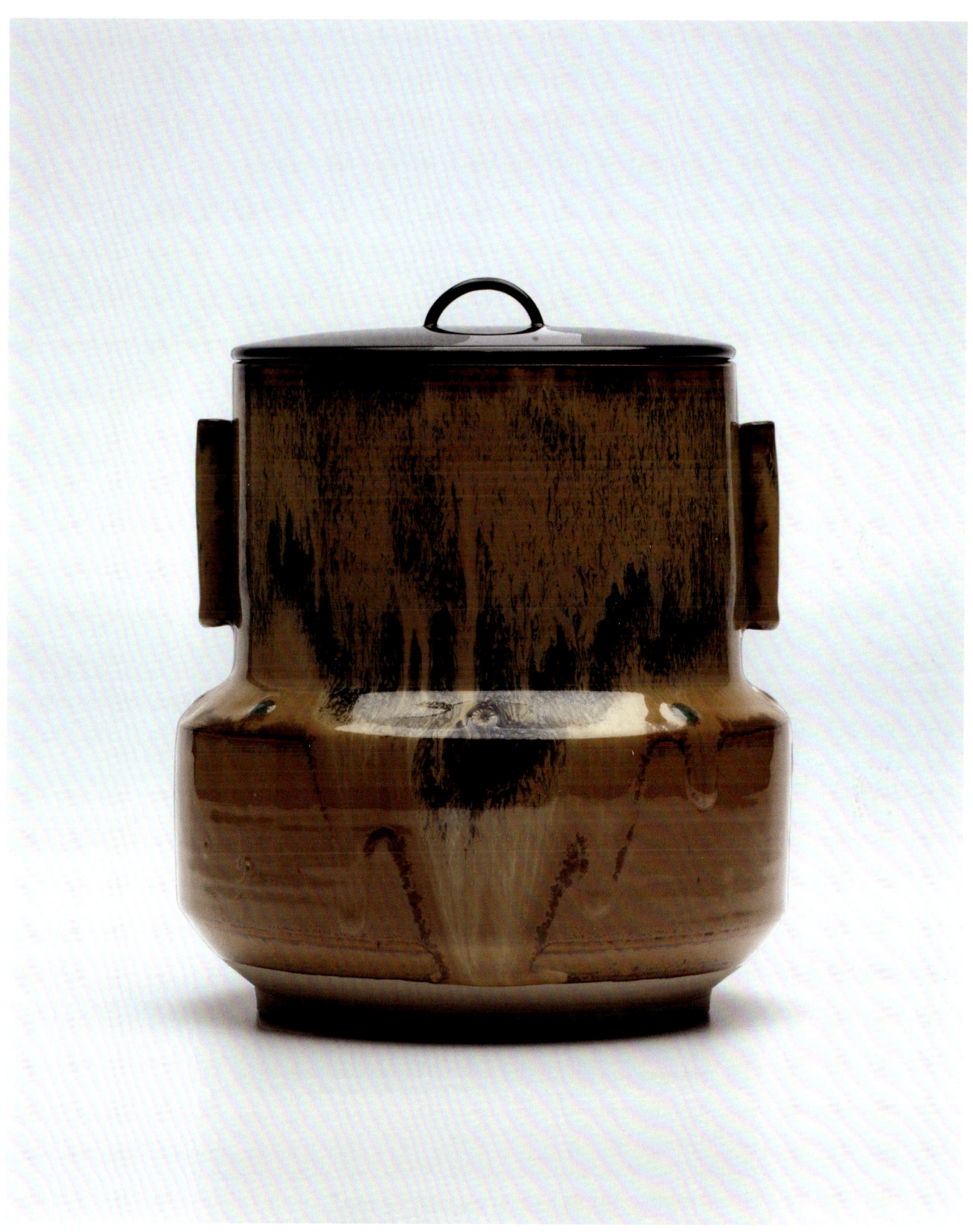

MIRAKU KAMEI XV
Axel-form Water Container with Lacquer Lid
2020
Yellow glaze
XV181

15代亀井味楽
うるし蓋付水指
2020年
黄釉

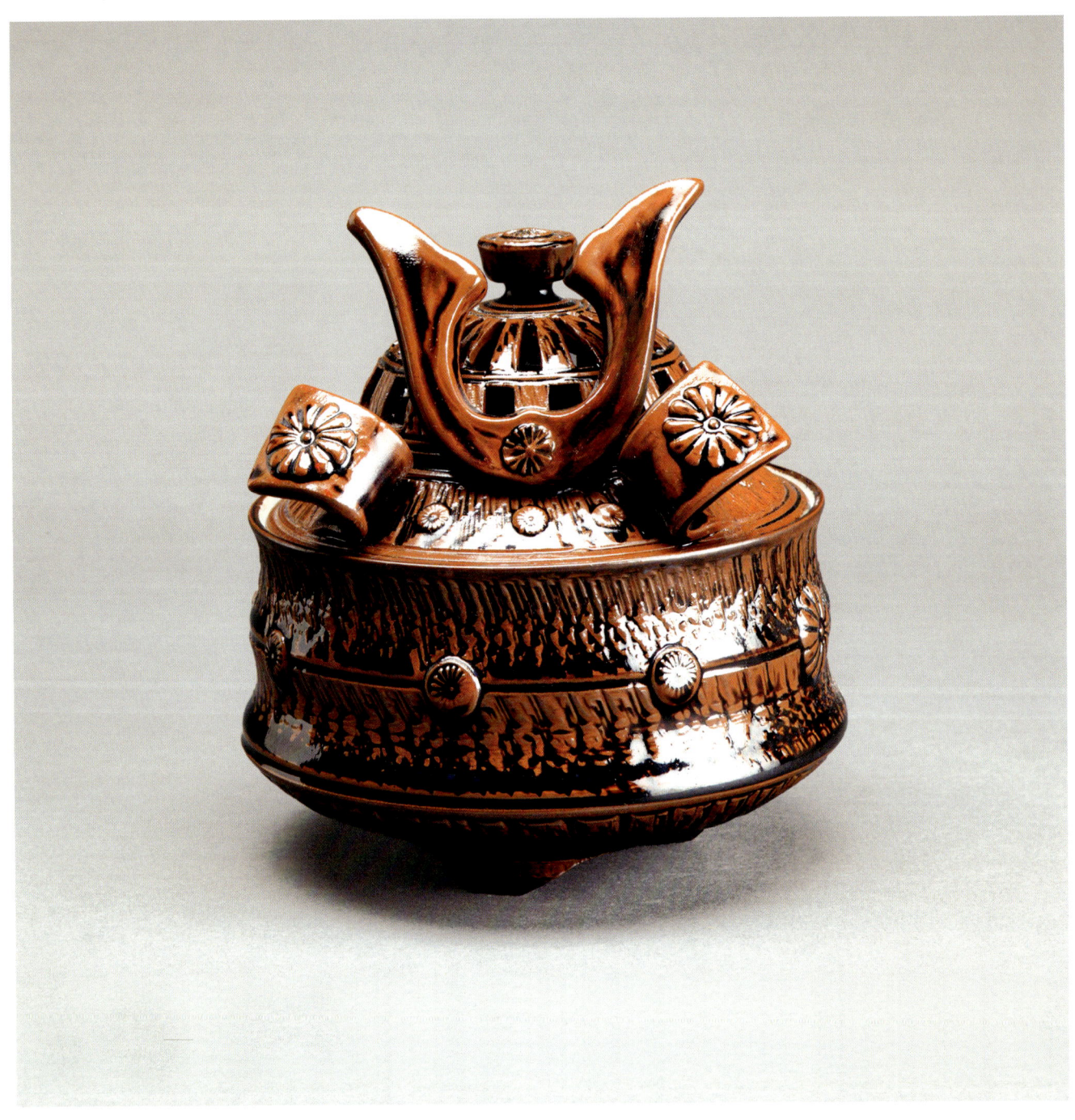

MIRAKU KAMEI XV
Helmet-form Incense Burner
2016
Ame glaze
XV149

15代亀井味楽
兜型香炉
2016年
飴釉

Takatori ware is known for its thin structure, which keeps items like water containers light even when filled.

高取焼はその薄さで知られている。水を入れても水指は重くならない。

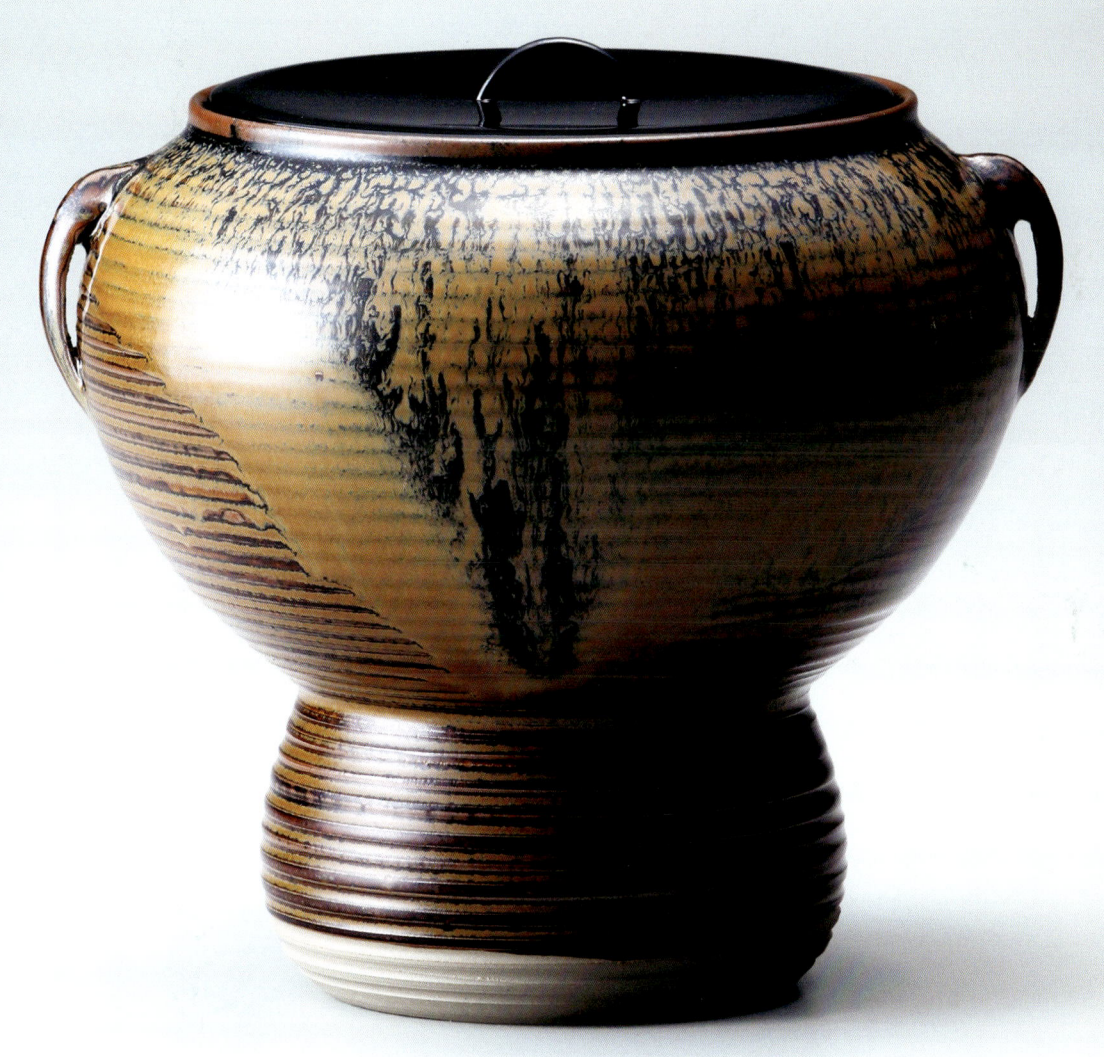

**MIRAKU KAMEI XV**
**Inverted Gourd-form Water Container with Lacquer Lid**
2014
Yellow and black glaze
XV15

15代亀井味楽
単瓢うるし蓋付水指
2014年
黄釉に黒流し

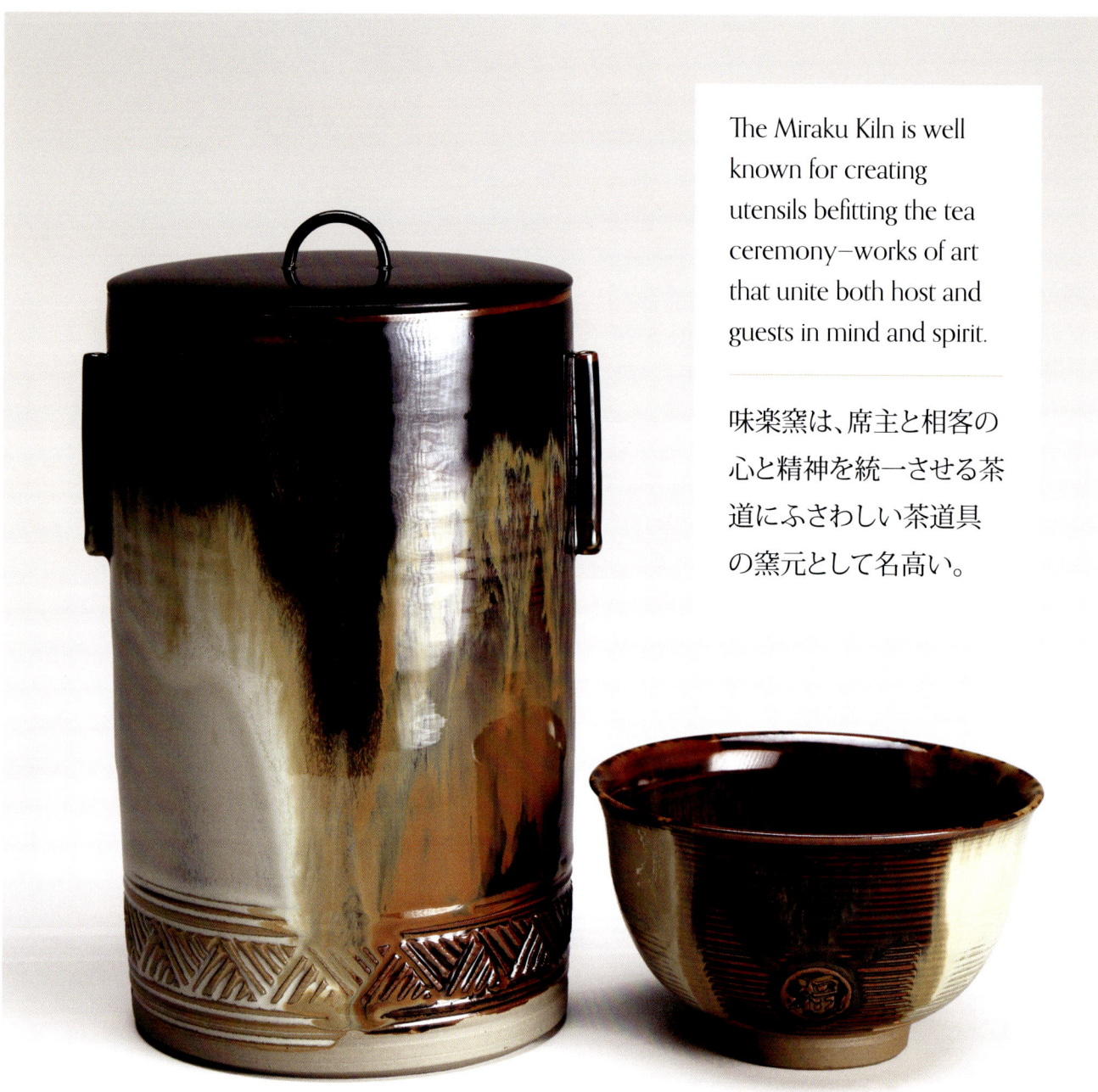

The Miraku Kiln is well known for creating utensils befitting the tea ceremony—works of art that unite both host and guests in mind and spirit.

味楽窯は、席主と相客の心と精神を統一させる茶道にふさわしい茶道具の窯元として名高い。

| | |
|---|---|
| **MIRAKU KAMEI XV** | 15代亀井味楽 |
| **Water Container with Lacquer Lid and Pipe Ear Handles** | うるし蓋付水指 |
| 2014 | 2014年 |
| Kakewake glaze | 掛分 |
| XV69 | |
| | |
| Tea Bowl | 茶盌 |
| 2014 | 2014年 |
| Kakewake glaze | 掛分 |
| XV61 | |

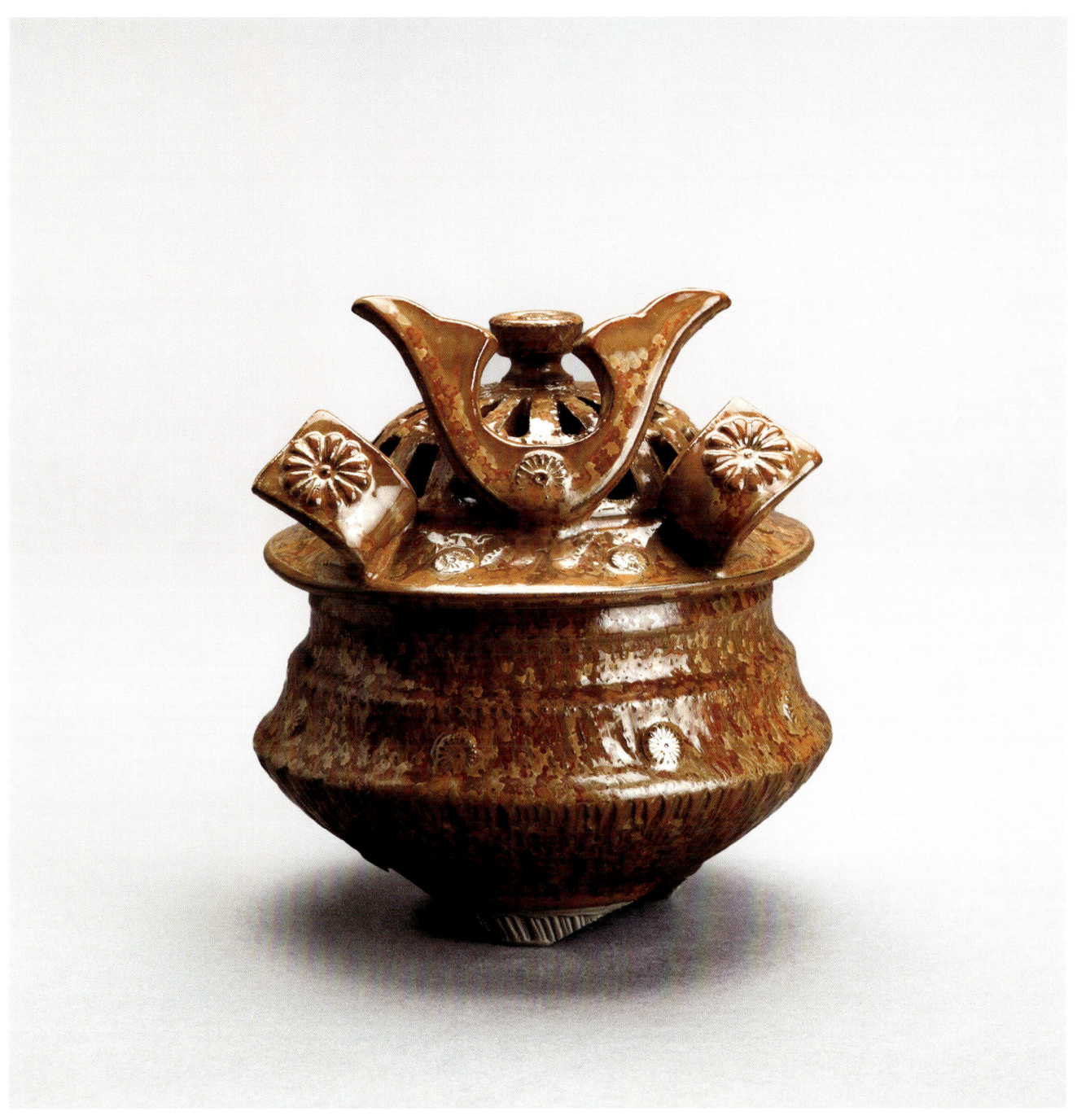

MIRAKU KAMEI XV
Helmet-form Incense Burner
2013
"Gold Flower" glaze
XV2

15代亀井味楽
兜型香炉
2013年
金華紋釉

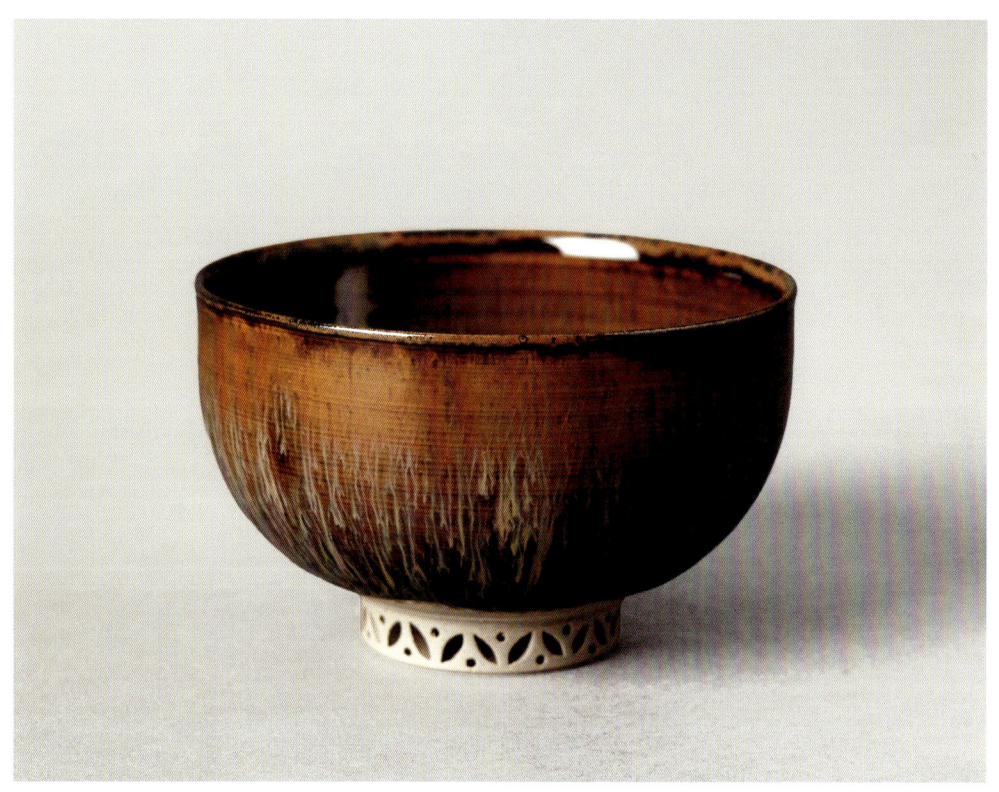

MIRAKU KAMEI XV
Tea Bowl with Shippō (openwork) on Foot
2014
Yellow glaze
XV58

15代亀井味楽
七宝透高台茶盌
2014年
黄釉

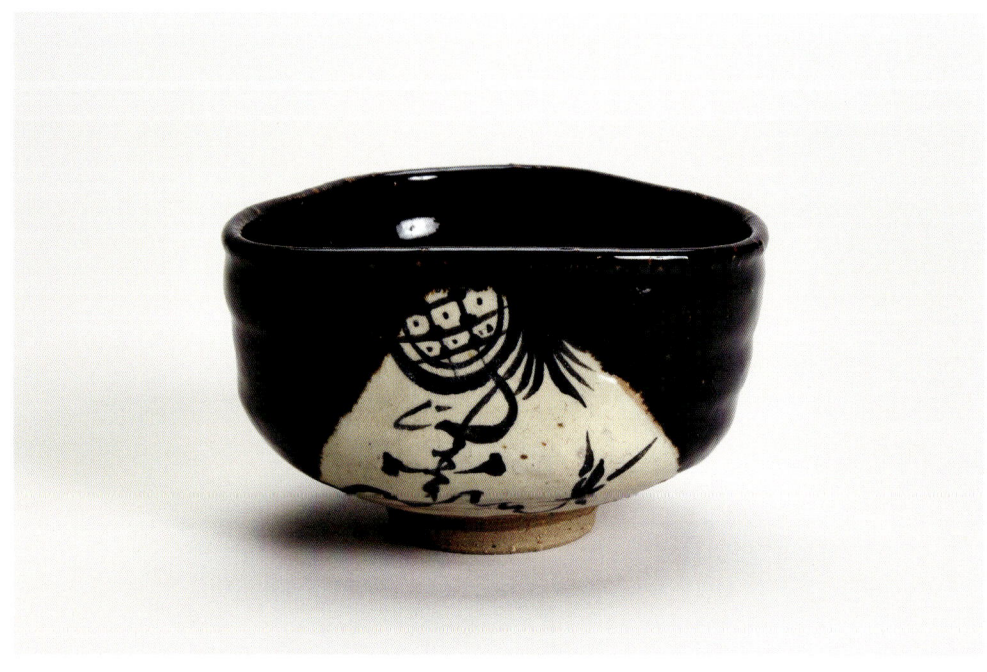

MIRAKU KAMEI XV
Tea Bowl
2022
Oribe and black glaze
XV193

15代亀井味楽
茶盌
2022年
織部釉および黒釉

"Teaism is a cult founded on the adoration of the beautiful among the sordid facts of everyday existence. It inculcates purity and harmony, the mystery of mutual charity, the romanticism of the social order. It is essentially a worship of the Imperfect, as it is a tender attempt to accomplish something possible in this impossible thing we know as life."

*The Book of Tea* (1906)
by Okakura Kakuzō

「茶道は日常生活の俗事の中に存する美しきものを崇拝することに基づく一種の儀式であって、純粋と調和、相互愛の神秘、社会秩序のローマン主義を諄々と教えるものである。茶道の要義は「不完全なもの」を崇拝するにある。いわゆる人生というこの不可解なもののうちに、何か可能なものを成就しようとするやさしい企てであるから。」

岡倉覚三　「茶の本」（1906年）村上博訳

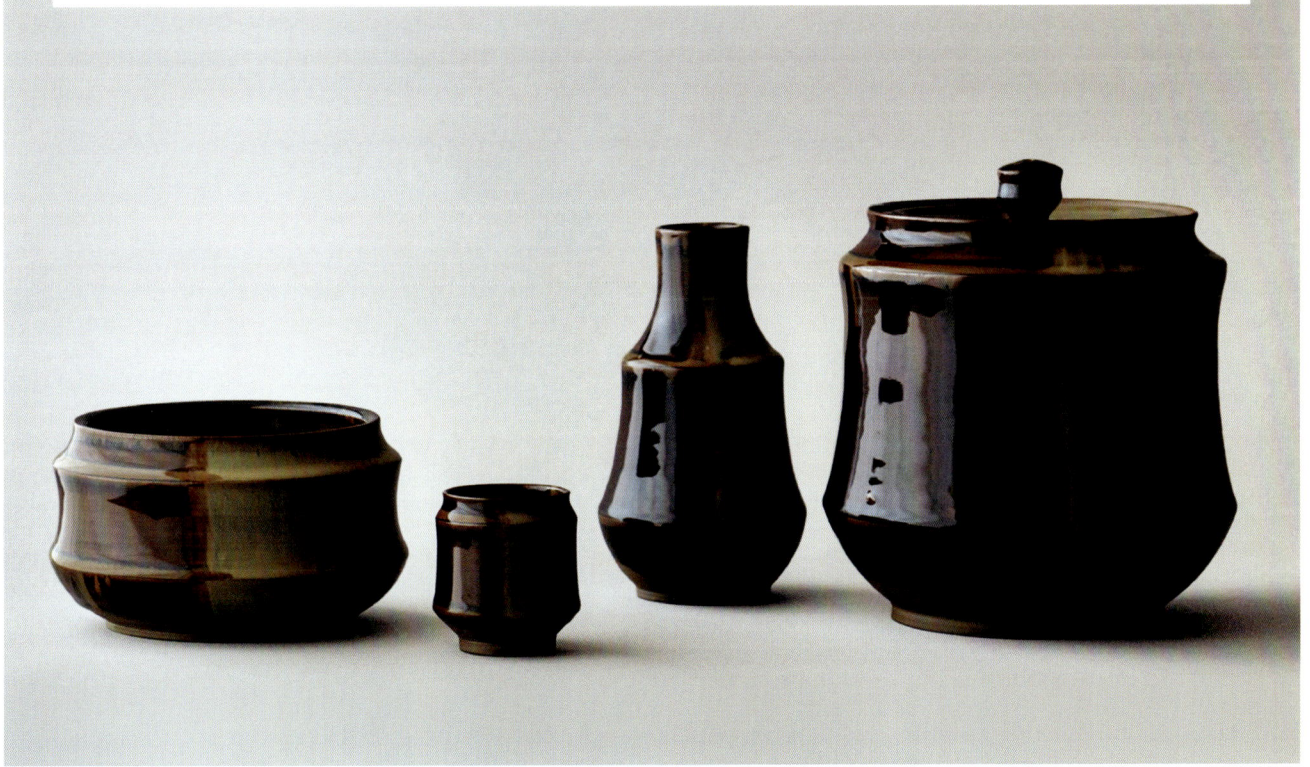

**MIRAKU KAMEI XV**
**Set of Tea Utensils**
**2013**
**Yellow and black glaze**

15代亀井味楽
皆具
2013年
黄釉に黒流し

"Nothing is more hallowing than the union of kindred spirits in art. At the moment of meeting, the art lover transcends himself. At once he is and is not. He catches a glimpse of Infinity, but words cannot voice his delight, for the eye has no tongue. Freed from the fetters of matter, his spirit moves in the rhythm of things."

*The Book of Tea* (1906)
by Okakura Kakuzō

「芸術において、類縁の精神が合一するほど世にも神聖なものはない。その会するやたちまちにして芸術愛好者は自己を超越する。彼は存在すると同時に存在しない。彼は永劫を瞥見するけれども、目には舌なく、言葉をもってその喜びを声に表わすことはできない。彼の精神は、物質の束縛を脱して、物のリズムによって動いている。」

岡倉覚三　「茶の本」（1906年）村上博訳

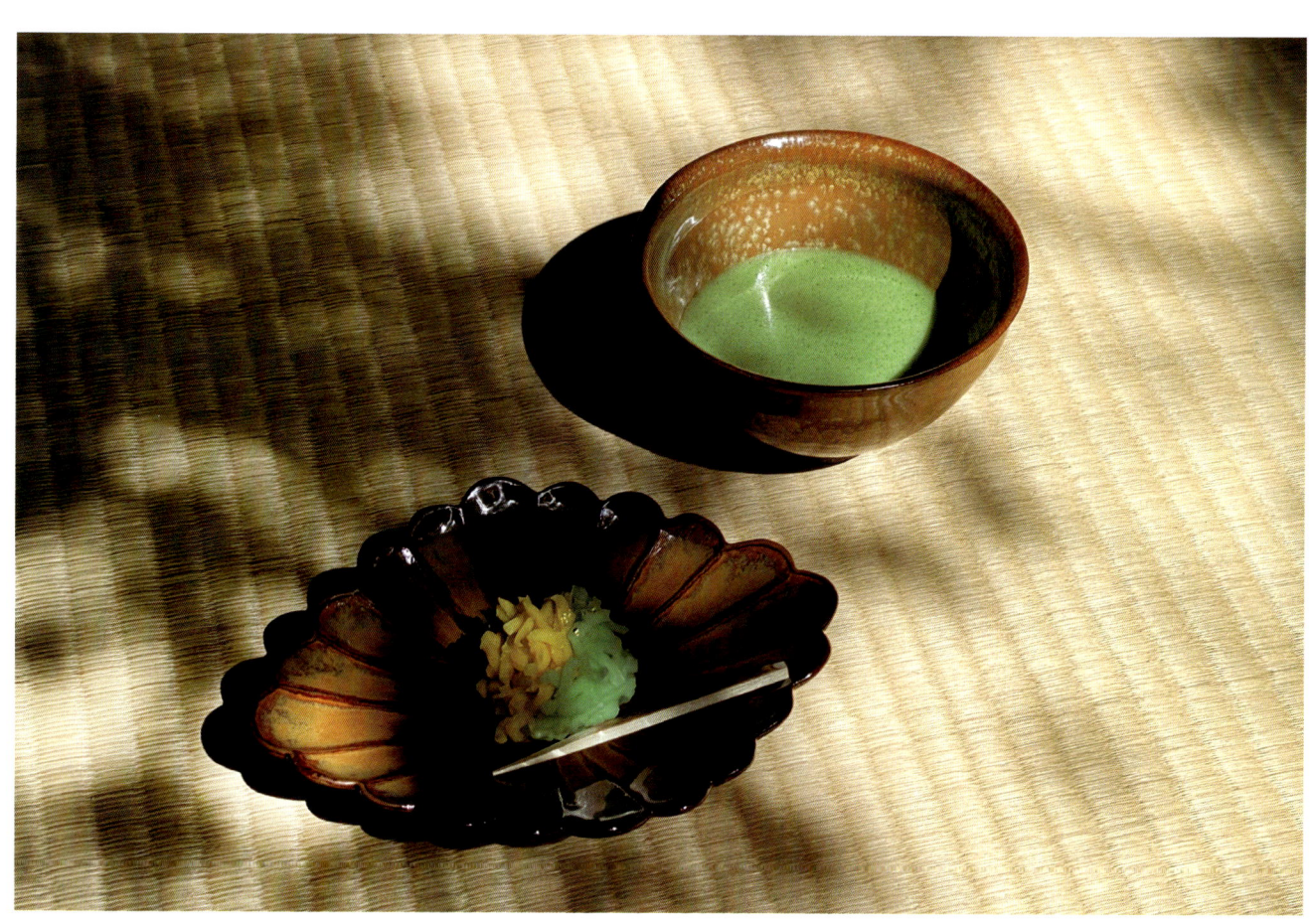

MIRAKU KAMEI XV
Small Rhombus Plate
2013
"Gold Flower" glaze

15代亀井味楽
菱形小皿
2013年
金華紋釉

Tea Bowl
2013
"Gold Flower" glaze

茶盌
2013年
金華紋釉

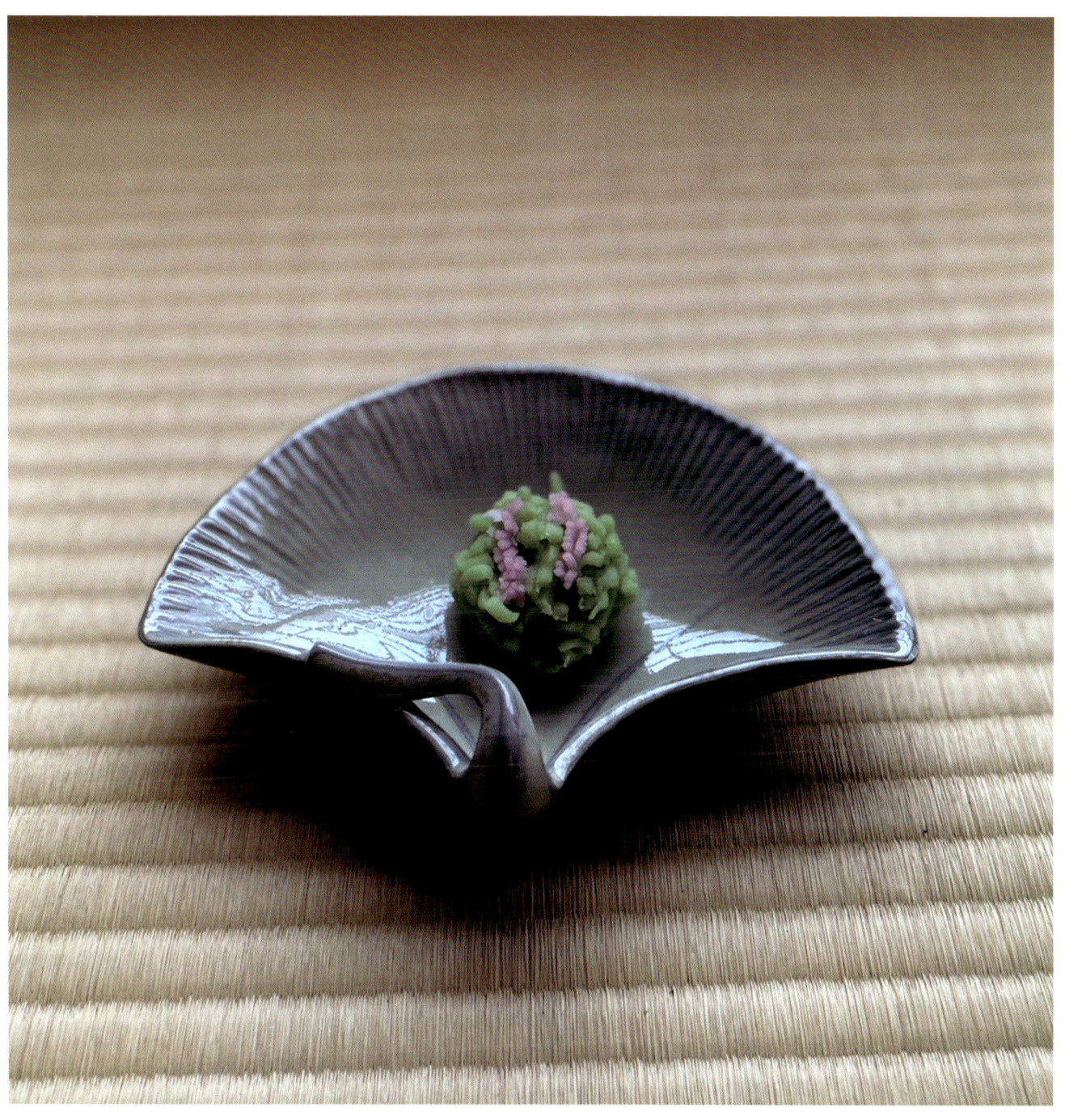

MIRAKU KAMEI XV | 15代亀井味楽
Ginkgo-form Plate | 銀杏型皿
2013 | 2013年
White glaze | 白釉

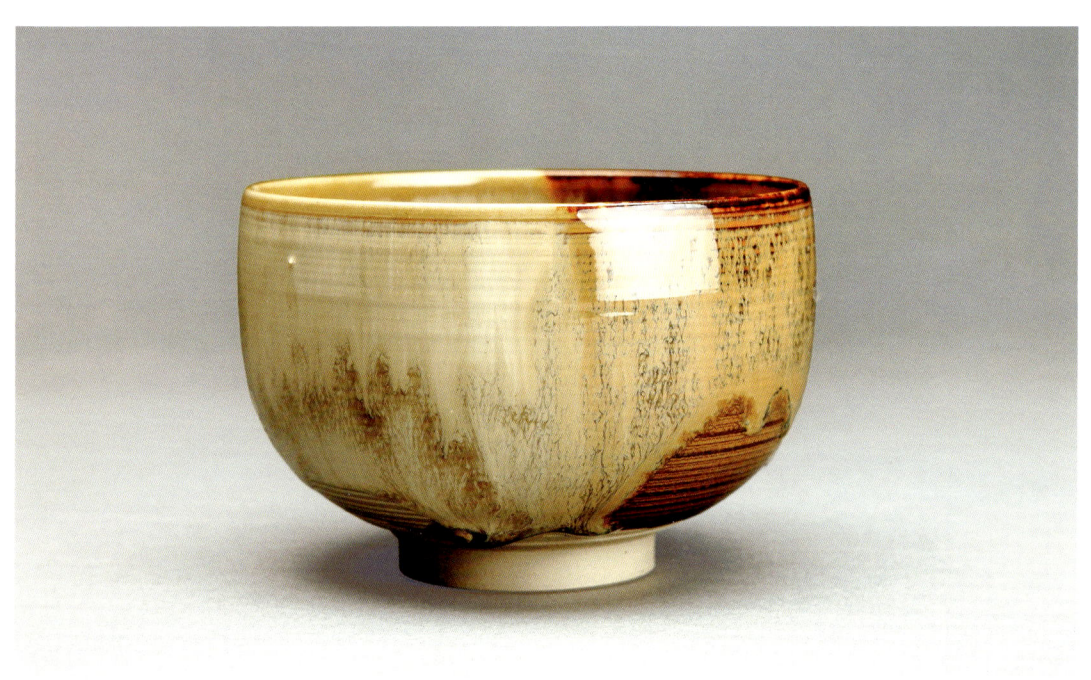

MIRAKU KAMEI XV | 15代亀井味楽
Tea Bowl | 茶盌
2016 | 2016年
Kakewake glaze | 掛分
XV106

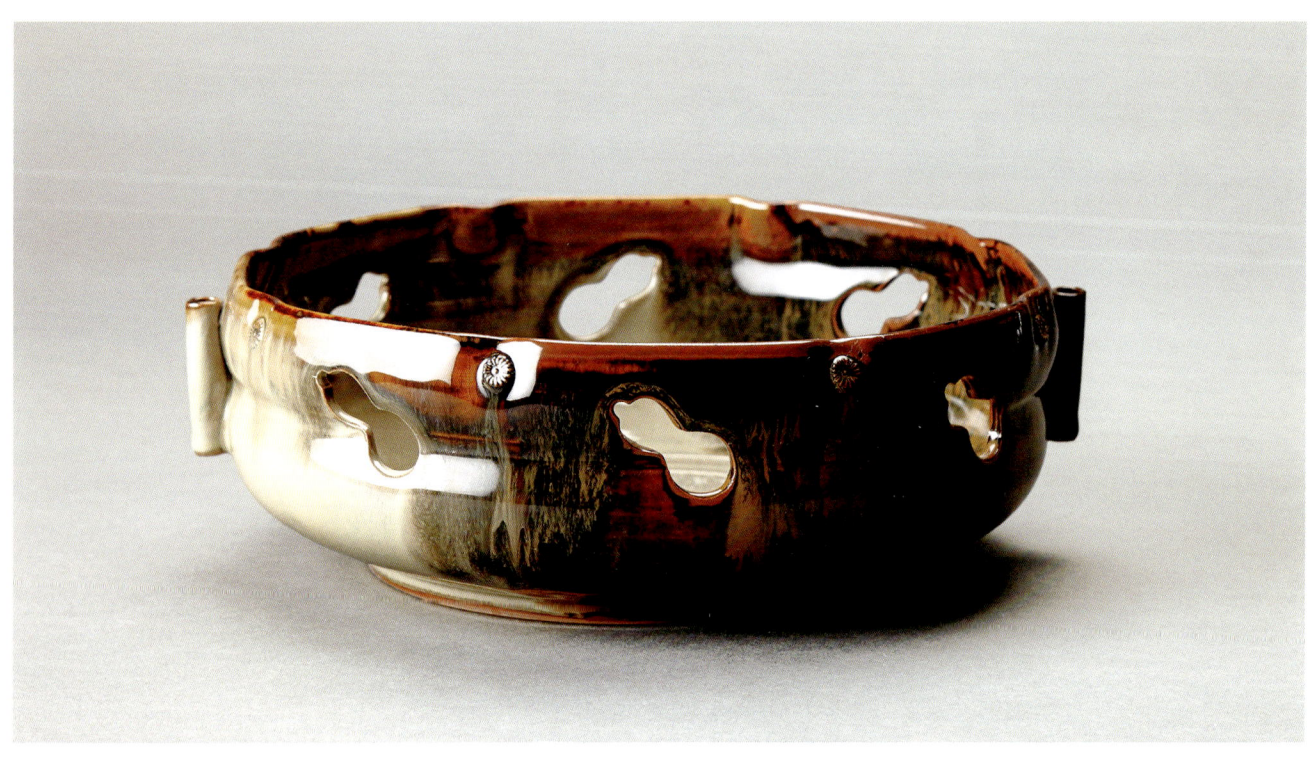

MIRAKU KAMEI XV | 15代亀井味楽
Sweets Tray with Six-gourd Design (openwork) | 六瓢透菓子器
2016 | 2016年
Kakewake glaze | 掛分
XV118

Sweets trays are selected for their harmony with the other tea utensils, the color and shape of sweets being served, and the season.

菓子器は、他の茶道具との調和、提供される菓子の色や形、そして季節に基づいて選択される。

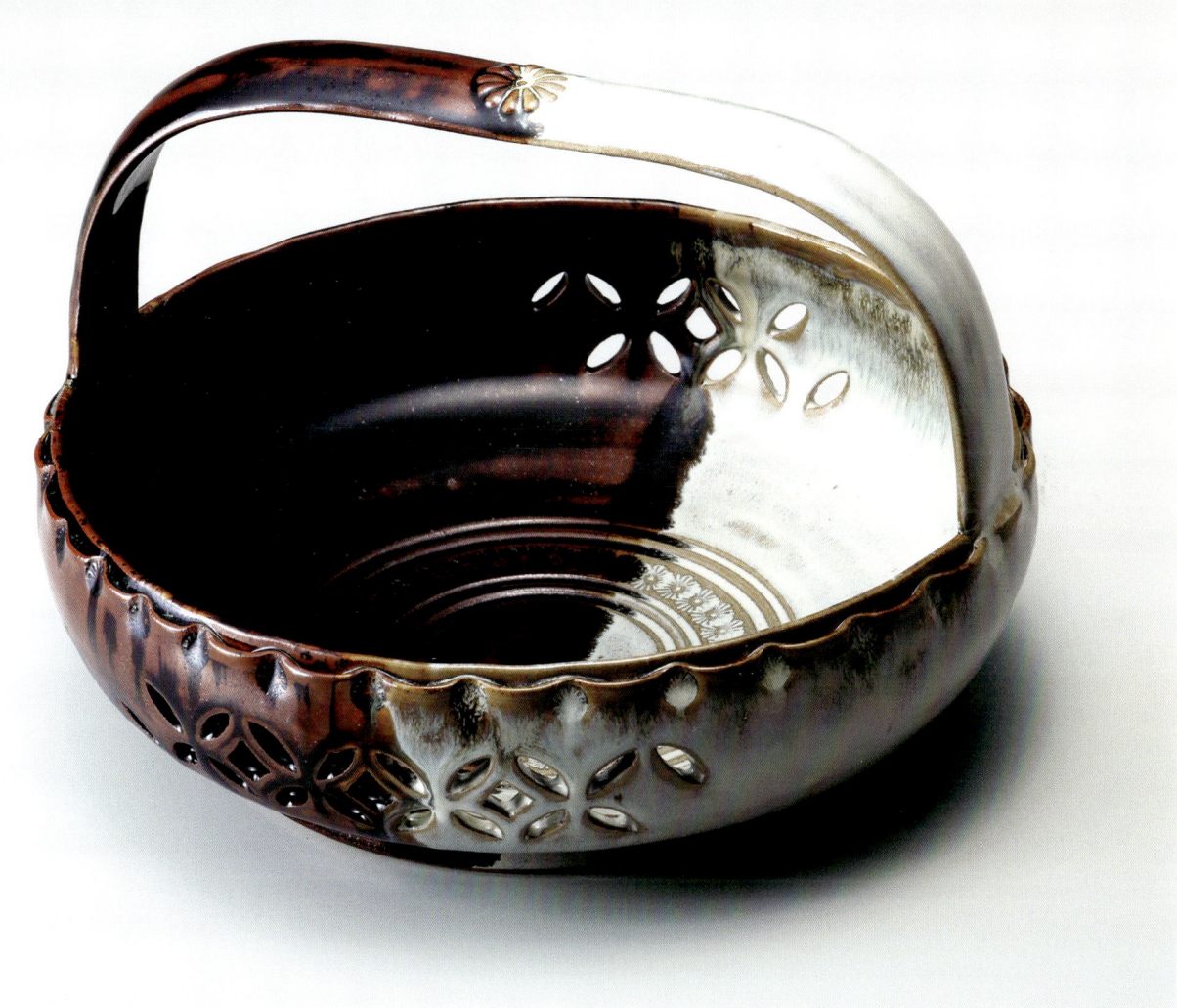

**MIRAKU KAMEI XV**
**Sweets Tray with Bridge Handle and Shippō (openwork)**
2014
Kakewake glaze
XV40

15代亀井味楽
取手付菓子器
2014年
掛分

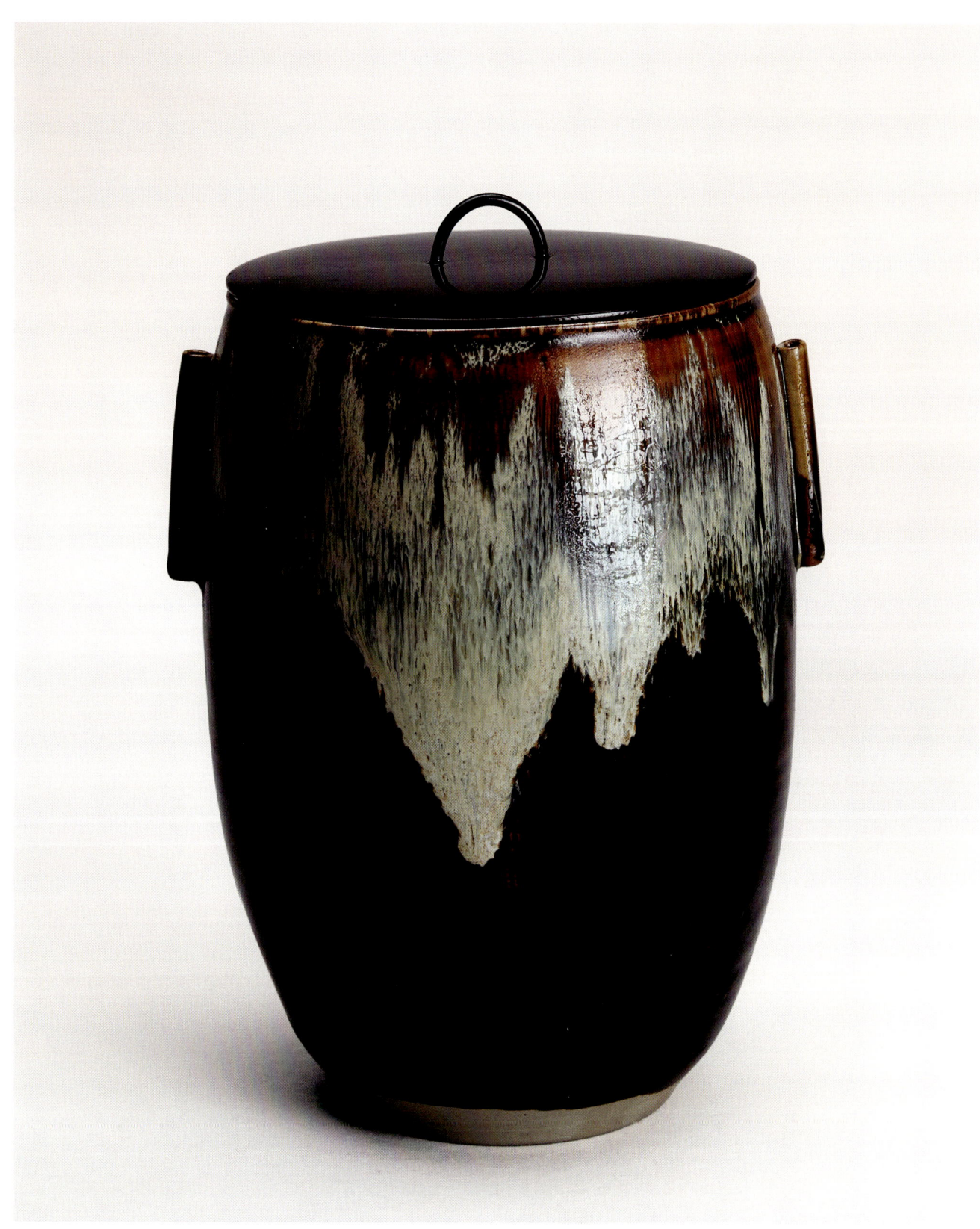

MIRAKU KAMEI XV
Water Container with Lacquer Lid,
Comb Pattern, and Pipe Ear Handles
2015
Ame glaze
XV70

15代亀井味楽
耳付うるし蓋付水指
2015年
飴釉

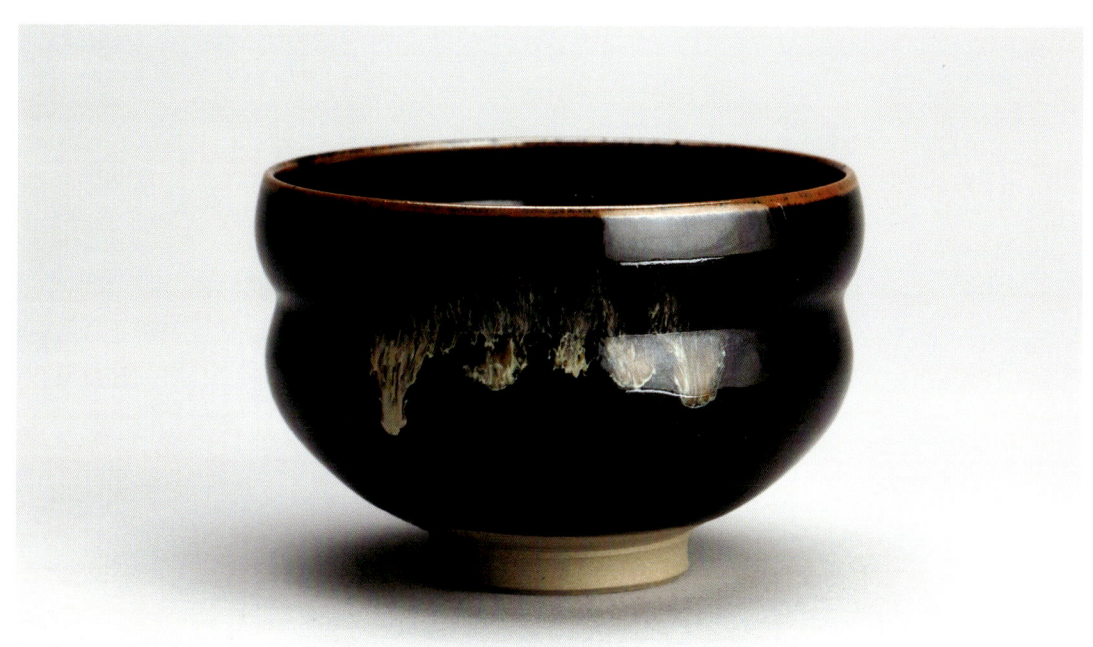

| MIRAKU KAMEI XV | 15代亀井味楽 |
| Tea Bowl | 茶碗 |
| 2018 | 2018年 |
| Black glaze | 黒釉 |
| XV165 | |

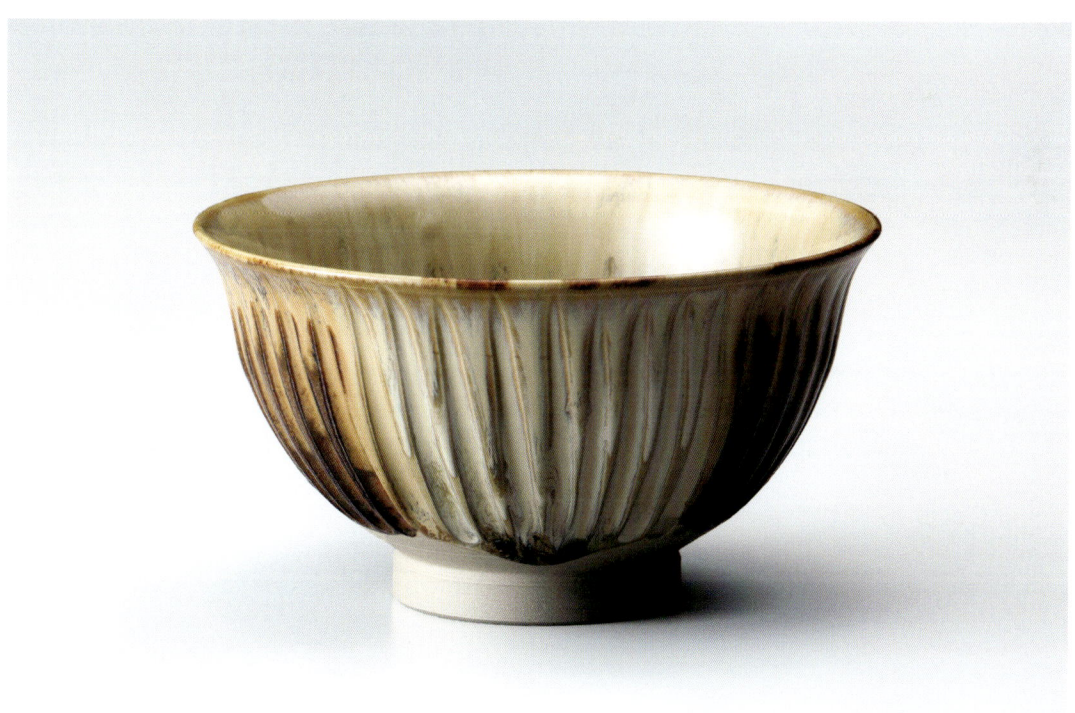

| MIRAKU KAMEI XV | 15代亀井味楽 |
| Tea Bowl with Ridged Decoration | 節目茶碗 |
| 2014 | 2014年 |
| Yellow glaze | 黄釉 |
| XV27 | |

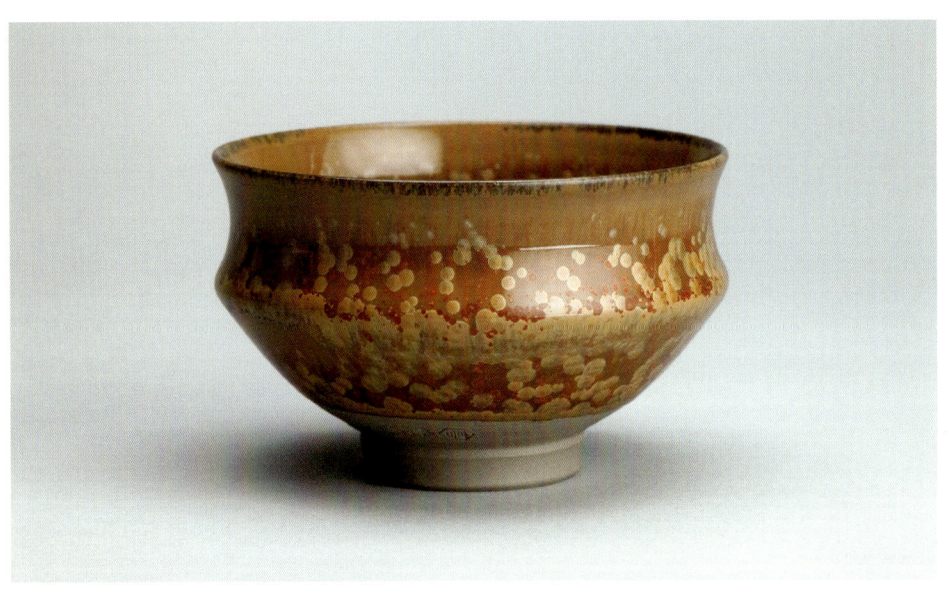

MIRAKU KAMEI XV
Tea Bowl
2018
"Gold Flower" glaze
XV161

15代亀井味楽
茶盌
2018年
金華紋釉

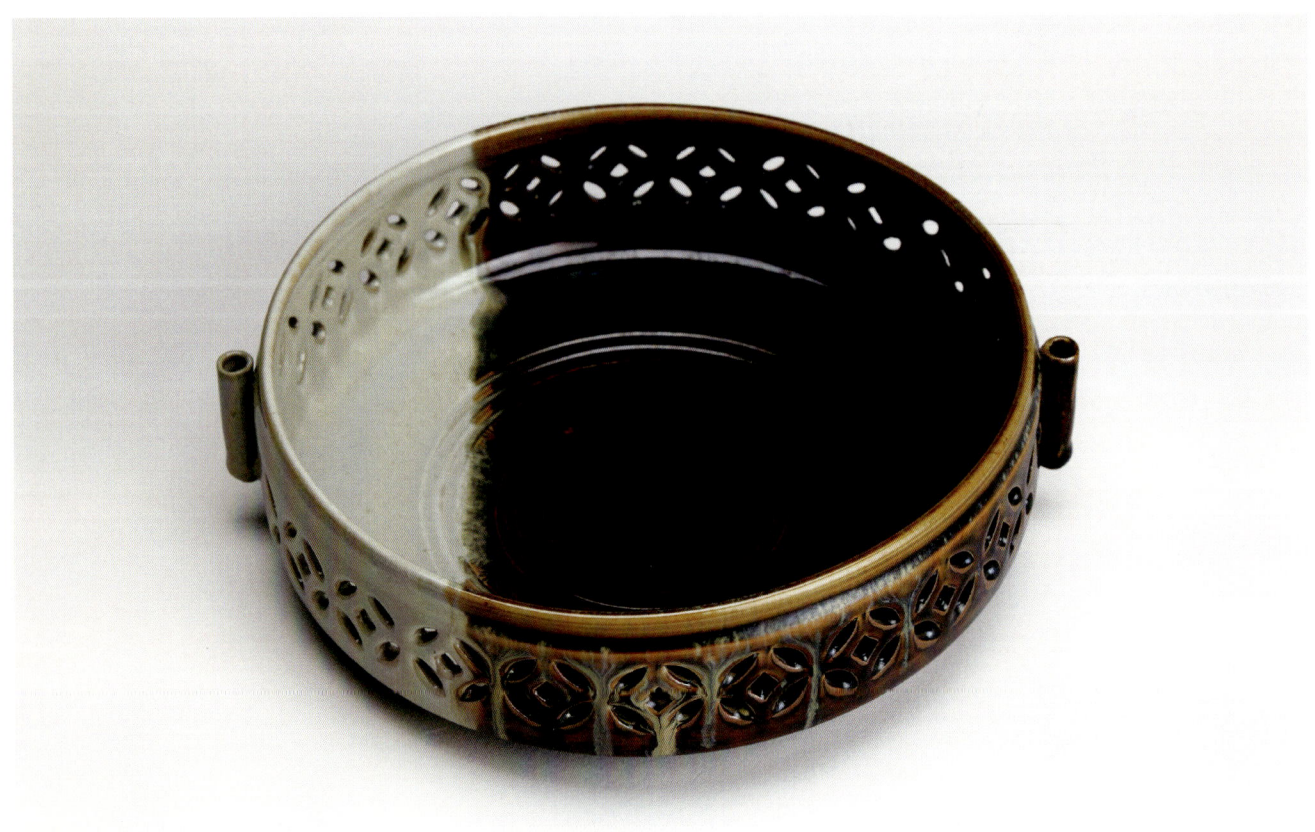

MIRAKU KAMEI XV
Sweets Tray with Shippō (openwork)
2014
Kakewake glaze
XV42

15代亀井味楽
七宝透菓子器
2014年
掛分

The innovation by the thirteenth generation of a double-walled openwork vessel is furthered by Miraku Kamei XV, who incorporated it in this tea bowl. The hot tea sits in the thin-walled inner bowl while the hands are protected by the outer layer. It proved challenging to create a double-walled tea bowl that adhered to traditional size and weight standards.

13代亀井味楽によって作られた二重構造を持つ透彫の器は、15代亀井味楽によってさらに進化した。15代はこの技術を茶盌に適用した。熱いお茶は内側の薄い茶盌に注がれるが、外側の層によって守られているため、茶盌を持つ手は熱さを感じない。伝統的な寸法と重量を保ちながら二重構造にするのは非常に困難である。

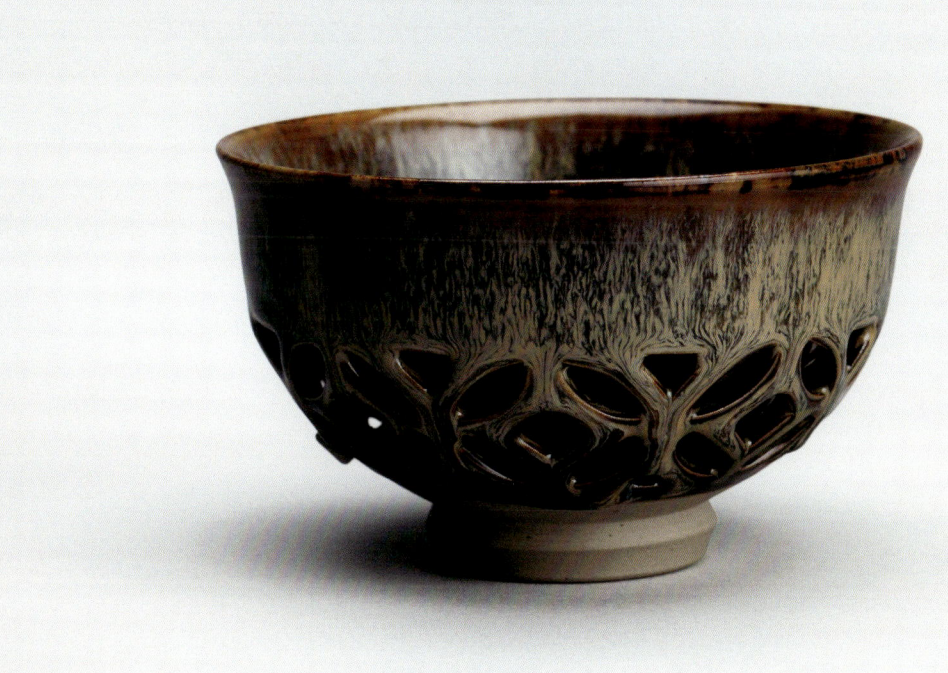

**MIRAKU KAMEI XV**
**Tea Bowl with Shippō (openwork)**
2018
Yellow glaze
XV160

15代亀井味楽
七宝透茶盌
2018年
黄釉

The "Gold Flower" glaze (*kinka* in Japanese) is a version of the yellow glaze exclusive to the Miraku Kiln.

「金華紋釉」は味楽窯でのみ使用されている黄釉である。

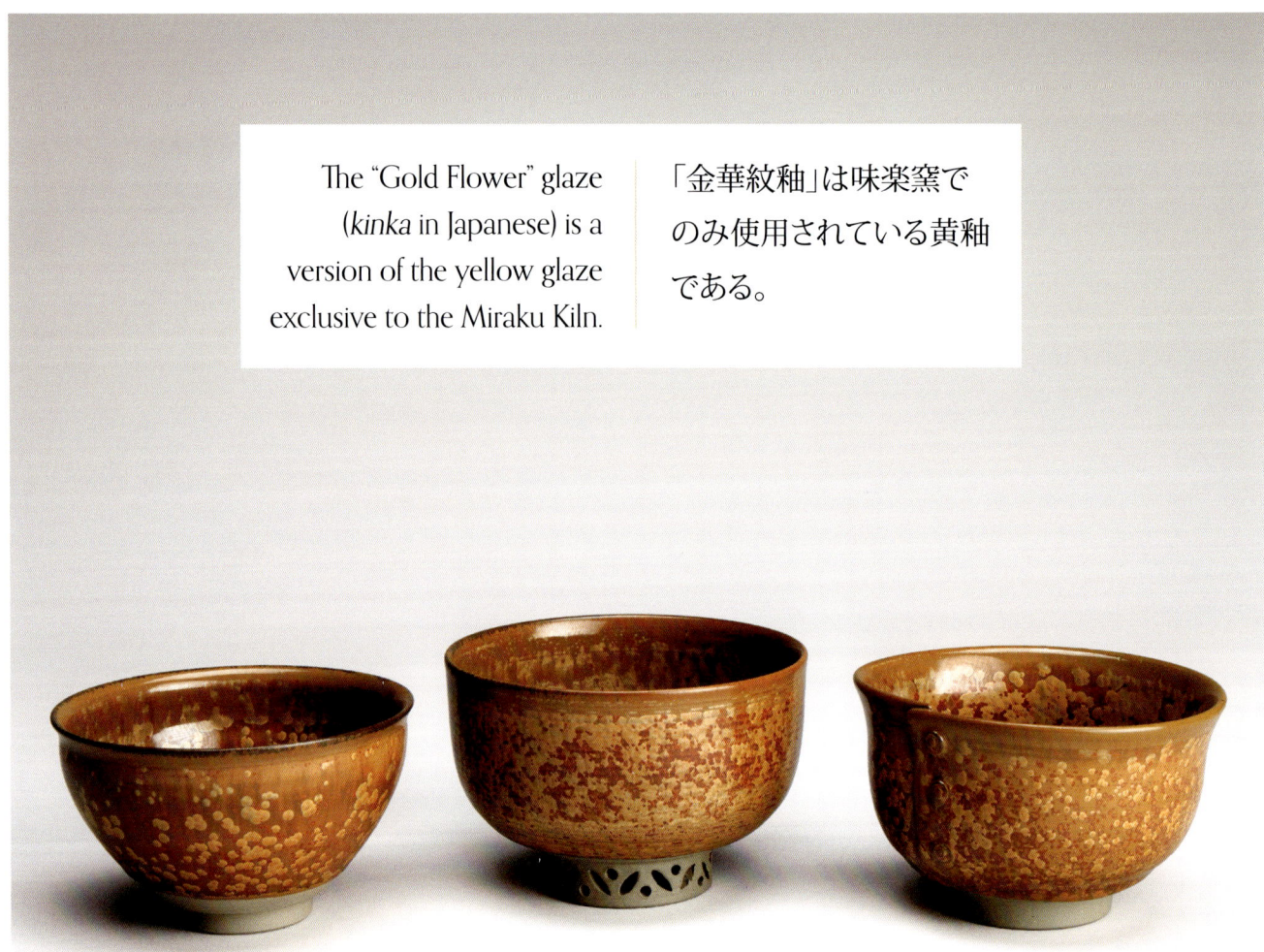

| | |
|---|---|
| **MIRAKU KAMEI XV** | 15代亀井味楽 |
| Tea Bowl | 茶盌 |
| 2018 | 2018年 |
| "Gold Flower" glaze | 金華紋釉 |
| XV175 | |
| | |
| Tea Bowl with Shippō (openwork) on Foot | 七宝透高台茶盌 |
| 2016 | 2016年 |
| "Gold Flower" glaze | 金華紋釉 |
| XV98 | |
| | |
| Tea Bowl with Seam | とじめ茶盌 |
| 2014 | 2014年 |
| "Gold Flower" glaze | 金華紋釉 |
| XV77 | |

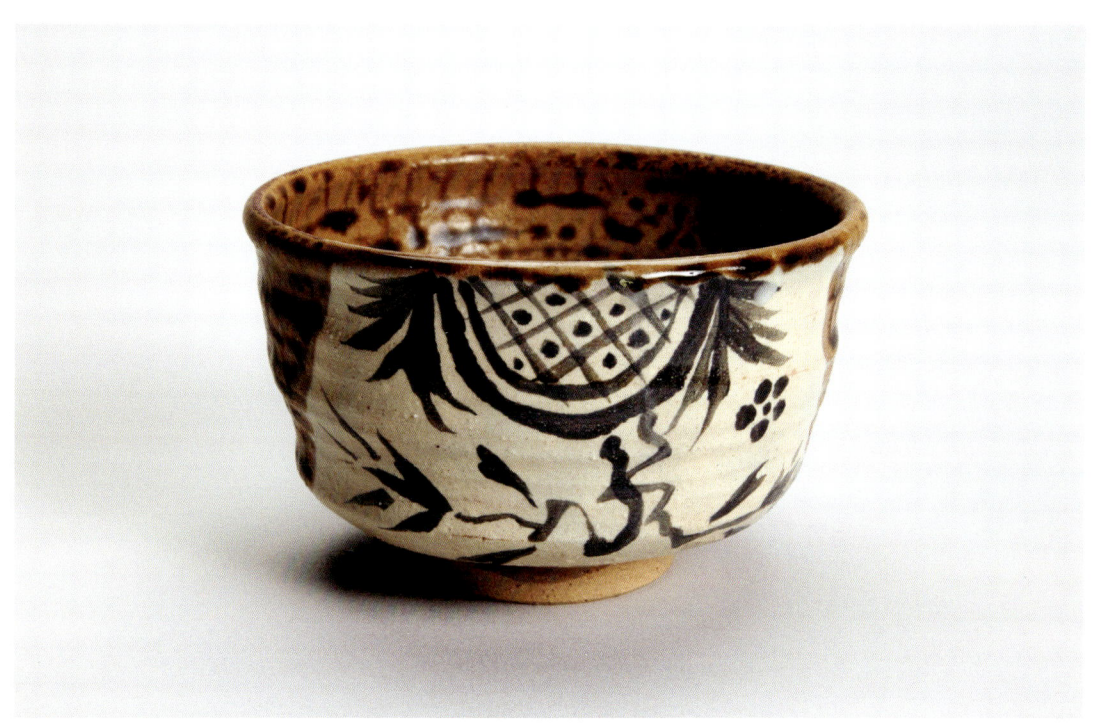

MIRAKU KAMEI XV | 15代亀井味楽
Tea Bowl | 茶盌
2022 | 2022年
Oribe and copper glaze | 織部釉および銅化釉
XV194 |

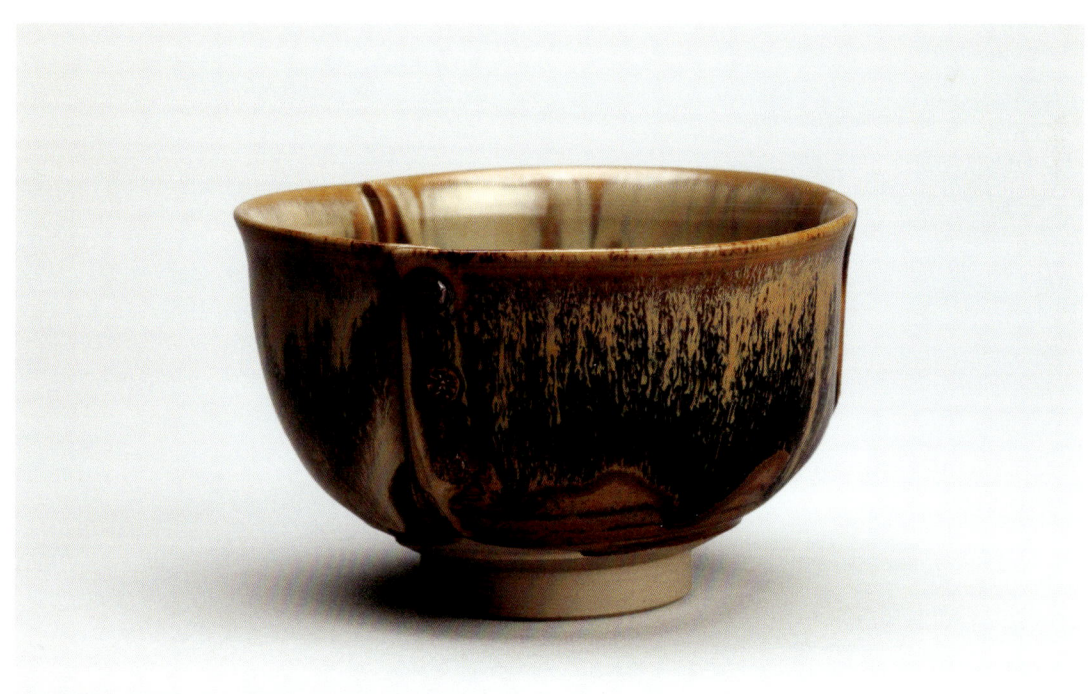

MIRAKU KAMEI XV | 15代亀井味楽
Tea Bowl with Seam | とじめ茶盌
2018 | 2018年
Kakewake glaze | 掛分
XV159 |

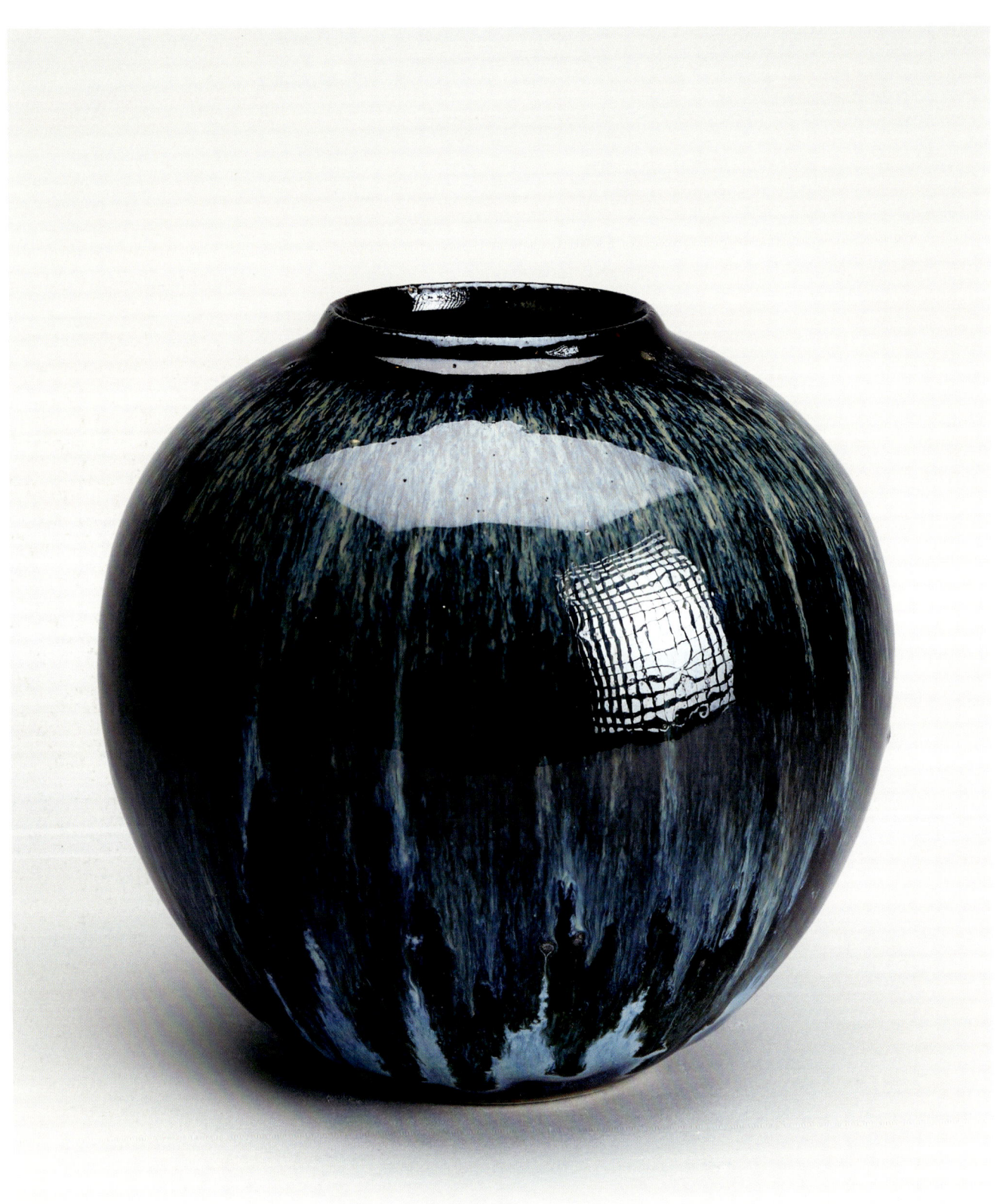

MIRAKU KAMEI XV　　15代亀井味楽
Jar　　壺
2024　　2024年
Black glaze　　黒釉
XV219

A thoughtfully made tea bowl is easy to hold in the hand and improves the flavor of the tea.

細心の注意を払って作られた茶盌は持ちやすく、茶の味わいを深める。

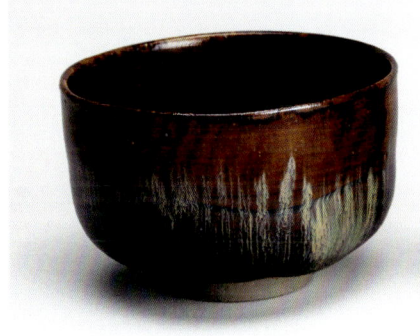 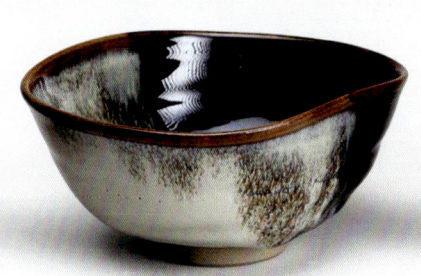 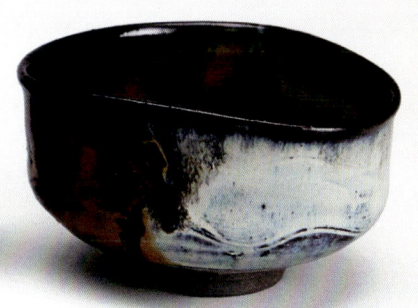

| | |
|---|---|
| **MIRAKU KAMEI XV** | 15代亀井味楽 |
| Tea Bowl | 茶盌 |
| 2024 | 2024年 |
| Yellow glaze | 黄釉 |
| XV215 | |
| | |
| Tea Bowl | 茶盌 |
| 2024 | 2024年 |
| Kakewake and oribe glaze | 掛分、織部釉 |
| XV214 | |
| | |
| Tea Bowl | 茶盌 |
| 2024 | 2024年 |
| Kakewake and oribe glaze | 掛分、織部釉 |
| XV211 | |

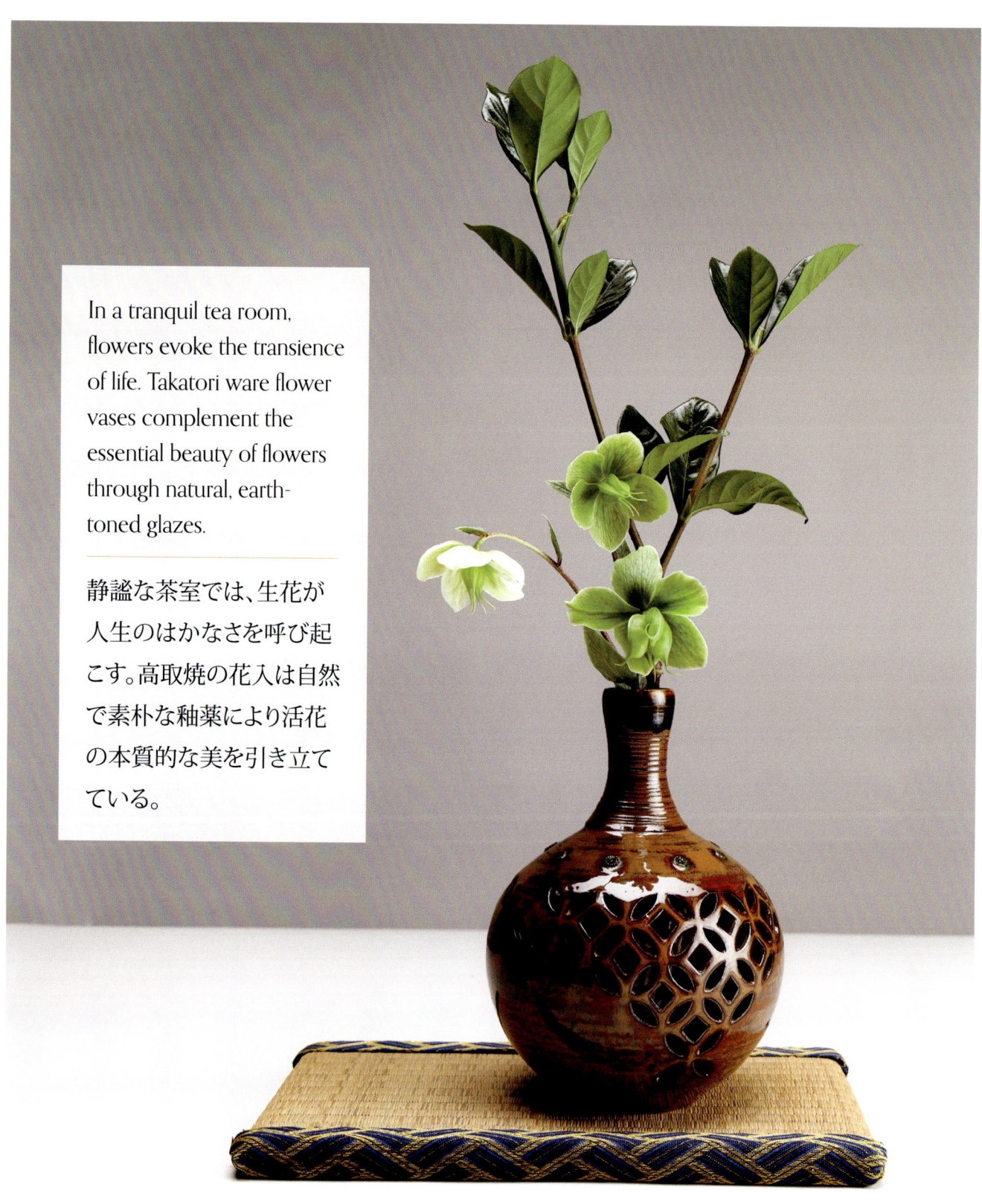

In a tranquil tea room, flowers evoke the transience of life. Takatori ware flower vases complement the essential beauty of flowers through natural, earth-toned glazes.

静謐な茶室では、生花が人生のはかなさを呼び起こす。高取焼の花入は自然で素朴な釉薬により活花の本質的な美を引き立てている。

**MIRAKU KAMEI XV**
**Flower Vase with Shippō (openwork)**
2014
Yellow glaze
XV45

15代亀井味楽
七宝透花入
2014年
黄釉

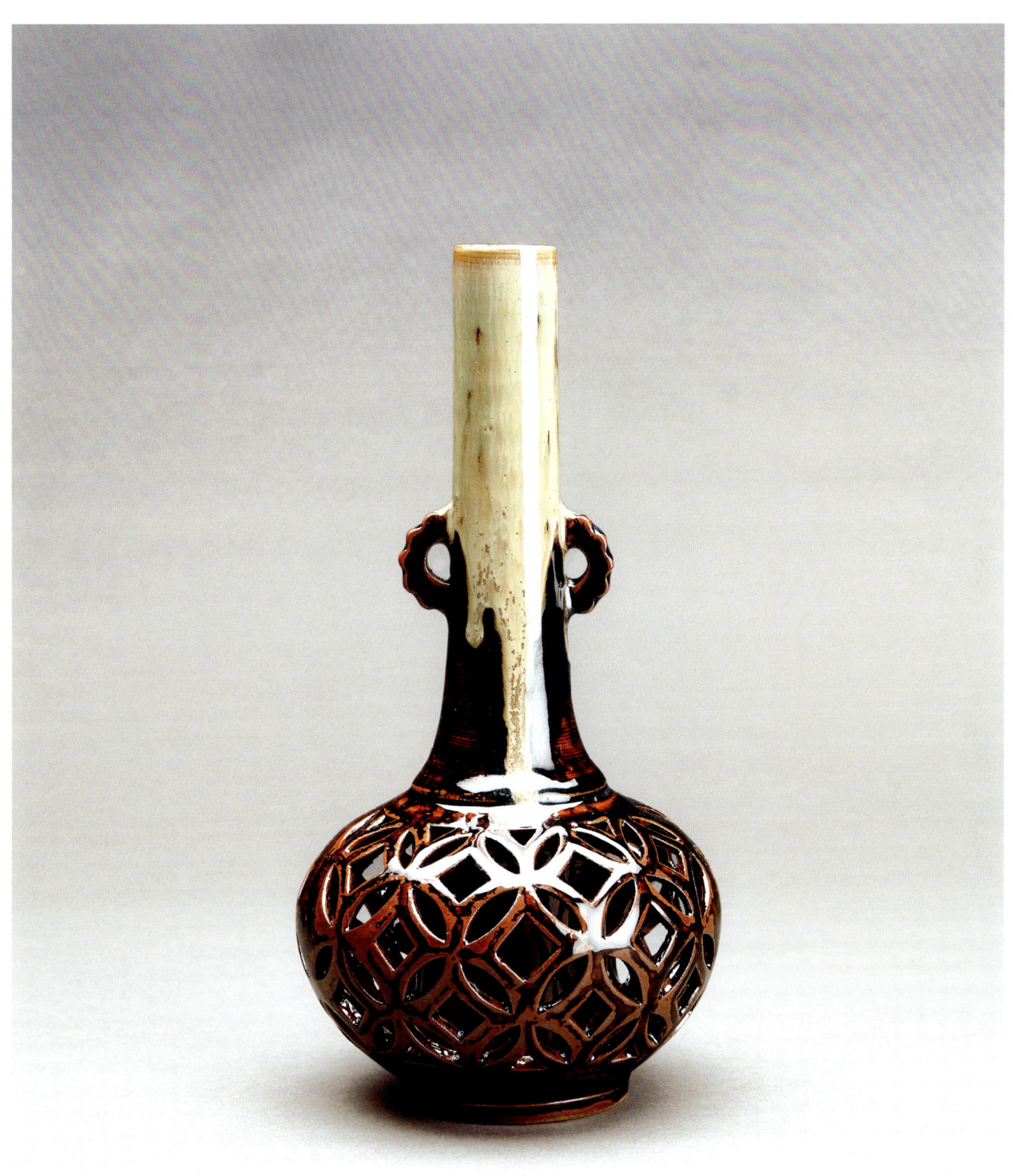

MIRAKU KAMEI XV | 15代亀井味楽
Flower Vase with Shippō (openwork) | 七宝透花入
2016 | 2016年
White and ame glaze | 白釉および飴釉
XV110

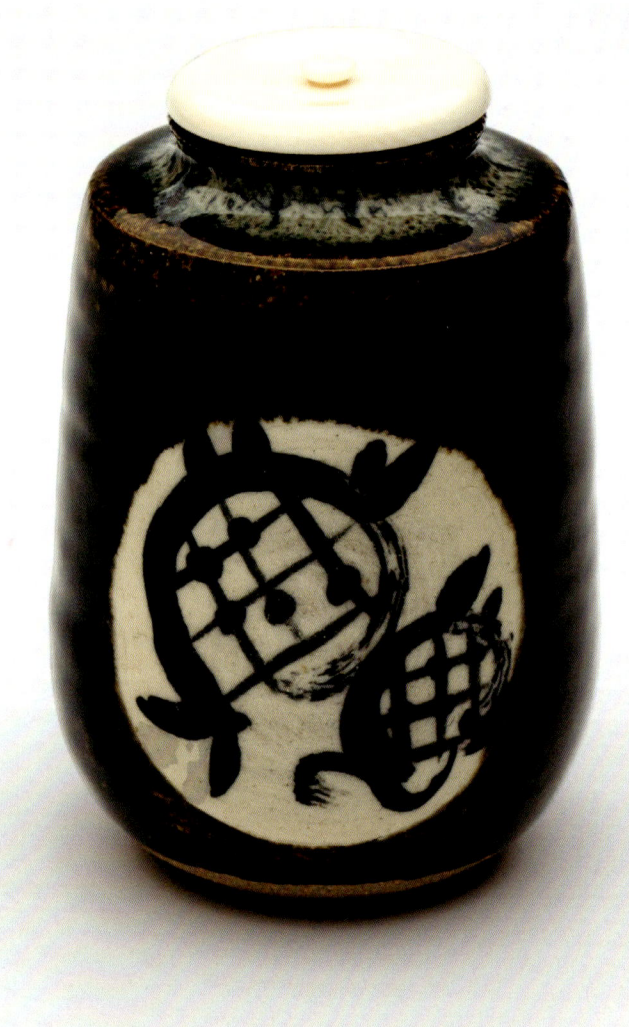

MIRAKU KAMEI XV | 15代亀井味楽
Tea Caddy | 茶入
2020 | 2020年
Oribe glaze | 織部釉
XV191 |

Painted designs appeared on Takatori ware in the early 17th century. Here, Miraku Kamei XV blends the classic flowing glazes of Takatori with bold pictorial markings inspired by the Oribe tradition.

絵付けされた高取焼は17世紀初頭にすでに存在していた。15代亀井味楽は、織部の伝統に着想を得て、高取焼の伝統的な釉薬に大胆な絵付けを施している。

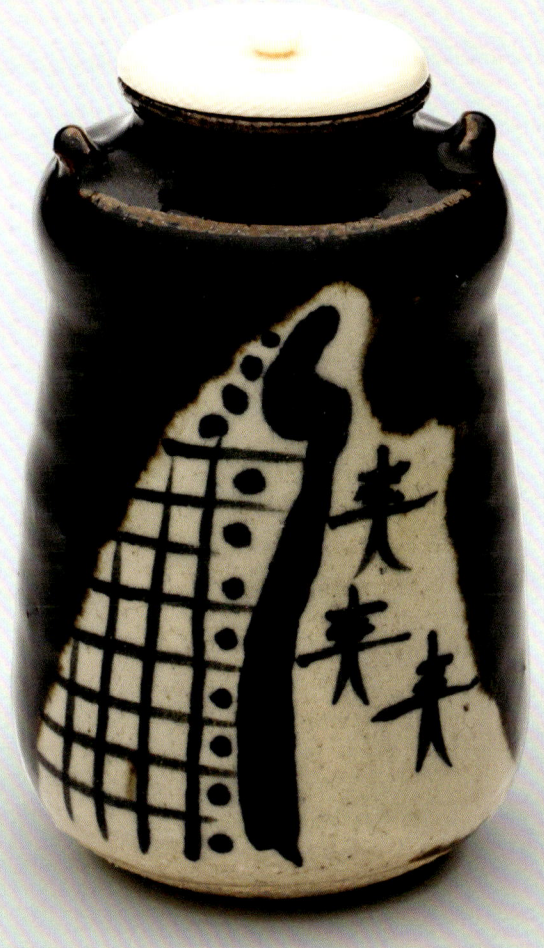

**MIRAKU KAMEI XV**
**Tea Caddy with Ear-shaped Handles**
2020
Oribe glaze
XV192

15代亀井味楽
耳付茶入
2020年
織部釉

*Katatsuki* (shouldered) tea caddies are the most emblematic Takatori ware pieces. In this piece, the thin-walled vessel is enhanced when one glaze is poured over another, an innovation characteristic of Miraku Kamei XV

肩衝茶入は高取焼の代表的な茶具の1つである。これは、15代亀井味楽ならではの革新的な技術によって生み出された薄造りの茶入で、黄釉の上に黒釉を掛けることにより、その深みが一層強調されている。

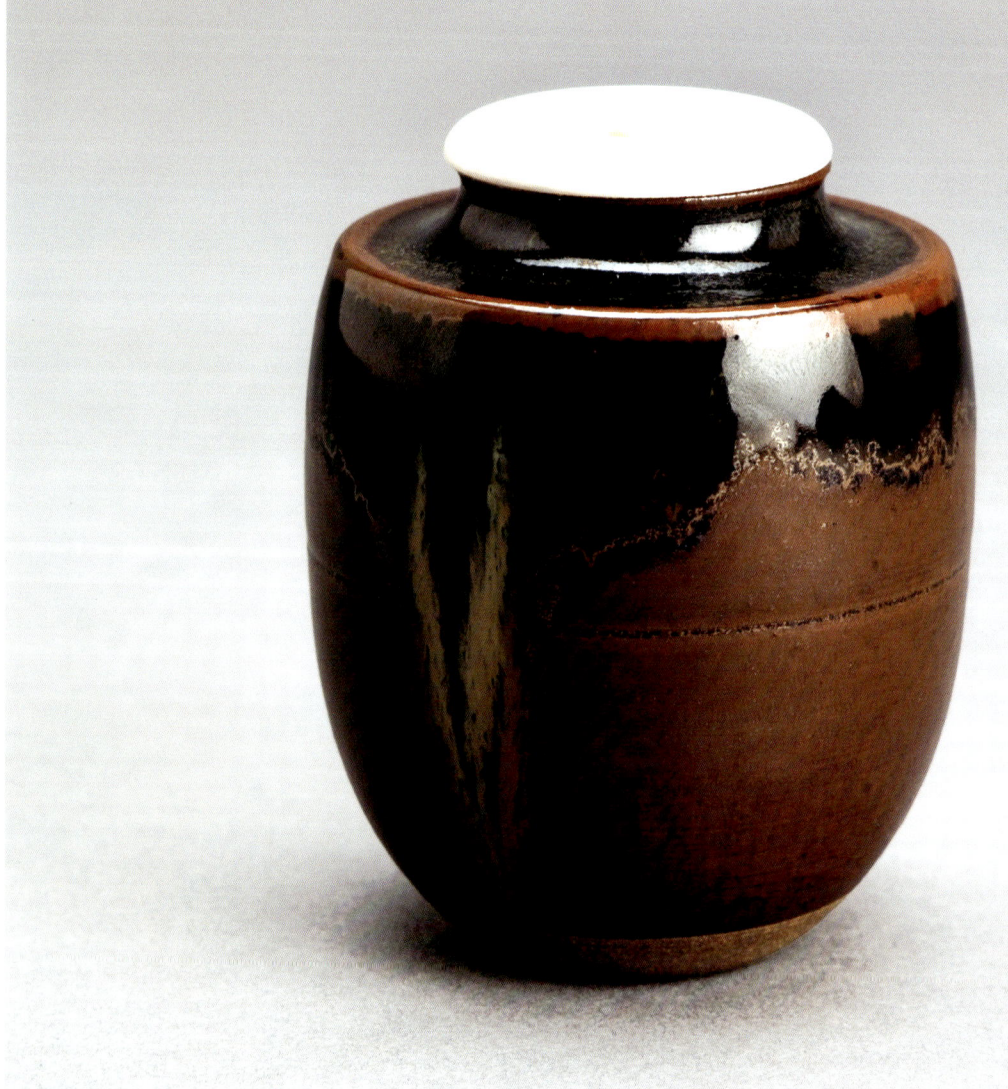

**MIRAKU KAMEI XV**
**Tea Caddy with Shoulder**
**2013**
**Yellow and black glaze**
**XV10**

15代亀井味楽
肩衝茶入
2013年
黄釉に黒流し

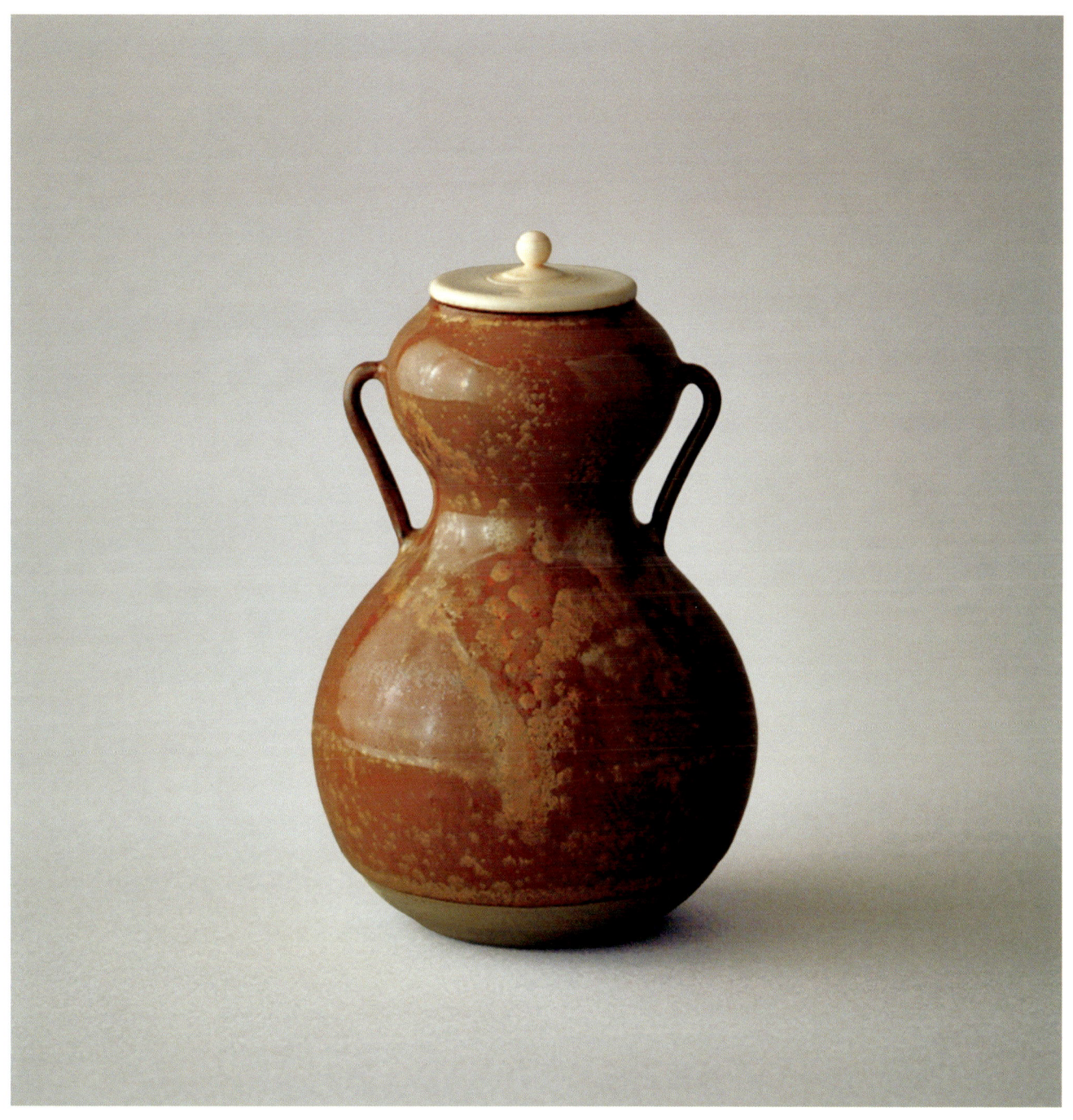

MIRAKU KAMEI XV
Gourd-form Tea Caddy with Ear-shaped Handles
2013
"Gold Flower" glaze

15代亀井味楽
瓢耳付茶入
2013年
金華紋釉

In Zen Buddhism, going from a square (4 corners) to a triangle (3 corners) to a circle (no corners) represents a person devoted to self-improvement who focuses the mind and lets go of excess and roughness.

禅において、しかく（四つの角）から、さんかく（三つの角）そしてまる（角なし）への移行は、精神に集中し、余計なものや粗雑なものを手放すことにより自己修養を行う人間を表している。

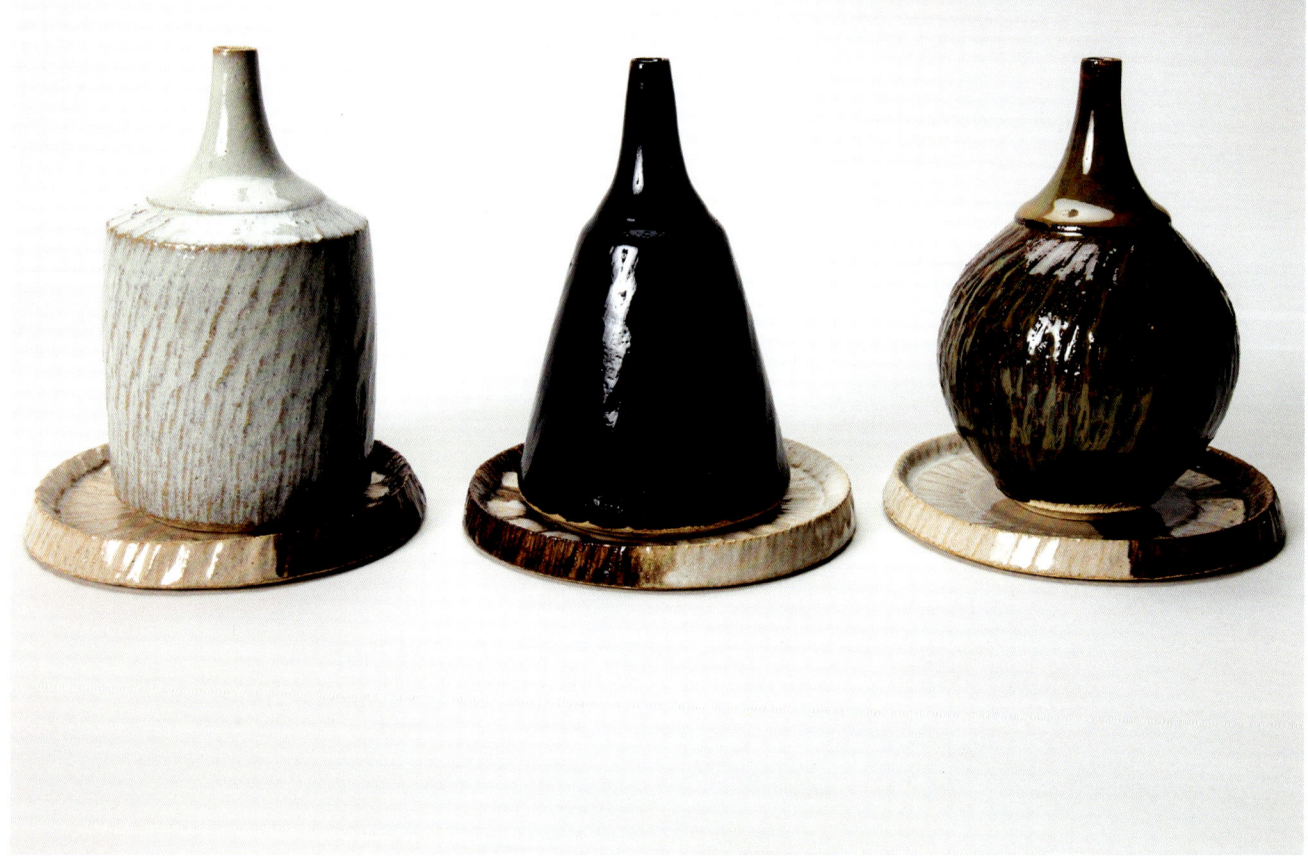

MIRAKU KAMEI XV
**Zen Series Flower Vases**
2022
**White glaze, black glaze, ame glaze**
XV205

15代亀井味楽
四点：皿および壺
2022年
白釉、黒釉、飴釉

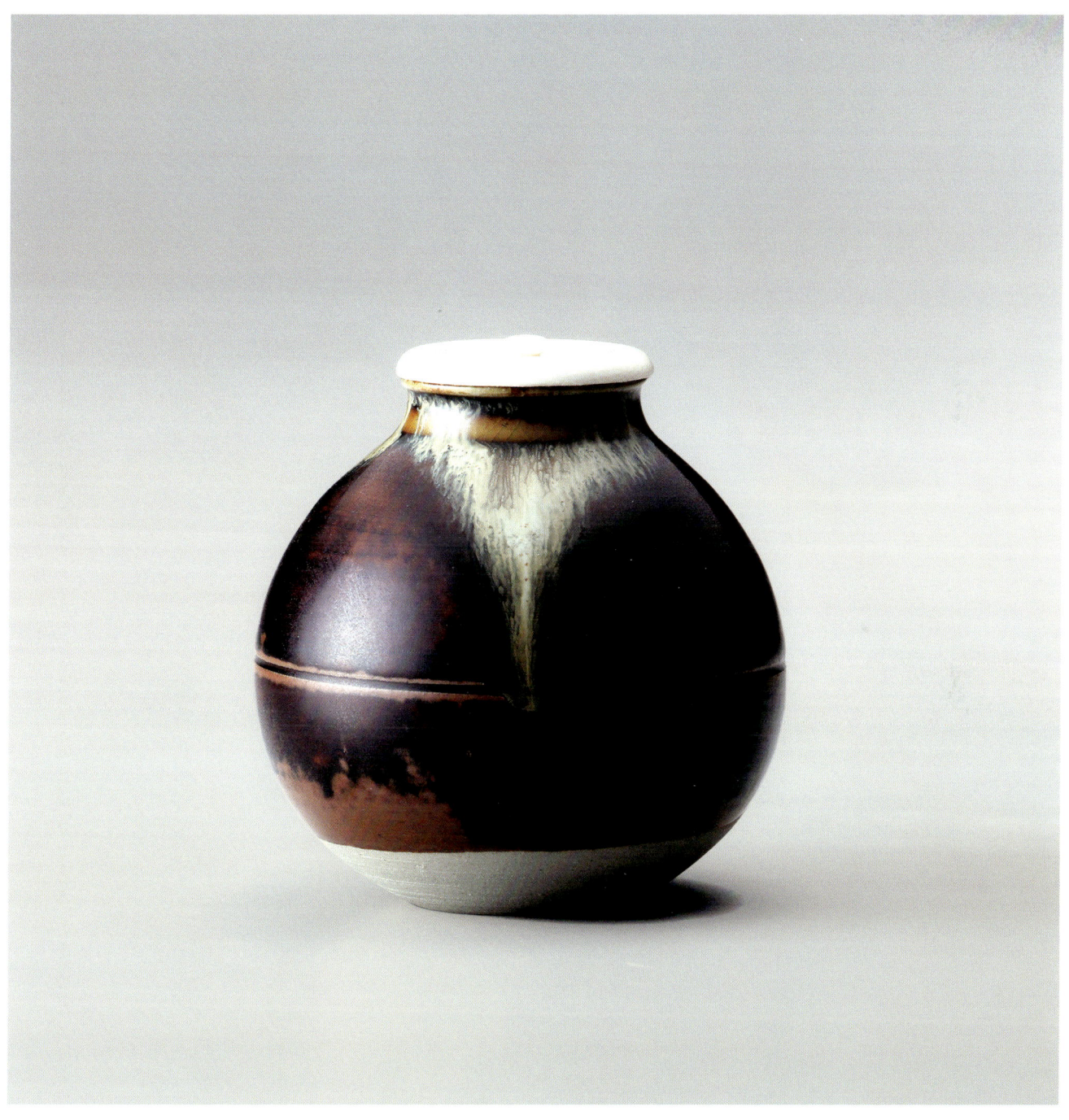

MIRAKU KAMEI XV
Eggplant-form Tea Caddy
2014
Ame and white glaze
XV12

15代亀井味楽
茄子形茶入
2014年
飴釉に白流し

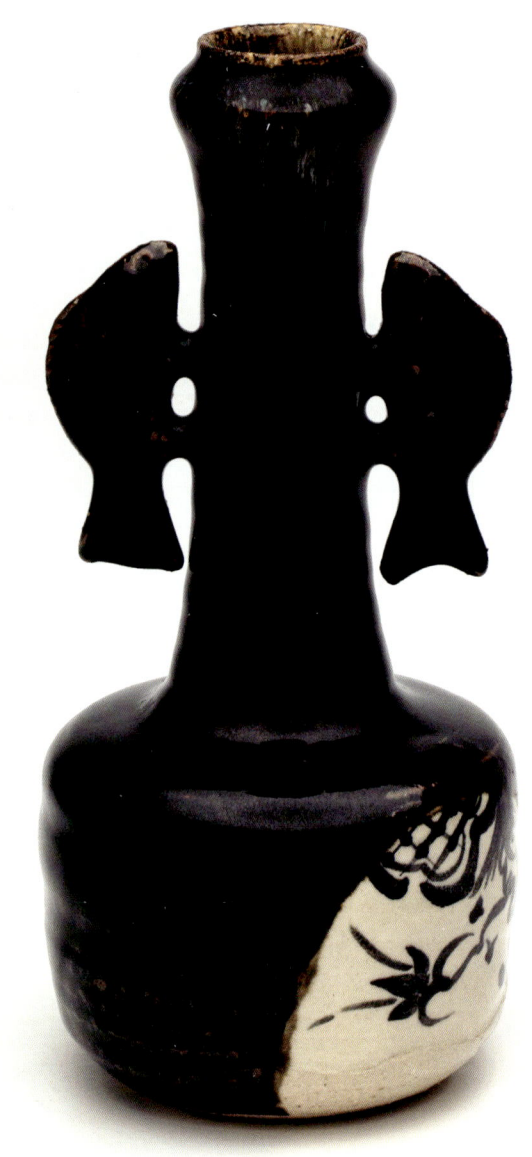

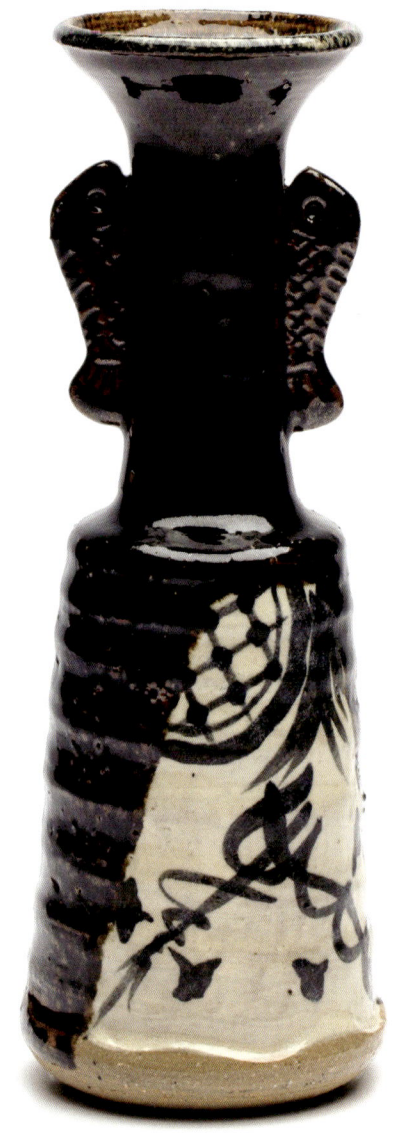

MIRAKU KAMEI XV
Hammer-form Flower Vase
with Carp-shaped Handles
2020
Oribe glaze
XV187

15代亀井味楽
鯉形耳付砧形花入
2020年
織部釉

MIRAKU KAMEI XV
Flower Vase with
Wide Mouth
2020
Oribe glaze
XV184

15代亀井味楽
広口花入
2020年
織部釉

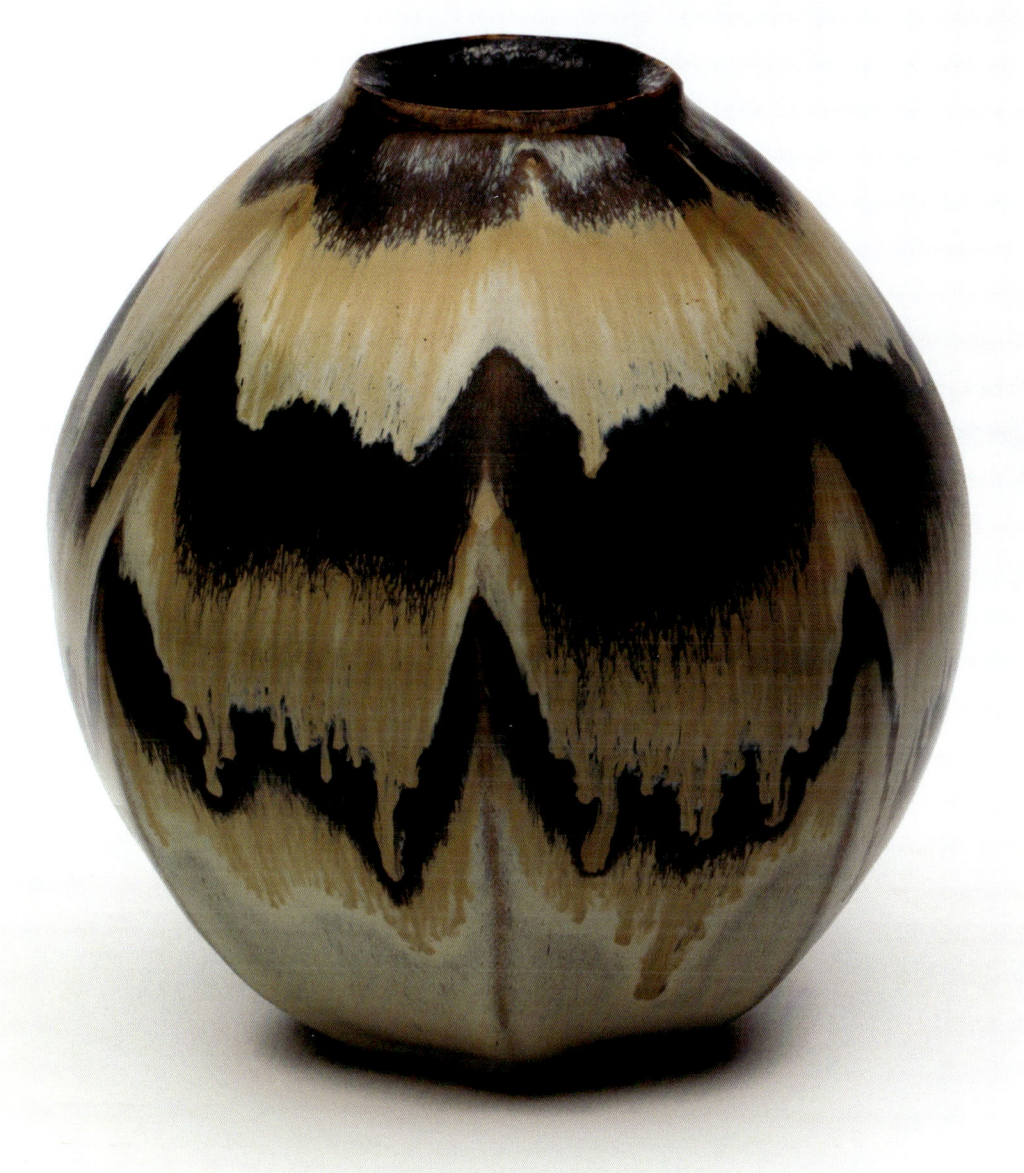

*Yu sai* is a technique in which significant amounts of multiple glazes are poured onto the piece to create gradation.

釉彩とは複数の釉薬を作品に掛けることによりグラデーションを作り出す技法である。

MIRAKU KAMEI XV
Jar
2020
Yu sai
XV178

15代亀井味楽
壺
2020年
釉彩

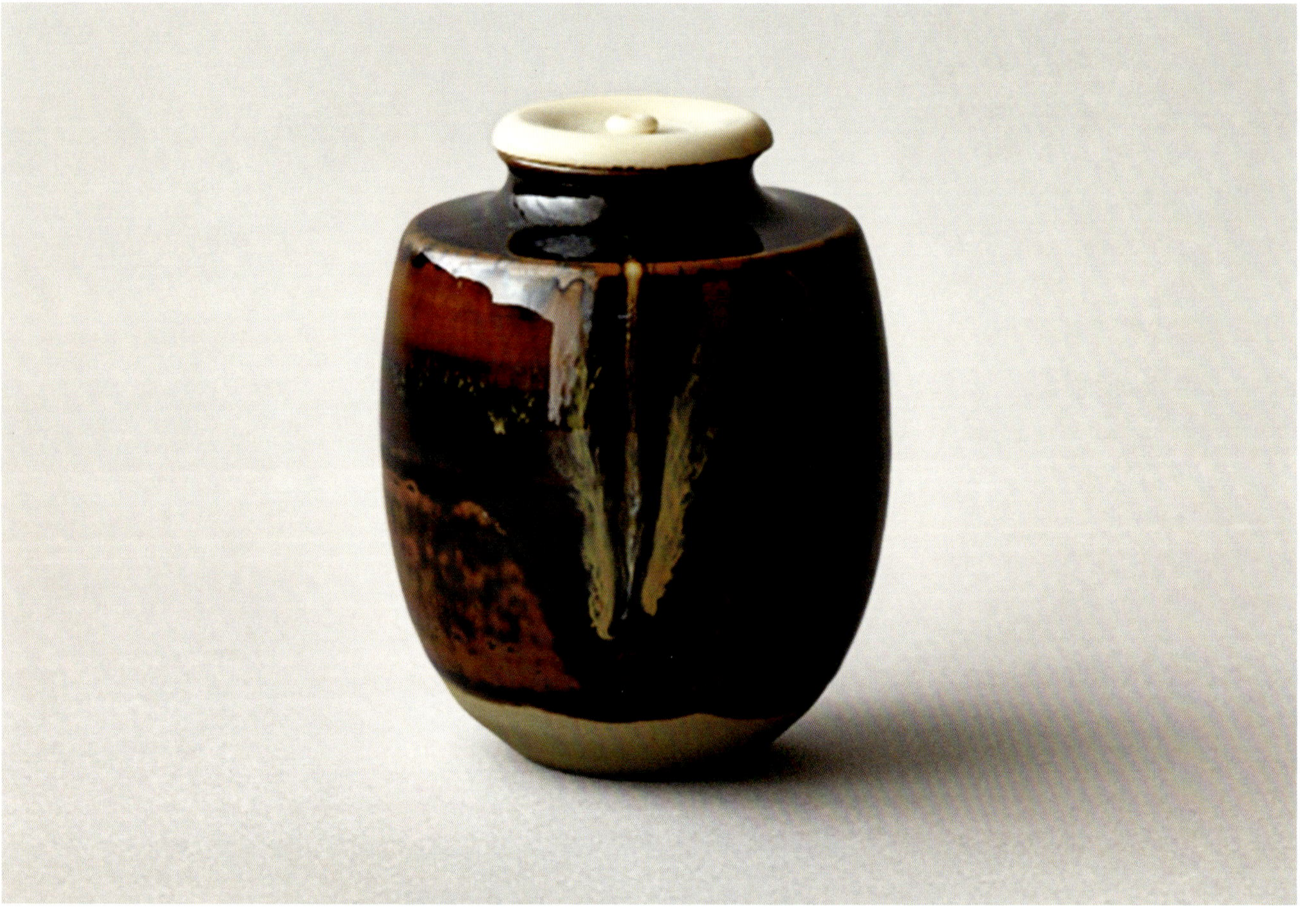

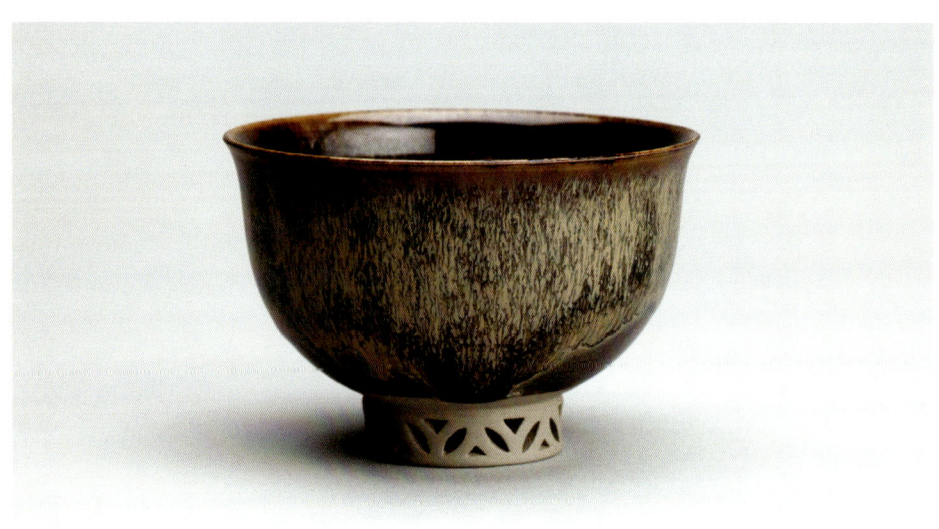

MIRAKU KAMEI XV
Tea Caddy with Shoulder
2014
Yellow and black glaze

15代亀井味楽
肩衝茶入
2014年
黄釉に黒流し

MIRAKU KAMEI XV
Tea Bowl with Shippō (openwork) on Foot
2018
Yellow glaze
XV163

15代亀井味楽
七宝透高台茶盌
2018年
黄釉

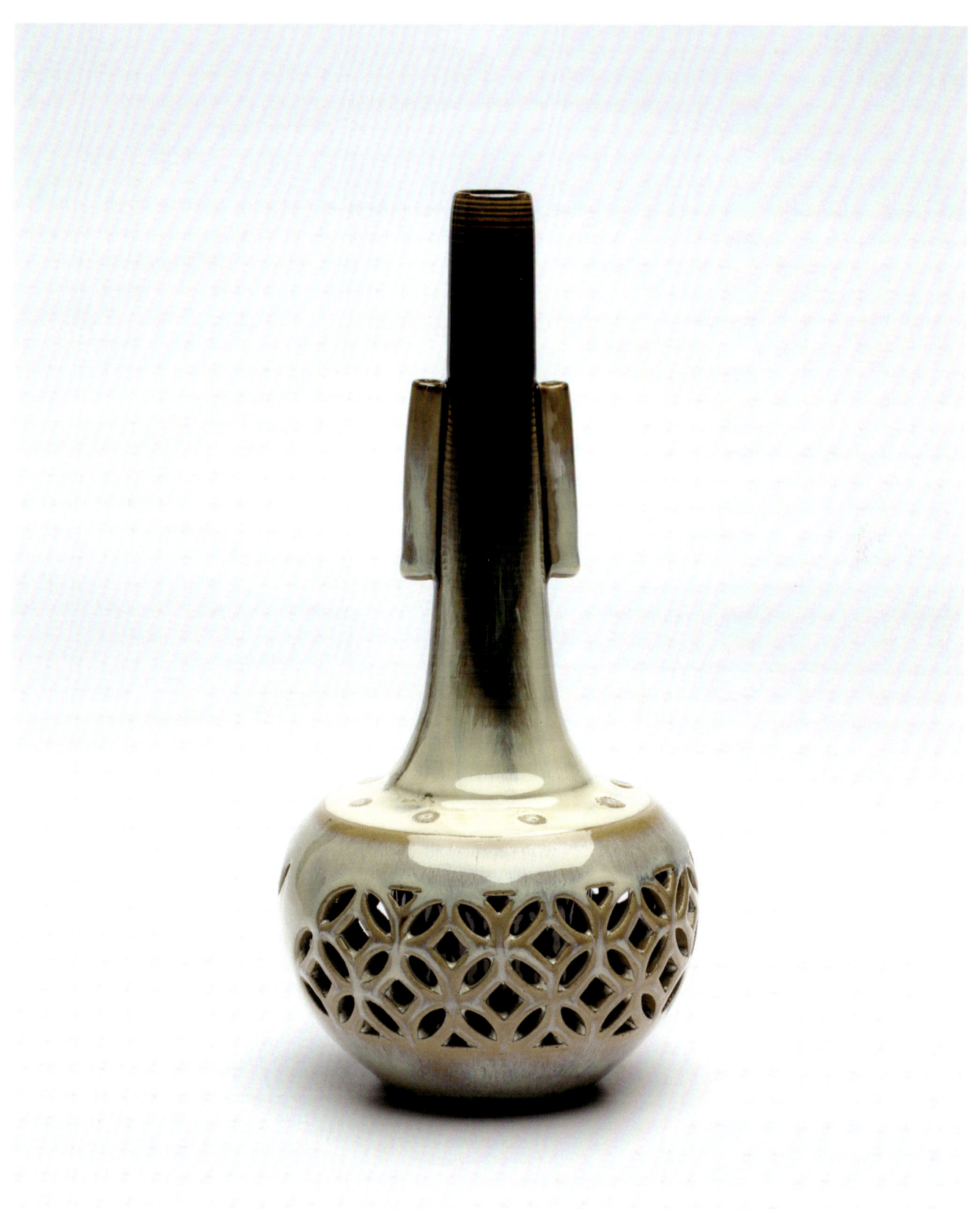

MIRAKU KAMEI XV
Flower Vase with Pipe Ear Handles and Shippō (openwork)
2020
White glaze
XV185

15代亀井味楽
七宝透耳付花入
2020年
白釉

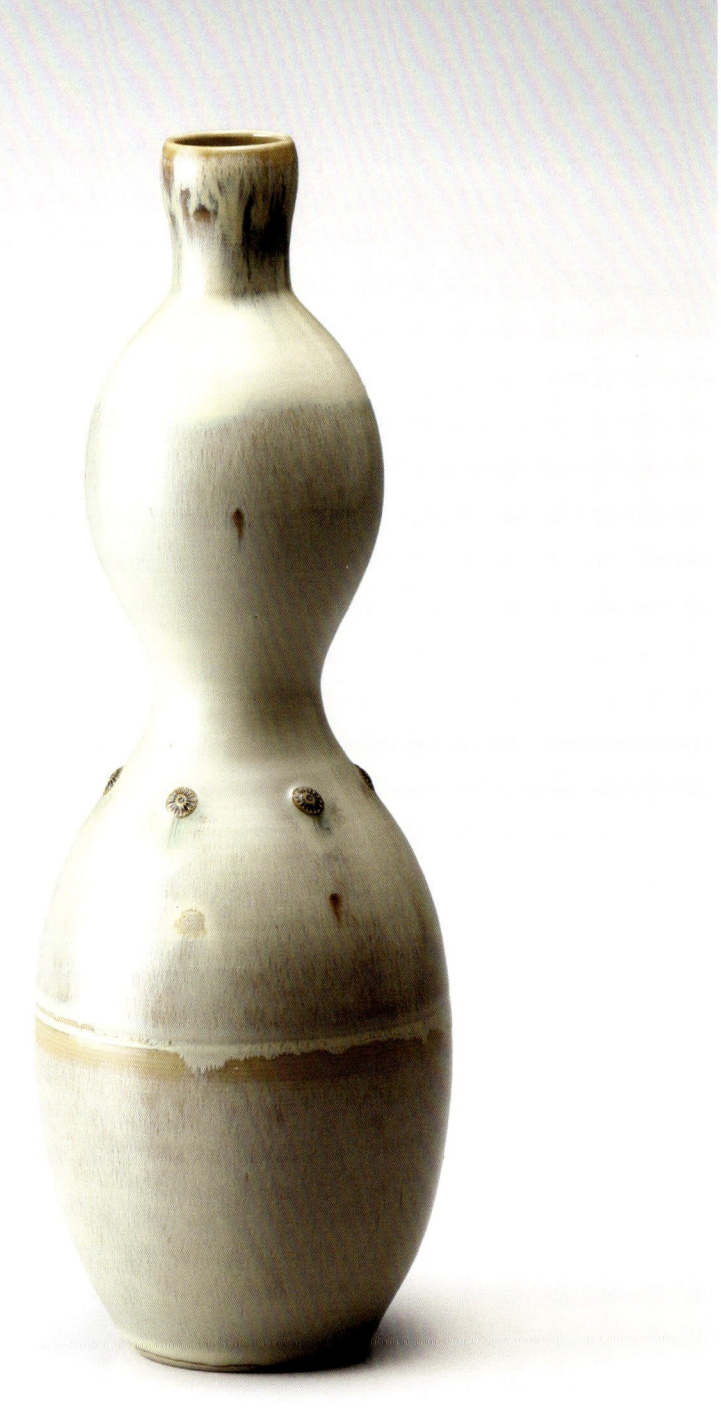

Depending on the atmosphere within the kiln, a traditional white glaze can express itself as white, yellowish-white, or blueish-white.

伝統的な白釉は、窯内の状態によって白、黄色がかった白、青みがかった白を発色する。

MIRAKU KAMEI XV
Gourd-form Flower Vase
2014
White glaze
XV39

15代亀井味楽
瓢形花入
2014年
白釉

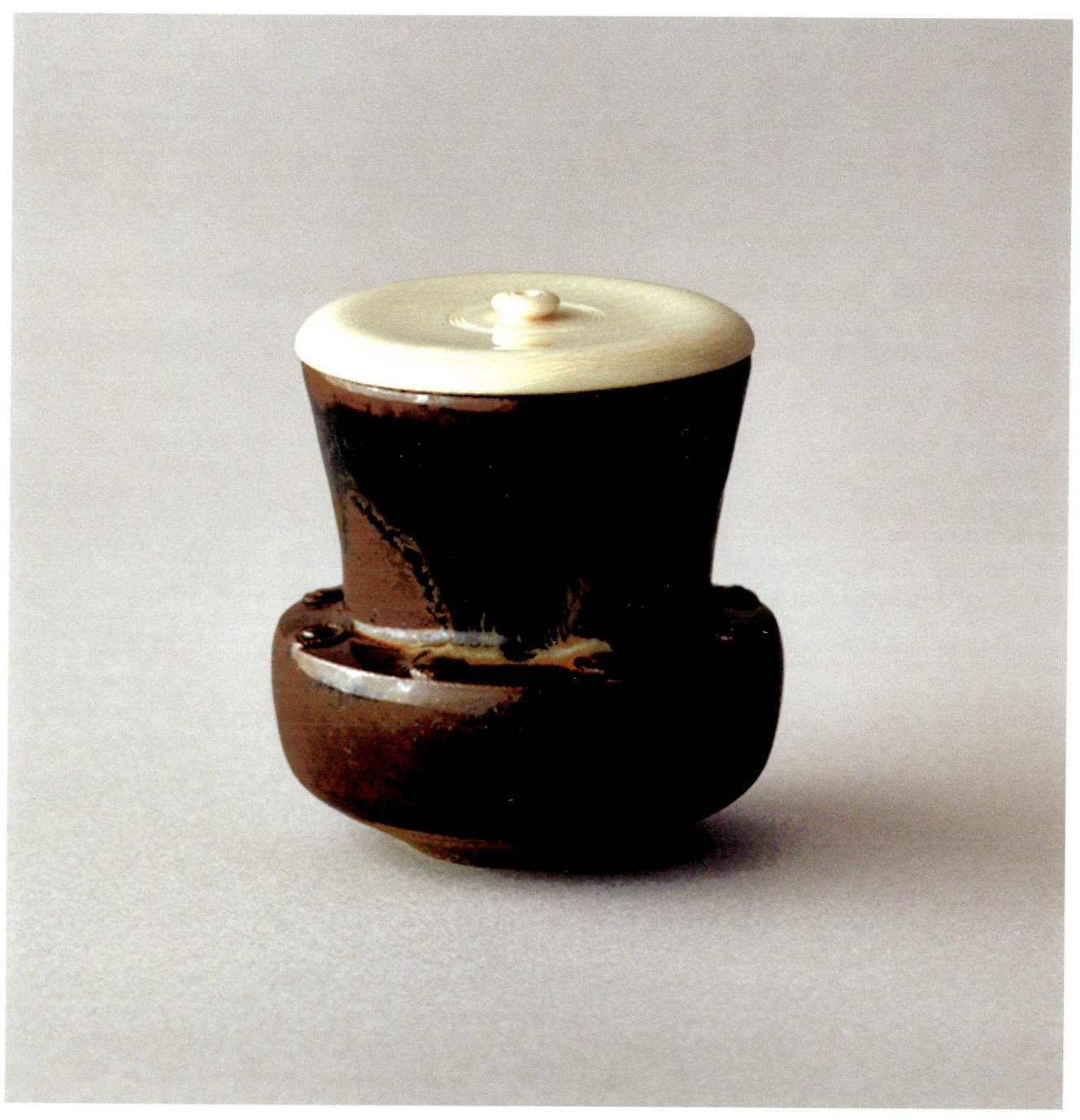

MIRAKU KAMEI XV                15代亀井味楽
Monkfish-form Tea Caddy        鮟鱇型茶入
2013                           2013年
Yellow and black glaze         黄釉に黒流し

Miraku Kamei XV mastered a technique to achieve unprecedented thinness in his tea caddies, which he brings to other vessels such as this flower vase.

15代亀井味楽は前例のない薄さの茶入を作る技法を習得している。この技法は花入など他のうつわにも適用されている。

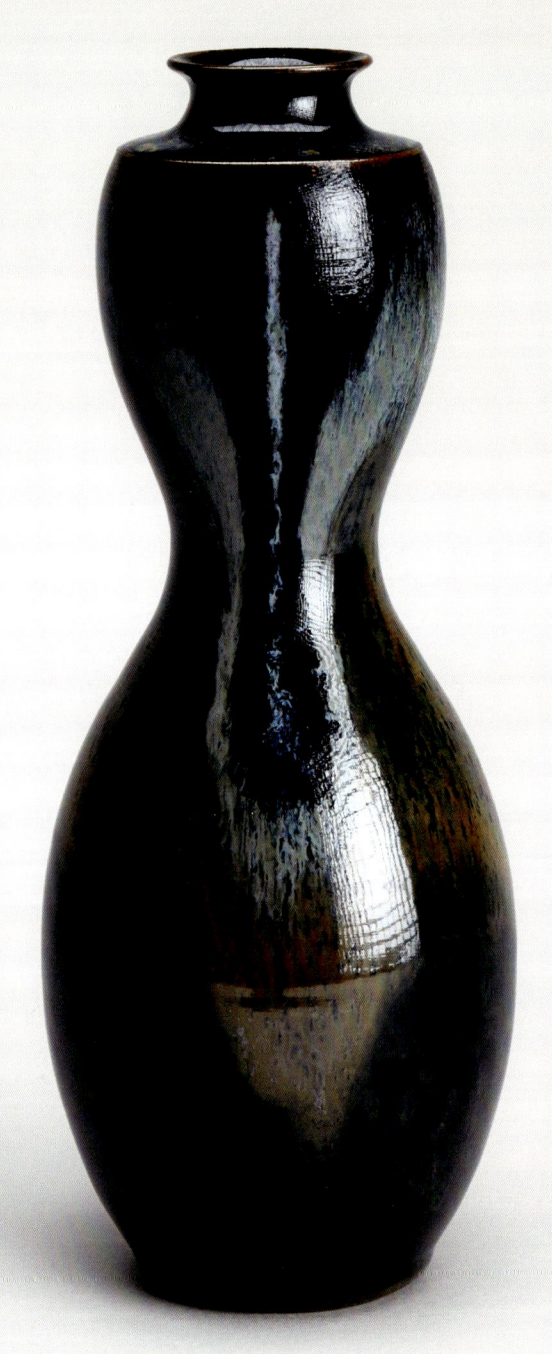

**MIRAKU KAMEI XV**
**Gourd-form Flower Vase**
2024
**Yellow glaze**
**XV216**

15代亀井味楽
瓢形花入
2024年
黄釉

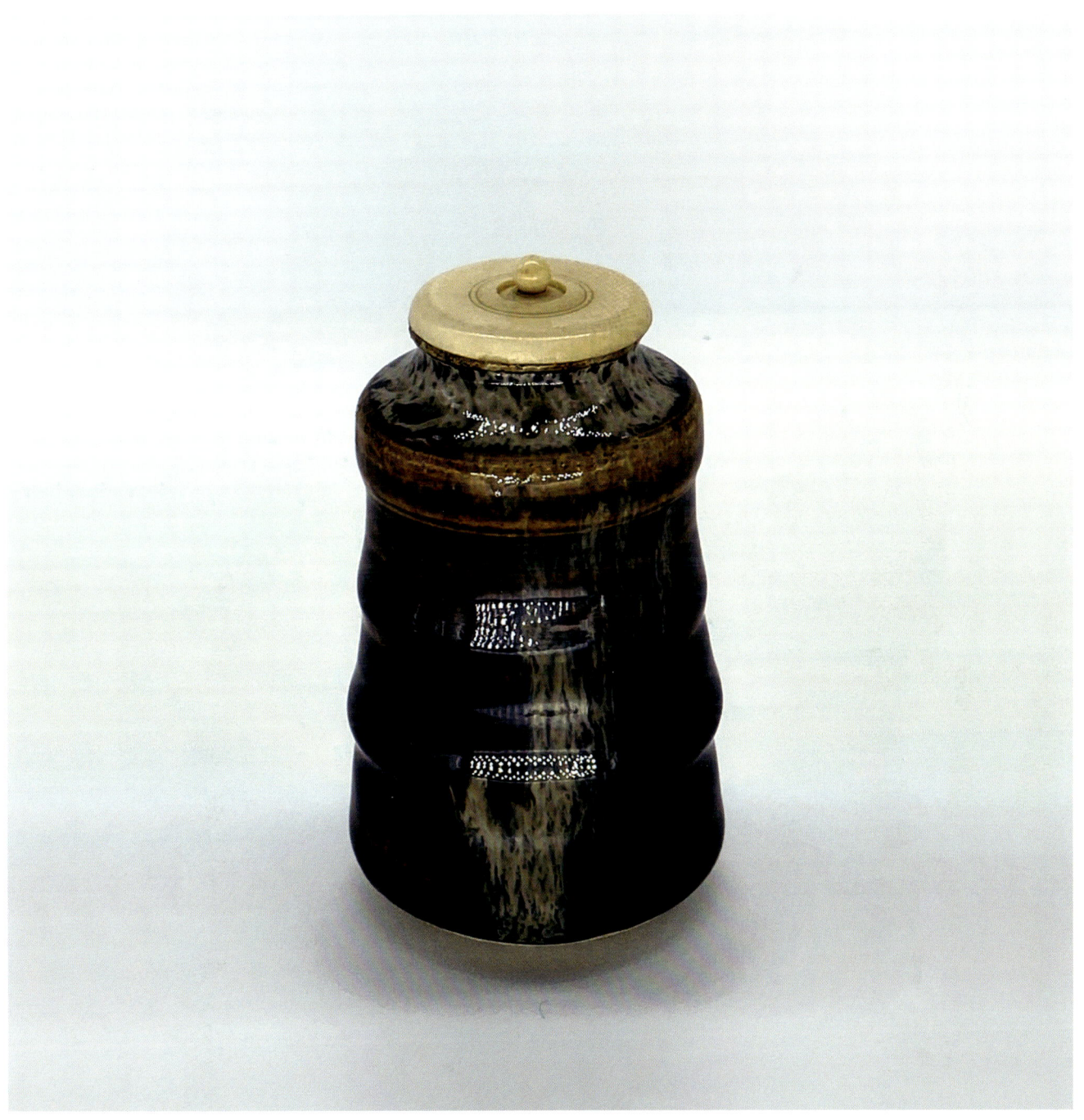

MIRAKU KAMEI XV | 15代亀井味楽
Tea Caddy | 茶入
2022 | 2022年
Yellow and black glaze | 黄釉に黒流し

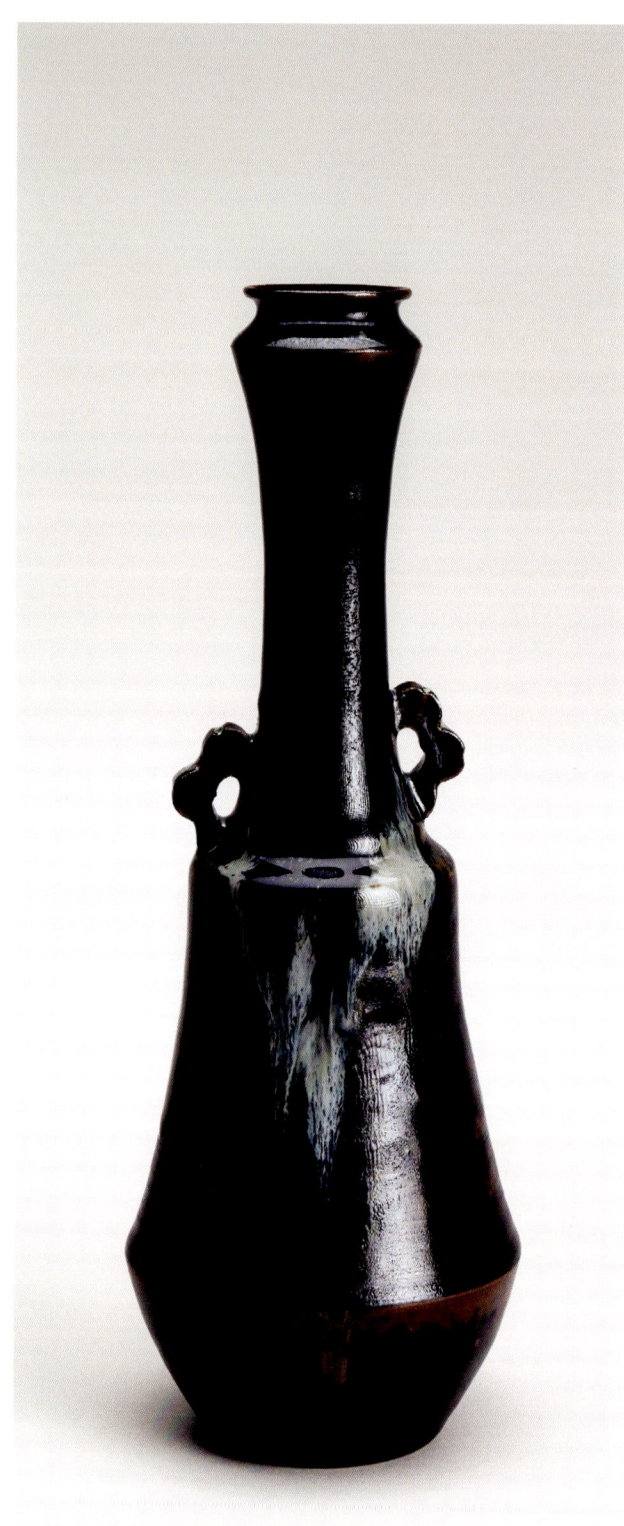

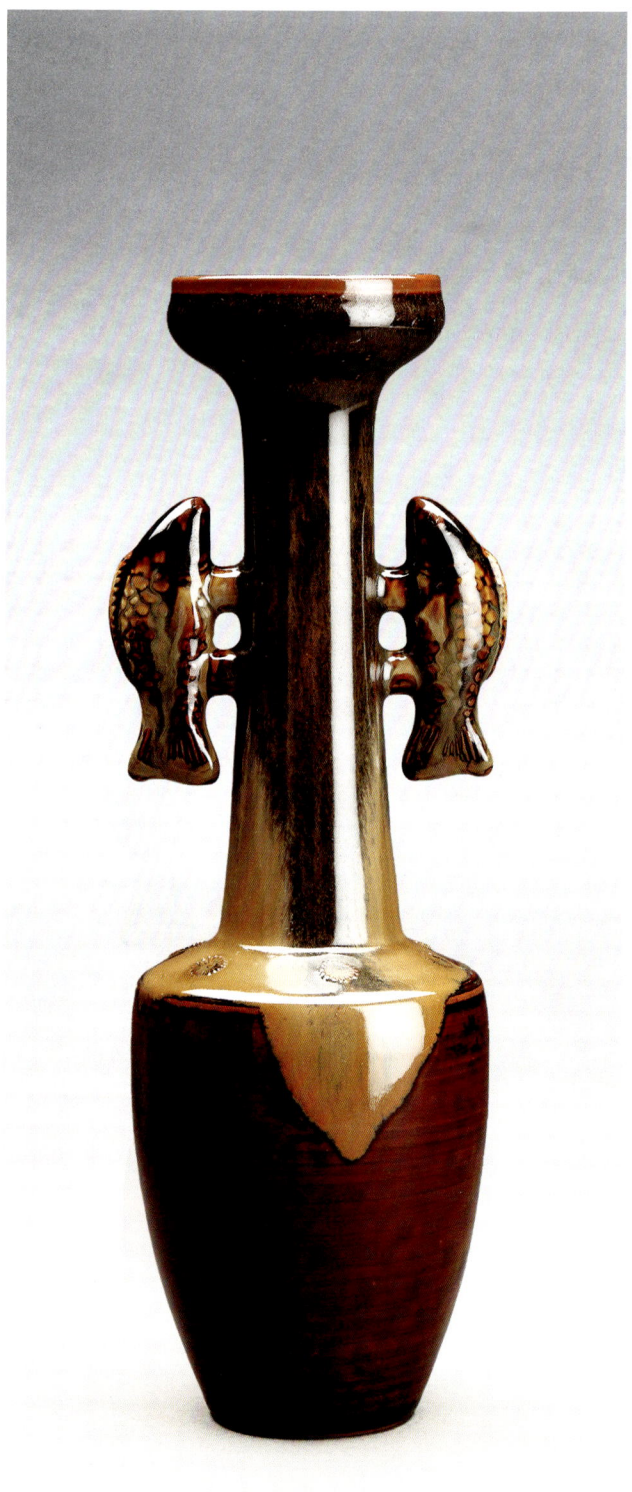

MIRAKU KAMEI XV
Flower Vase with
Ear-shaped Handles
2024
Ame glaze
XV217

15代亀井味楽
耳付花入
2024年
飴釉

MIRAKU KAMEI XV
Flower Vase with
Carp-shaped Handles
2016
Yellow glaze
XV112

15代亀井味楽
鯉形耳付花入
2016年
黄釉

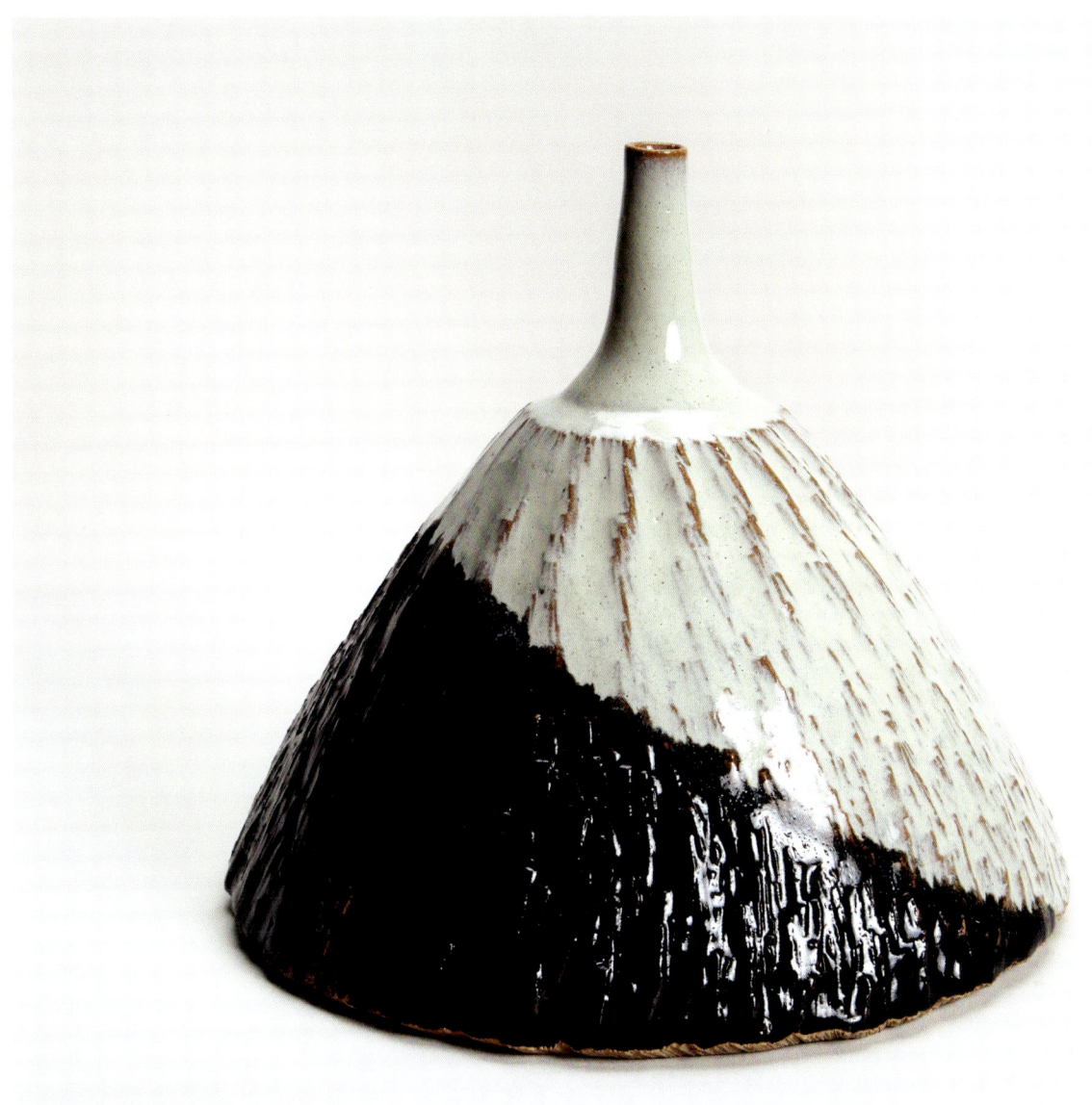

Inspired by Mt Fuji, the craggy surface of this mountain-shaped jar is finished in a black glaze with white overlay to mimic the snow-capped peak.

富士山から着想を得たごつごつした表面の山型の壺は、黒釉仕上げで、頂上の雪を表すような白釉が施されている。

MIRAKU KAMEI XV
Triangle Jar
2022
Kakewake glaze
XV206

15代亀井味楽
三角壺
2022年
掛分

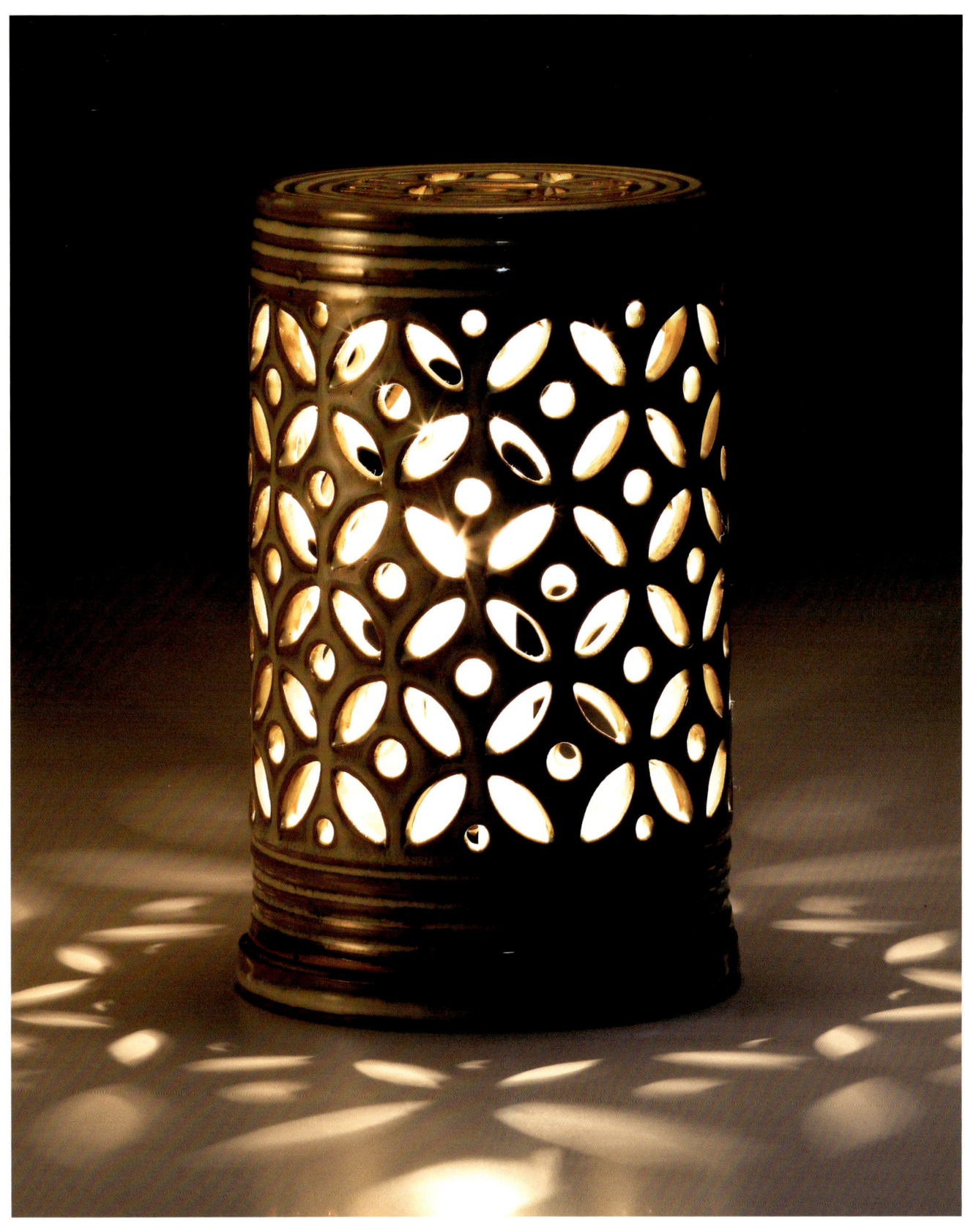

MIRAKU KAMEI XV
Lantern with Shippō (openwork)
2014
Yellow glaze
XV47

15代亀井味楽
七宝透灯篭
2014年
黄釉

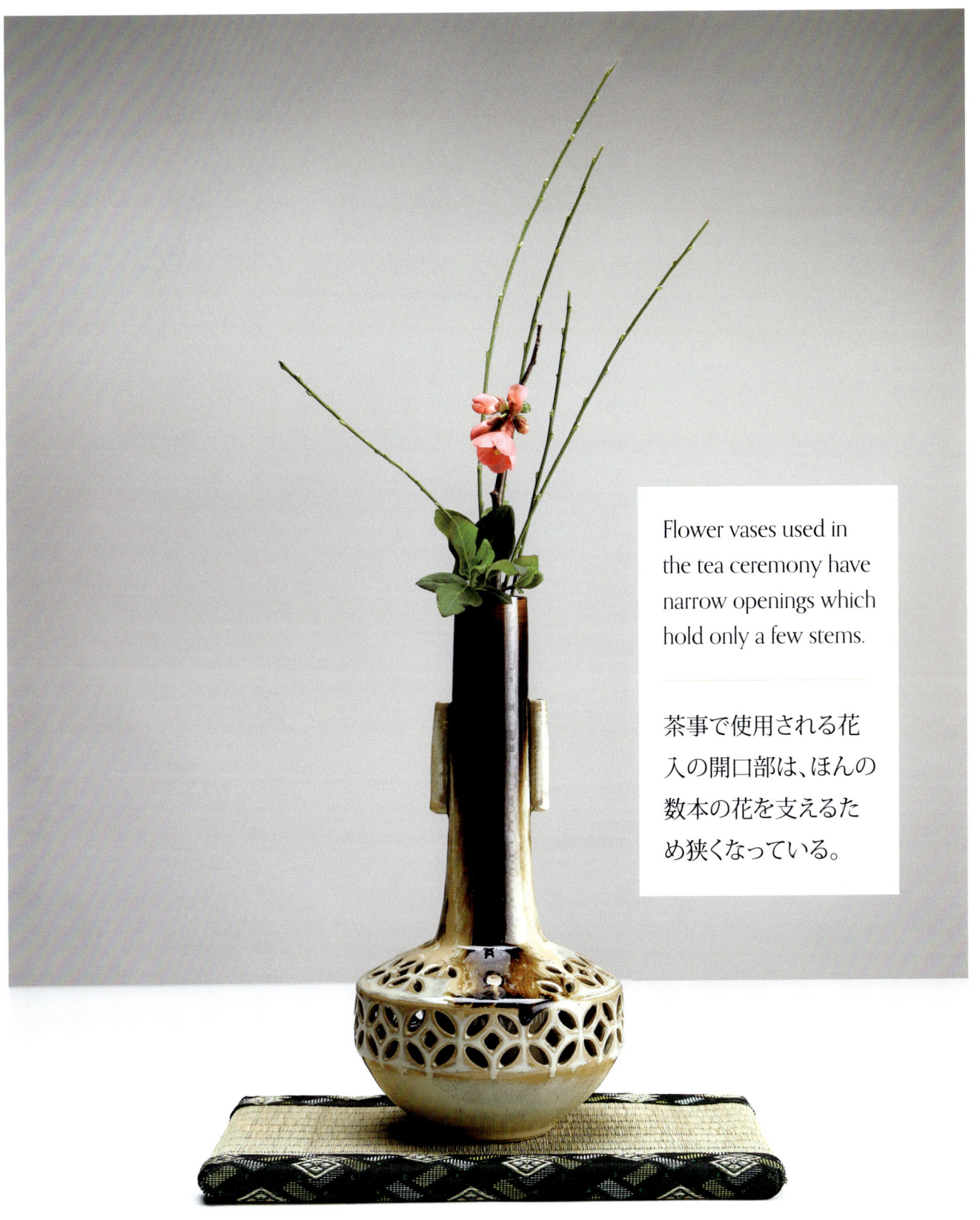

Flower vases used in
the tea ceremony have
narrow openings which
hold only a few stems.

茶事で使用される花
入の開口部は、ほんの
数本の花を支えるた
め狭くなっている。

MIRAKU KAMEI XV
Flower Vase with Pipe Ear Handles and Shippō (openwork)
2016
White and black glaze
XV109

15代亀井味楽
七宝透耳付花入
2016年
白釉に黒流し

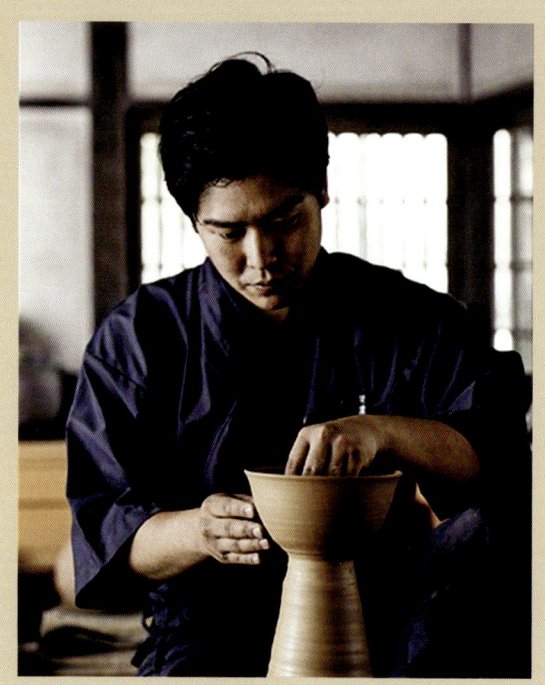

Hisaaki Kamei | 亀井久彰
2021 | 令和3年

# Hisaaki Kamei | 亀井久彰

(to be XVI; Born 1991) | 1991年生まれ

The eldest son of Miraku Kamei XV, Hisaaki Kamei received a B.A. at the School of Business at Hosei University and graduated from the Forming Department, Kyoto Prefecture Pottery School. He is a Board Member of the Japan-France Tea Ceremony Association, teaches pottery at Fukuoka City Fukusho High School and Momochi Palace Culture Center, and has lectured in Cameroon and France. He uses new glazes such as *kyokkyu* (Aurora glaze) and *saiyu* (multicolor glaze), which he created based on the seven classic glazes of Takatori. In time, Hisaaki Kamei will take the title of Miraku Kamei XVI.

15代亀井味楽の長男として生まれる。法政大学経営学部経営学科を卒業後、京都府立陶工高等技術専門校成形科総合コースを修了する。日仏茶道協会の理事であり、福岡市福翔高等学校およびモモチカルチャーセンターで陶芸を教え、カメルーンやフランスでも講演を行っている。亀井久彰氏は高取焼の7種類の伝統的な釉薬をもとに、極光釉や彩釉などの新しい釉薬を作り出している。

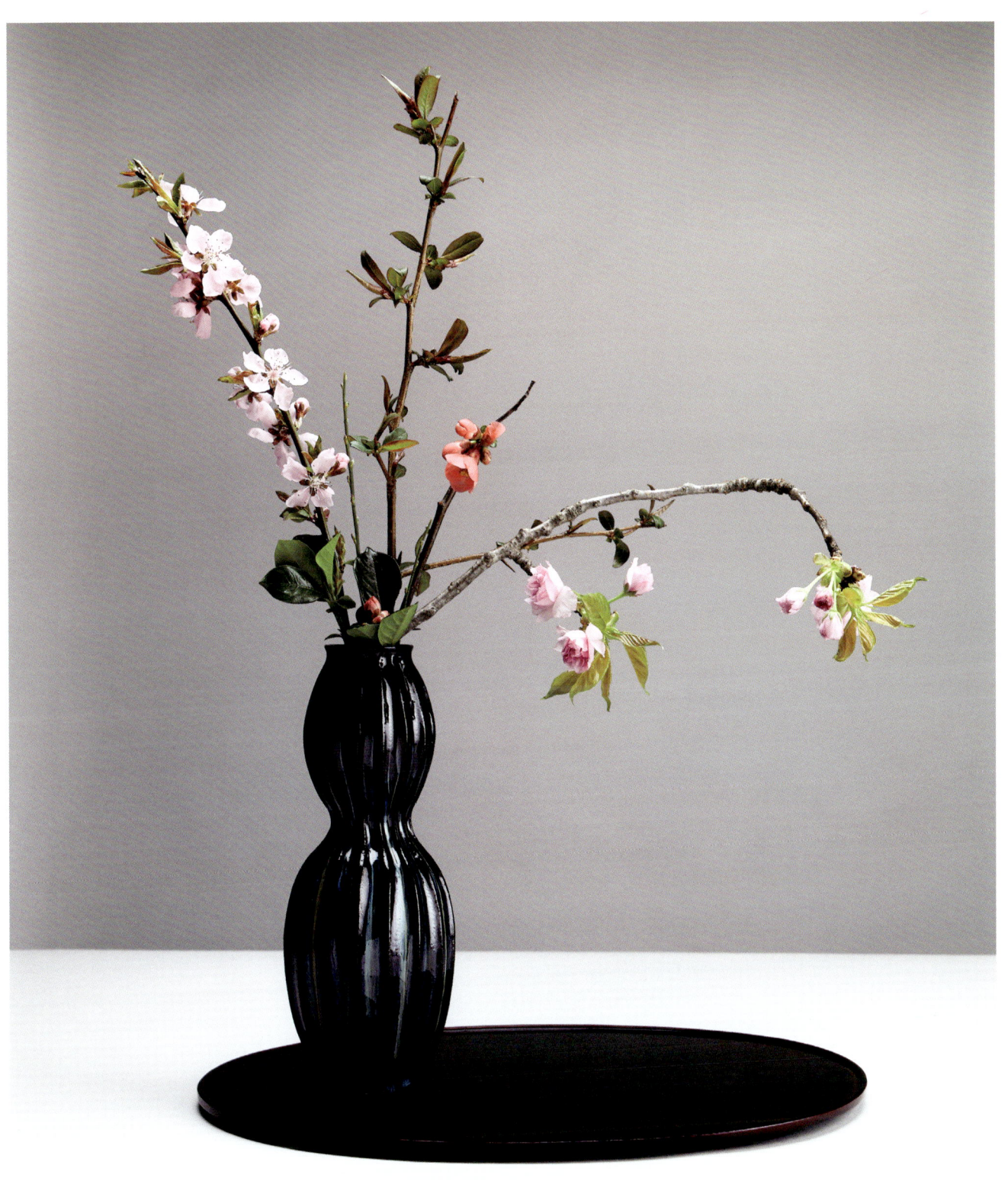

HISAAKI KAMEI     亀井久彰
Gourd-form Flower Vase     瓢形花入
2020     2020年
Aurora glaze     極光釉
HK29

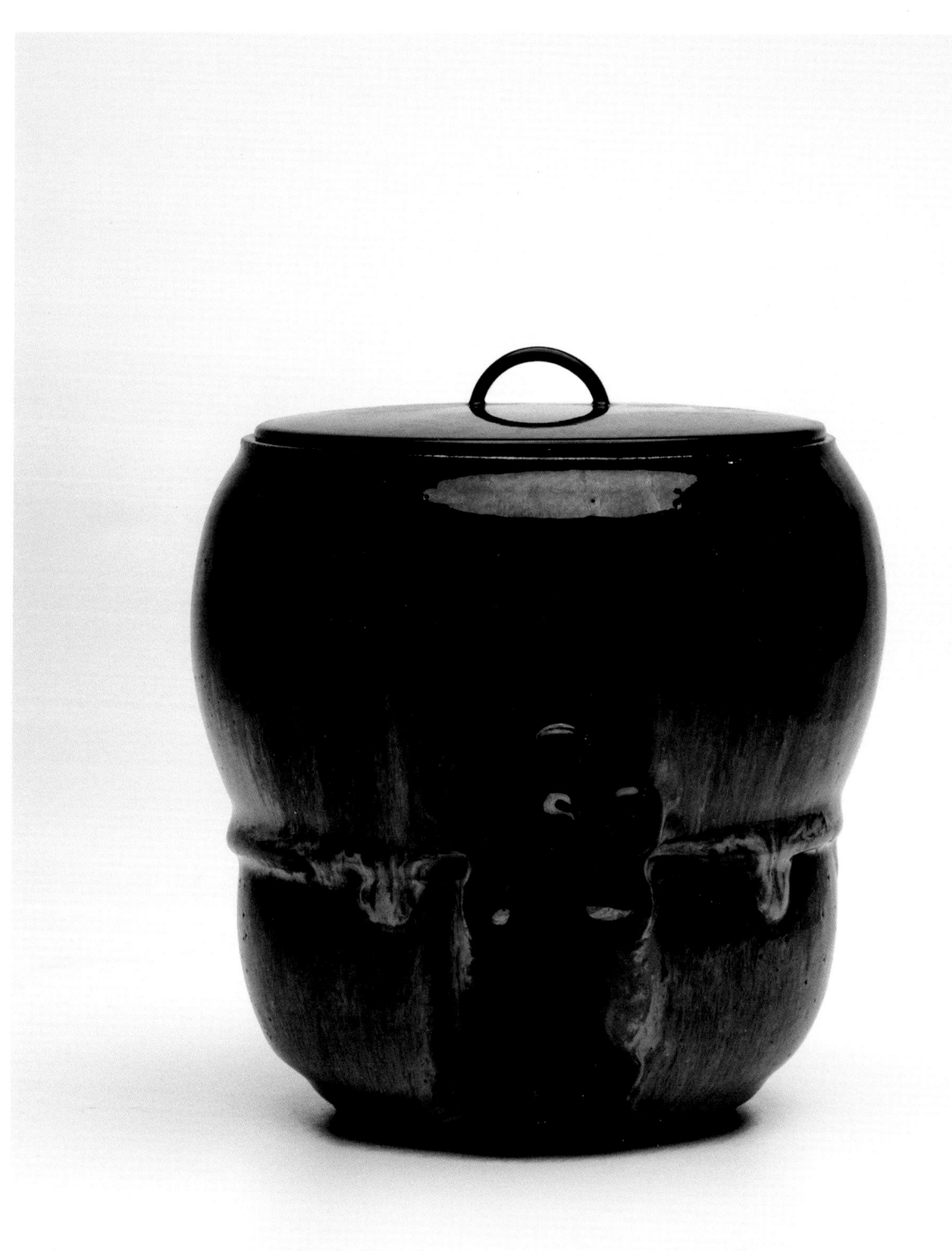

HISAAKI KAMEI     亀井久彰
Gourd-form Water Container with Plum Knot Decoration     瓢箪形梅結水指
2020     2020年
Aurora glaze     極光釉
HK27

The Aurora glaze was inspired by Hisaaki Kamei's fascination with the aurora borealis. He harnesses the sweeping glaze application typical of Takatori ware to capture the dynamism of that phenomenon.

極光釉は亀井久彰氏の北極光に対する強い興味から着想を得た釉薬である。亀井久彰氏は高取焼の典型的な釉薬の使用方法を適用し、極光のダイナミックな動きをとらえている。

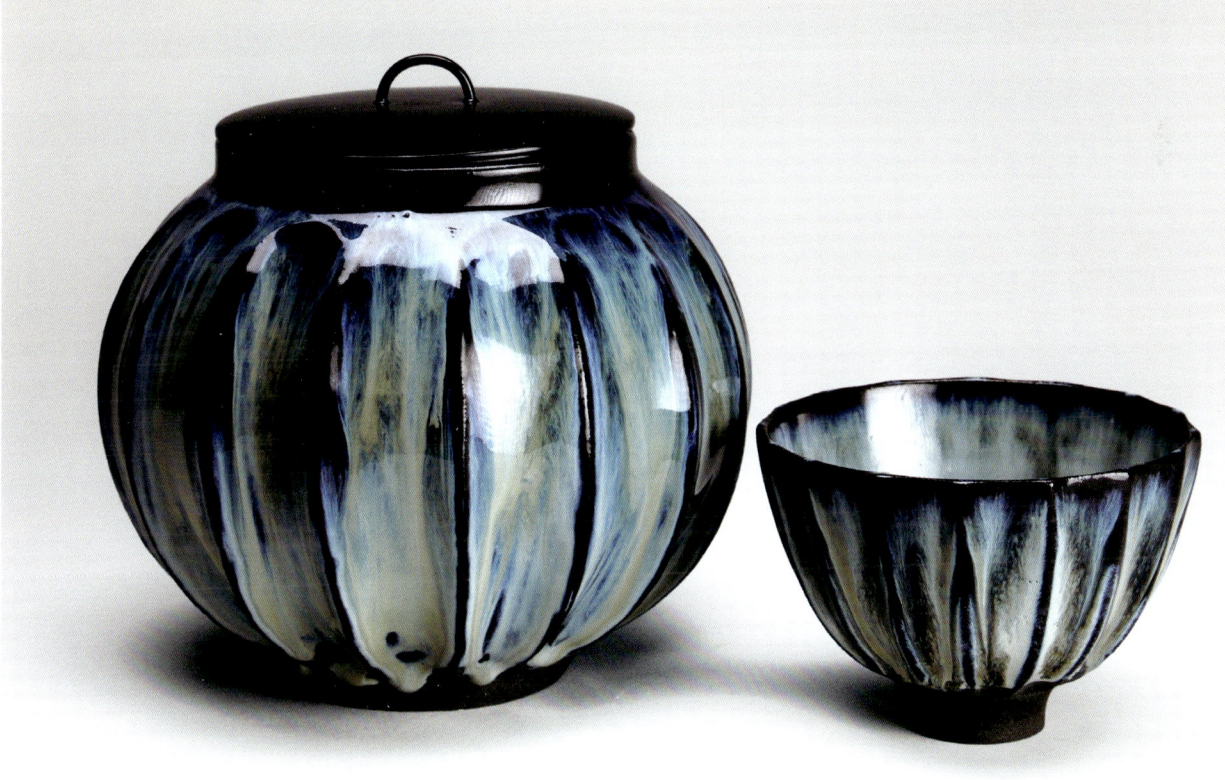

**HISAAKI KAMEI**
**Water Container with Lacquer Lid**
2018
Aurora glaze
HK22

亀井久彰
うるし蓋付水指
2018年
極光釉

**Tea Bowl**
2018
Aurora glaze
HK23

茶盌
2018年
極光釉

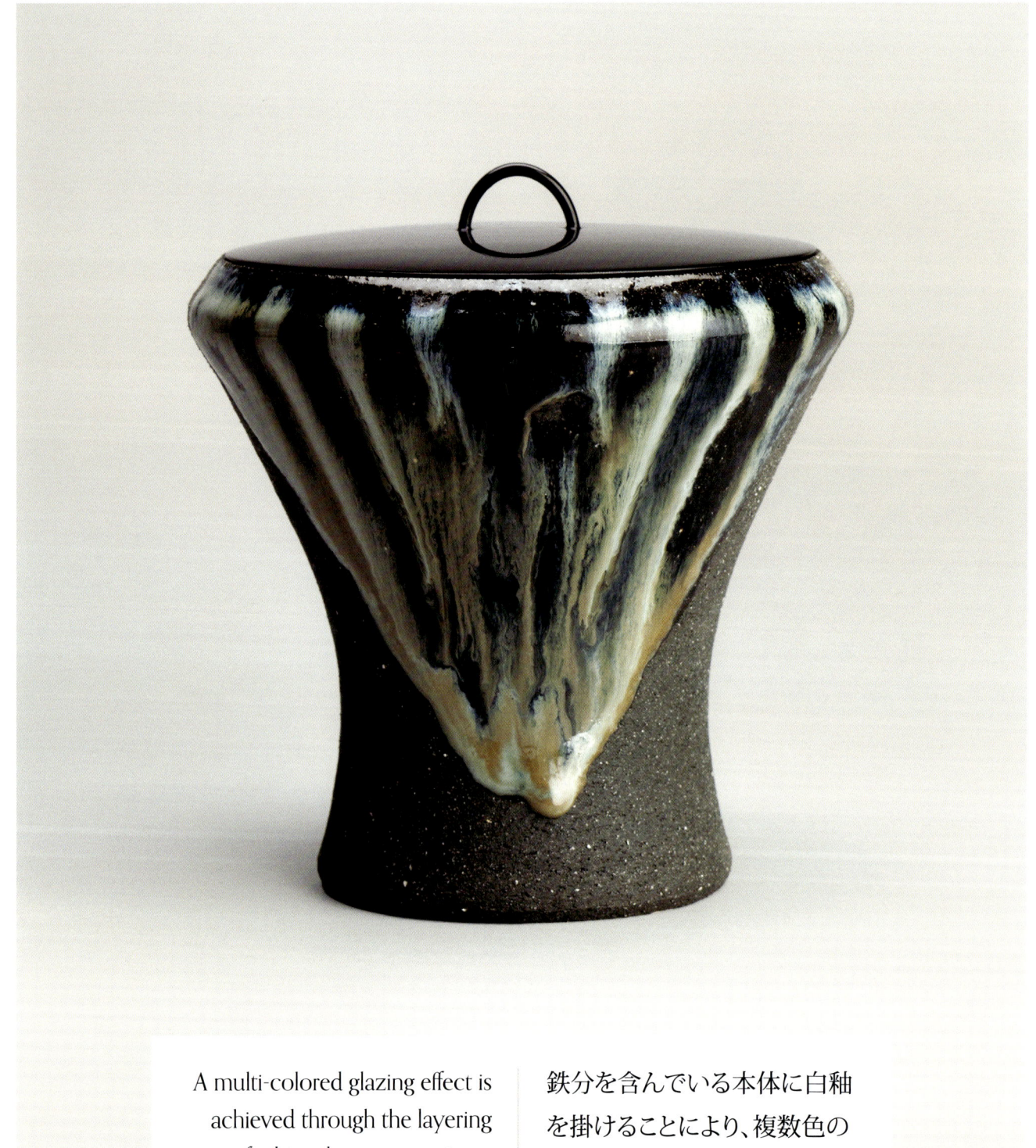

A multi-colored glazing effect is achieved through the layering of white glaze over an iron-bearing body.

鉄分を含んでいる本体に白釉を掛けることにより、複数色の釉薬効果を出している。

**HISAAKI KAMEI**
**Water Container with Lacquer Lid**
**2018**
**Aurora glaze**
**HK14**

亀井久彰
うるし蓋付水指
2018年
極光釉

Although blue is not one of the seven traditional glazes of Takatori ware, Hisaaki Kamei was inspired by the sky and water to achieve the color in his work.

青色は7種類ある高取焼の伝統的な釉薬ではないが、亀井久彰氏は青色を使って空と水を作品に表現している。

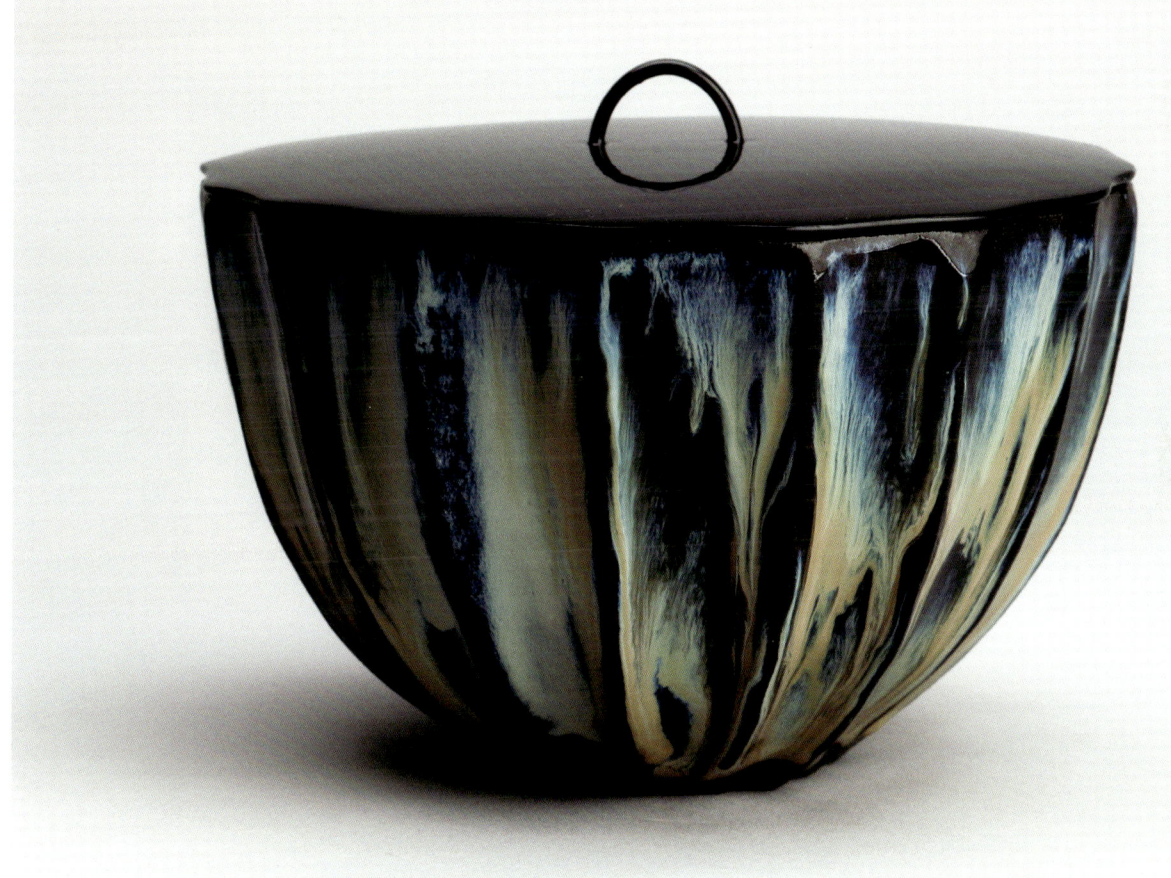

HISAAKI KAMEI
**Water Container with Lacquer Lid**
2018
Aurora glaze
HK15

亀井久彰
うるし蓋付水指
2018年
極光釉

*Icchin* involves loading slip (liquid clay) into a piping bag and trailing it onto the pot to create designs.

一珍とは泥漿（液体粘土）を絞り袋に入れ、陶器上に盛り付ける装飾技法である。

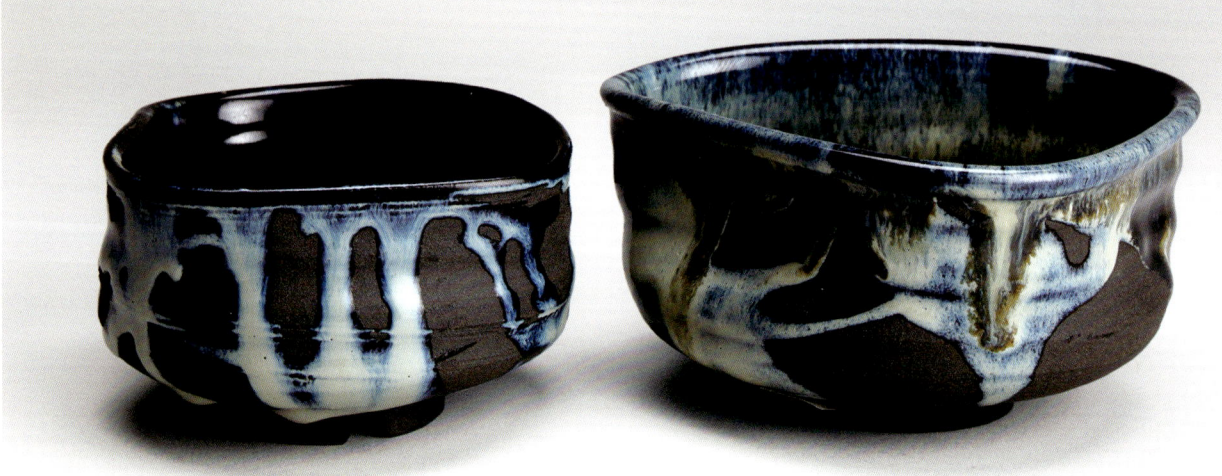

HISAAKI KAMEI
Tsutsugaki Tea Bowl with Icchin Decoration
2020
White glaze
HK36

亀井久彰
一珍筒描茶盌
2020年
白釉

Tsutsugaki Tea Bowl with Icchin Decoration
2020
White glaze
HK31

一珍筒描茶盌
2020年
白釉

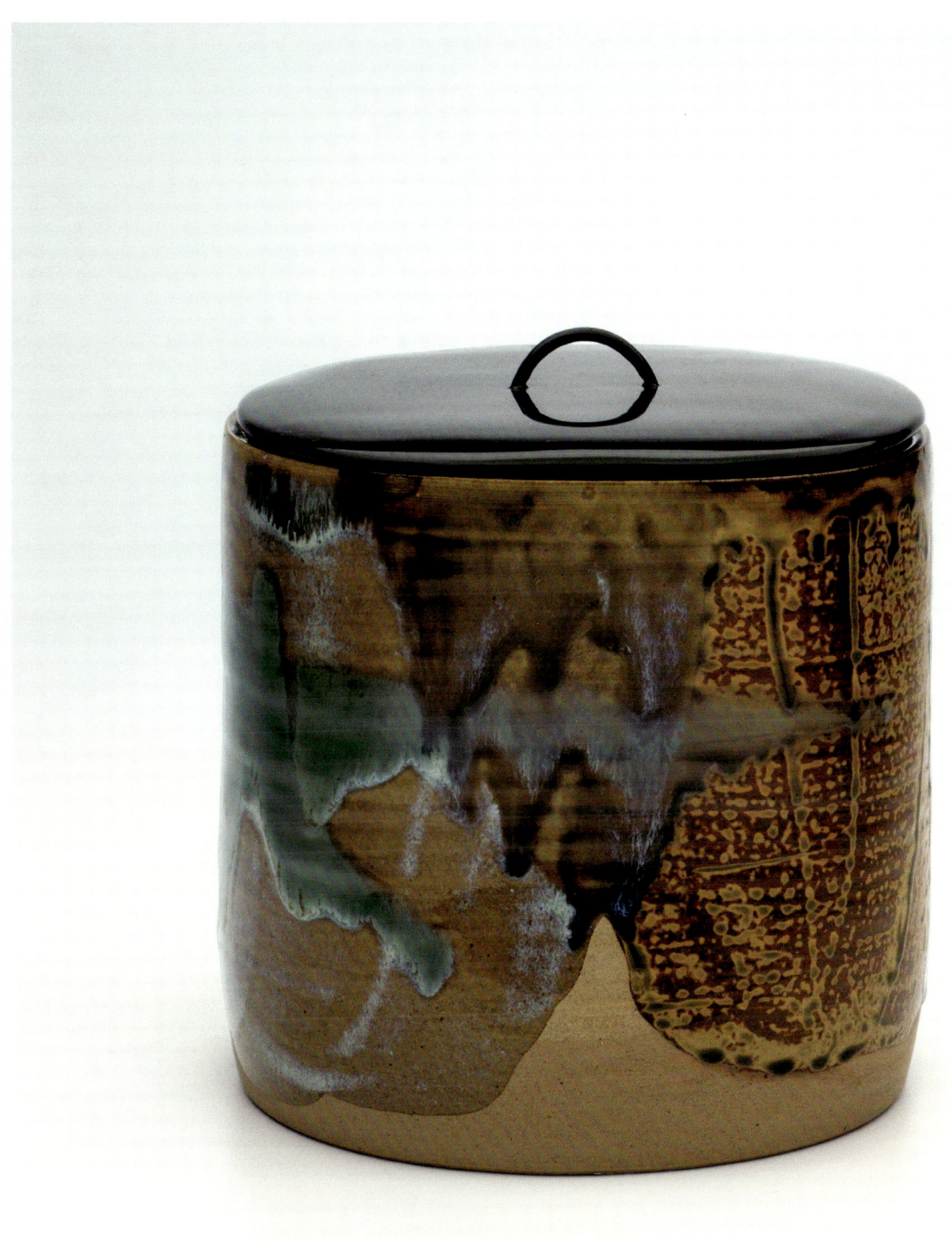

HISAAKI KAMEI | 亀井久彰
Water Container with Lacquer Lid | うるし蓋付水指
2020 | 2020年
Three-colored glaze | 三彩釉
HK26

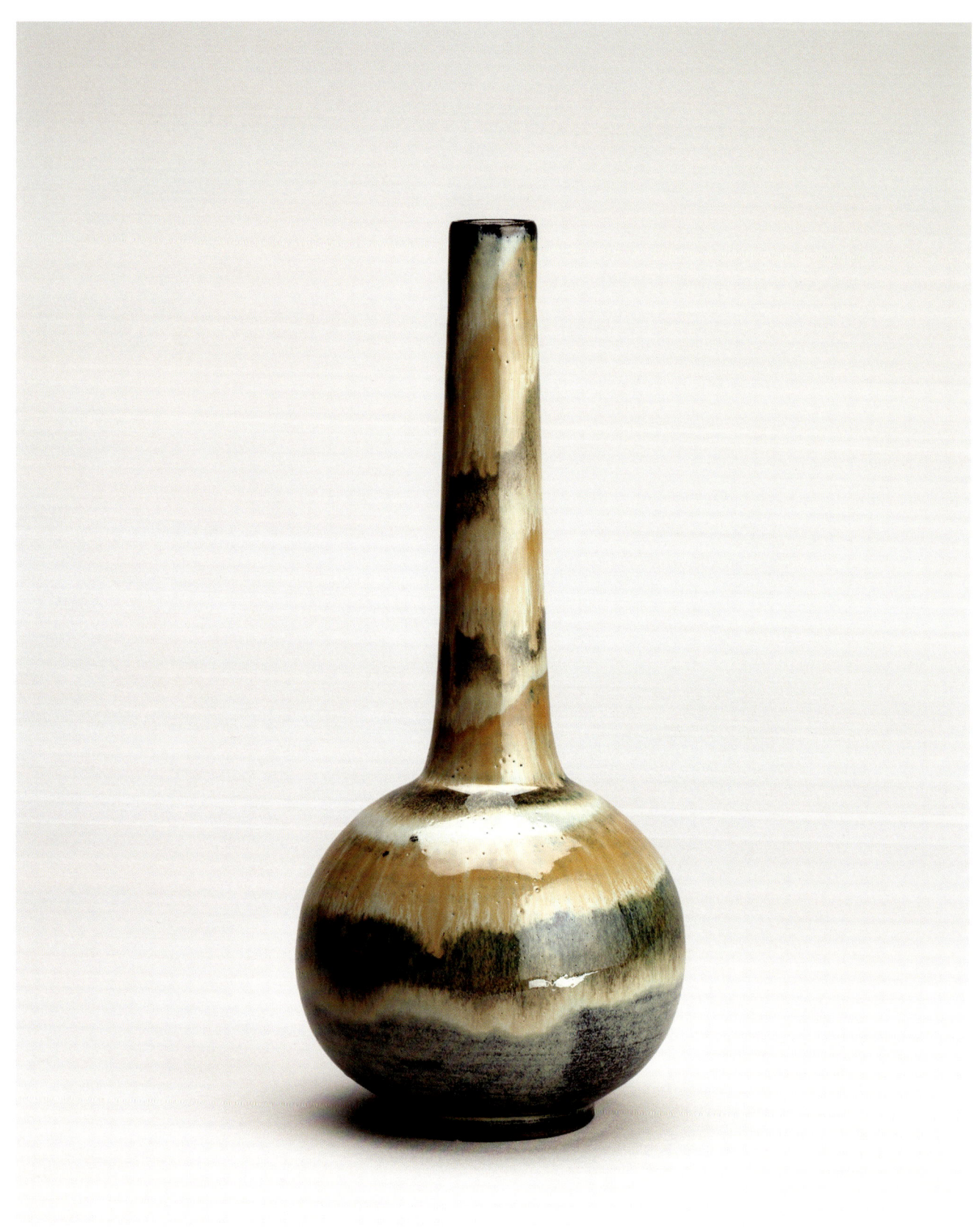

HISAAKI KAMEI    亀井久彰
Turnip-form Flower Vase    花入
2018    2018年
Yu sai    釉彩
HK11

This tea bowl is shaped to comfortably fit in the hands and pays homage to 400 years of Takatori tradition in its flowing glaze. The round base, square body, and triangular opening reflect Zen Buddhism.

この茶盌は高取焼400年にわたる伝統を尊重した釉薬を使い、持った時に手にすっぽりと収まるような形状となっている。円形の土台に四角い本体、そして三角の口を持つこの茶盌には禅宗の教えが反映されている。

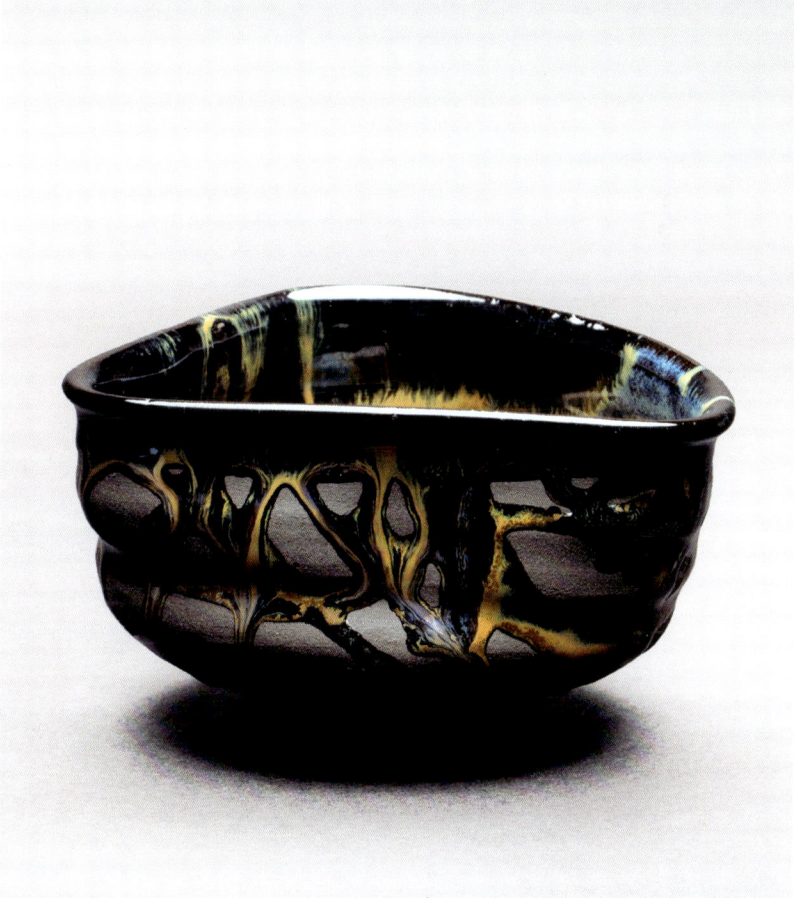

**HISAAKI KAMEI**
**Tsutsugaki Tea Bowl with Icchin Decoration**
2020
Kakewake glaze
HK32

亀井久彰
一珍筒描茶盌
2020年
掛分

Cutting and overlapping can be found in Japanese tea bowls dating back to the late 1700s, and while these bowls use traditional clay and glaze components, they are remarkably poetic departures from the mainstream.

1700年代後半には、日本の茶碗に切削や重ね付けなどがみられる。これらの茶盌には伝統的な土や釉薬が使われているが、主流を超えた非常に詩的な表現がみられる。

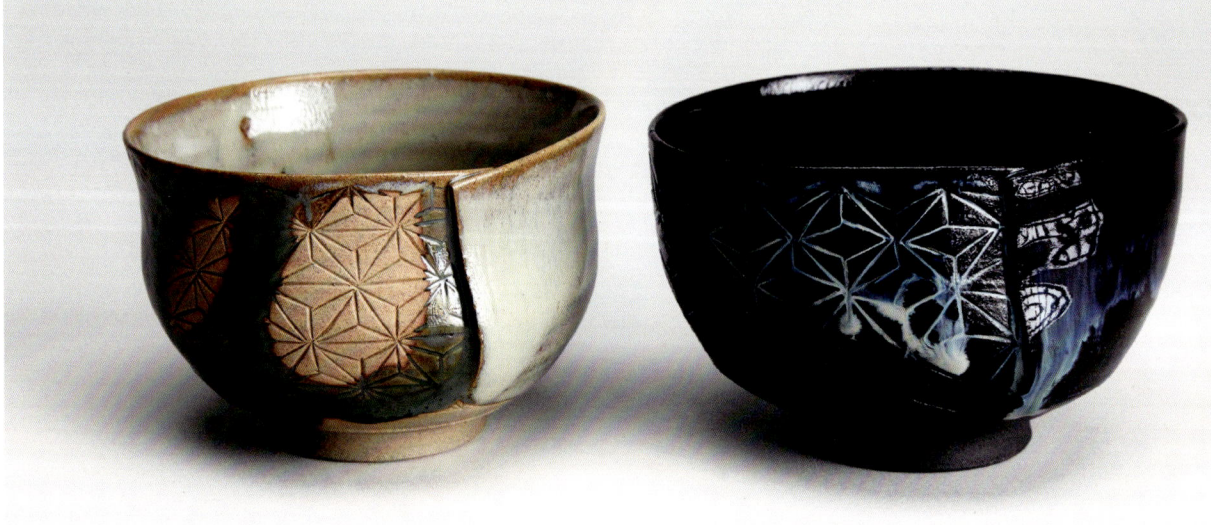

HISAAKI KAMEI
Tea Bowl with Hemp Leaf Pattern
2024
Verdigris glaze
HK63

亀井久彰
とじめ麻の葉柄茶盌
2024年
緑青釉

Tea Bowl with Hemp Leaf Pattern
2024
Aurora glaze
HK62

とじめ麻の葉柄茶盌
2024年
極光釉

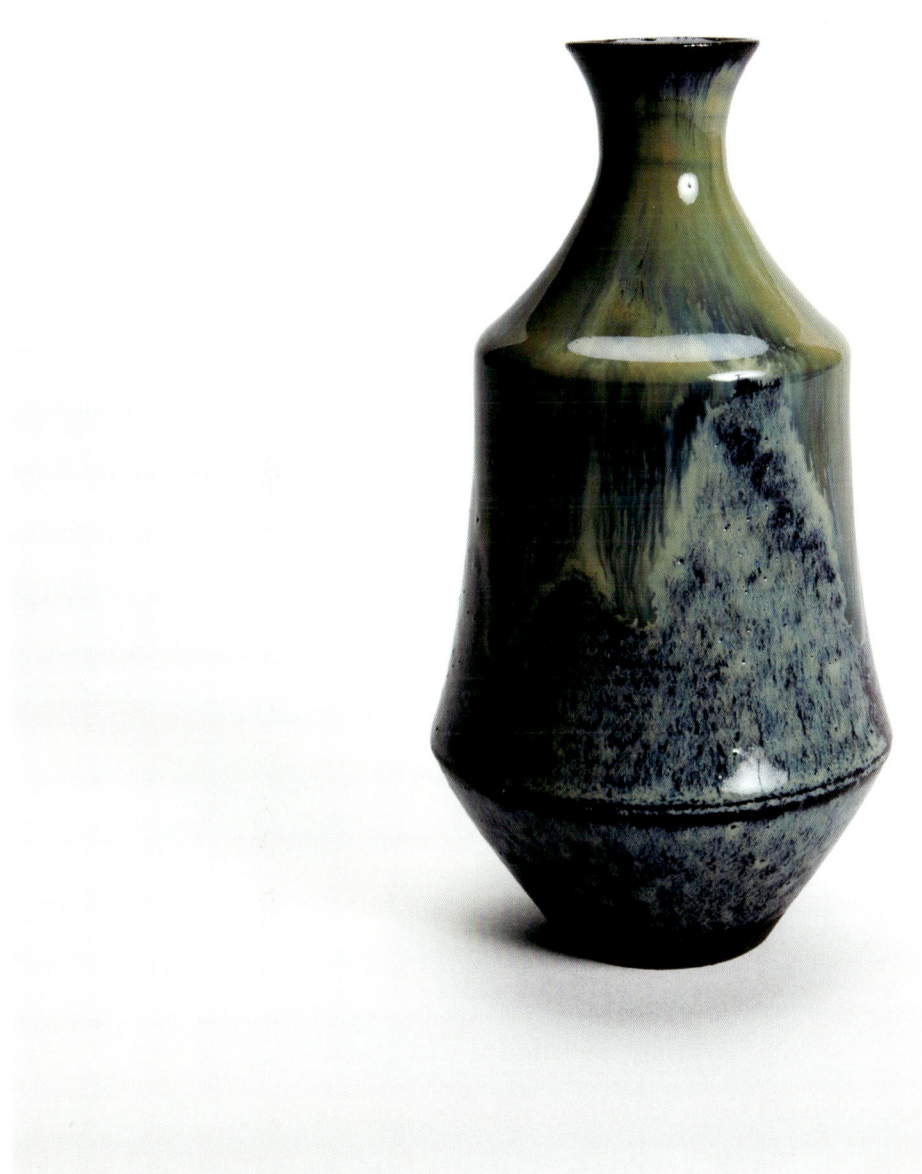

HISAAKI KAMEI   |   亀井久彰
Sake Bottle   |   酒器
2022   |   2022年
Aurora glaze   |   極光釉
HK53

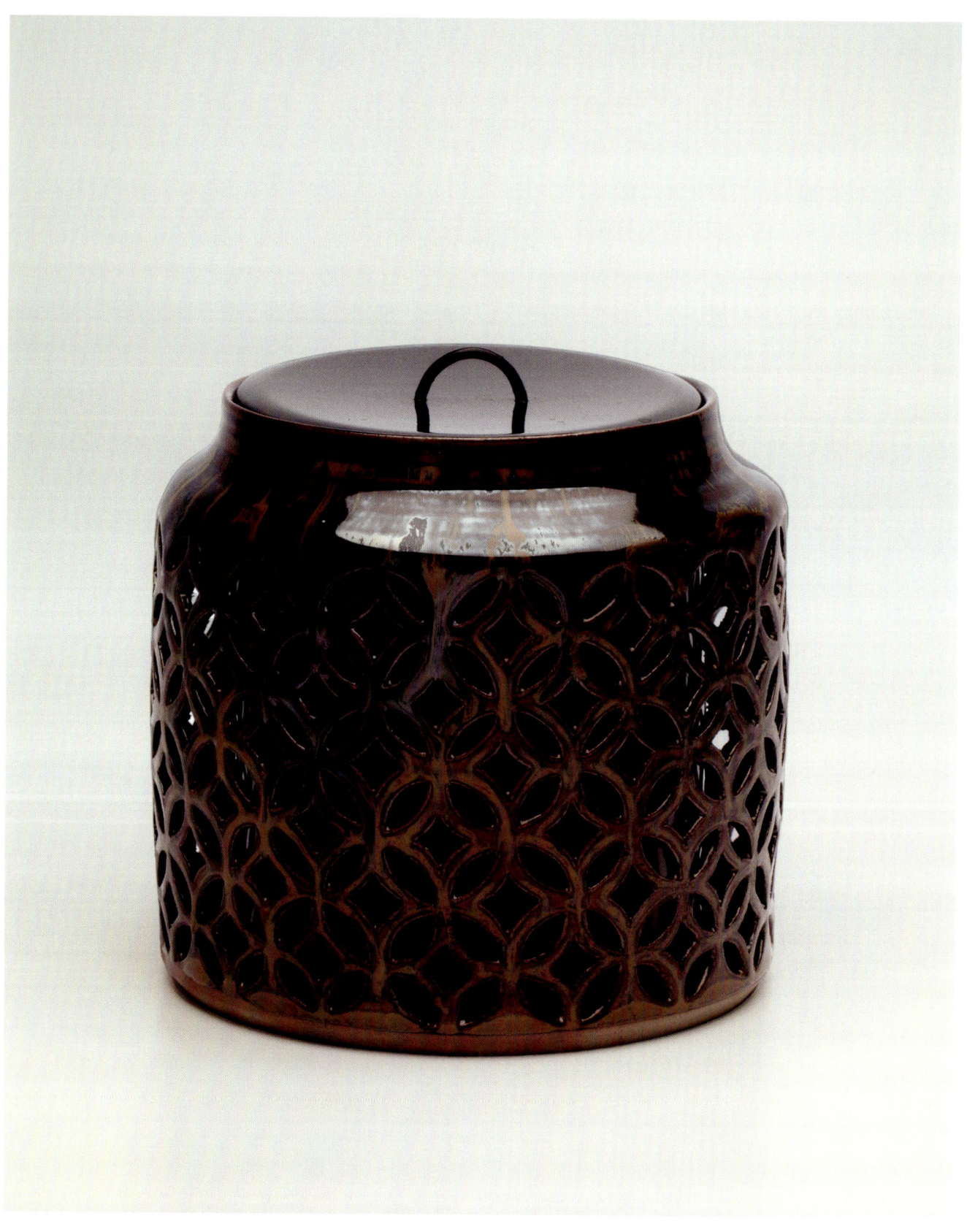

HISAAKI KAMEI
Water Container with Lacquer Lid and Shippō (openwork)
2020
Copper glaze
HK25

亀井久彰
七宝透うるし蓋付水指
2020年
銅化釉

Fukuoka is home to Shōfuku-ji, the first Zen temple. Its 133rd master suggested adding these characters to this bowl. The right character indicates nothingness and the left refers to "the thing." In Zen spirit, the two together represent the peacefulness of the mind.

聖福寺は福岡にある日本最初の禅寺である。133代住職である細川白峰はこの茶盌に書を加えることを提案した。右側の漢字は「無」、左側は「事」であり、禅では精神の平和を表す。

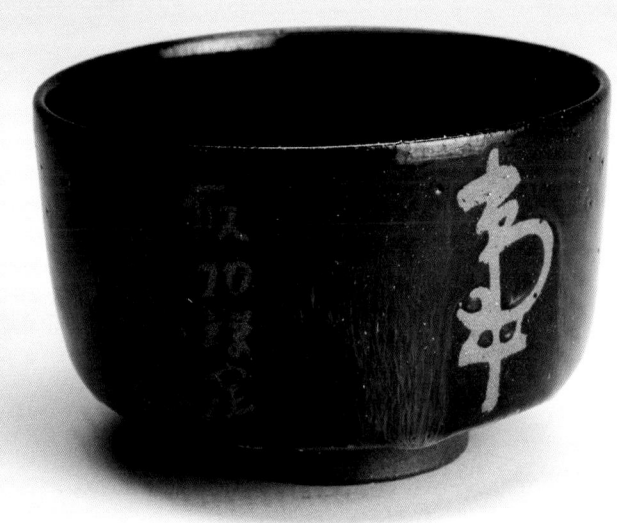

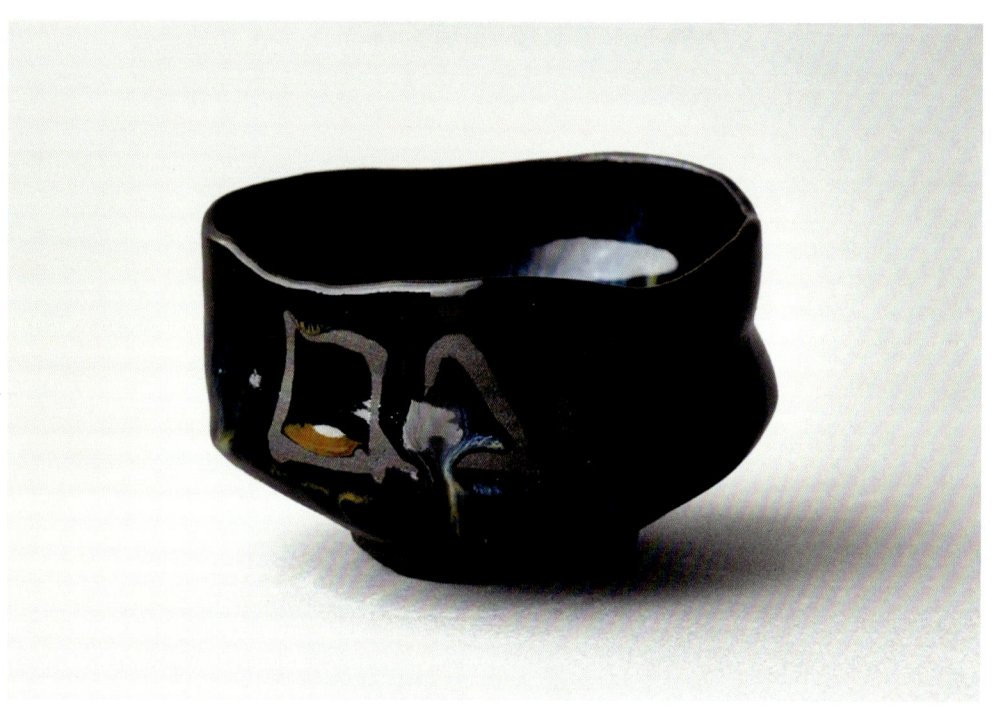

| HISAAKI KAMEI | 亀井久彰 |
| Tea Bowl | 茶盌 |
| 2018 | 2018年 |
| Zen painting by Shiramine Hosokawa, | 福岡聖福寺133世 細川白峰老師による禅画 |
| 133rd head priest of the temple Shōfuku-ji, | 掛分 |
| Fukuoka, Japan | |
| Kakewake glaze | |

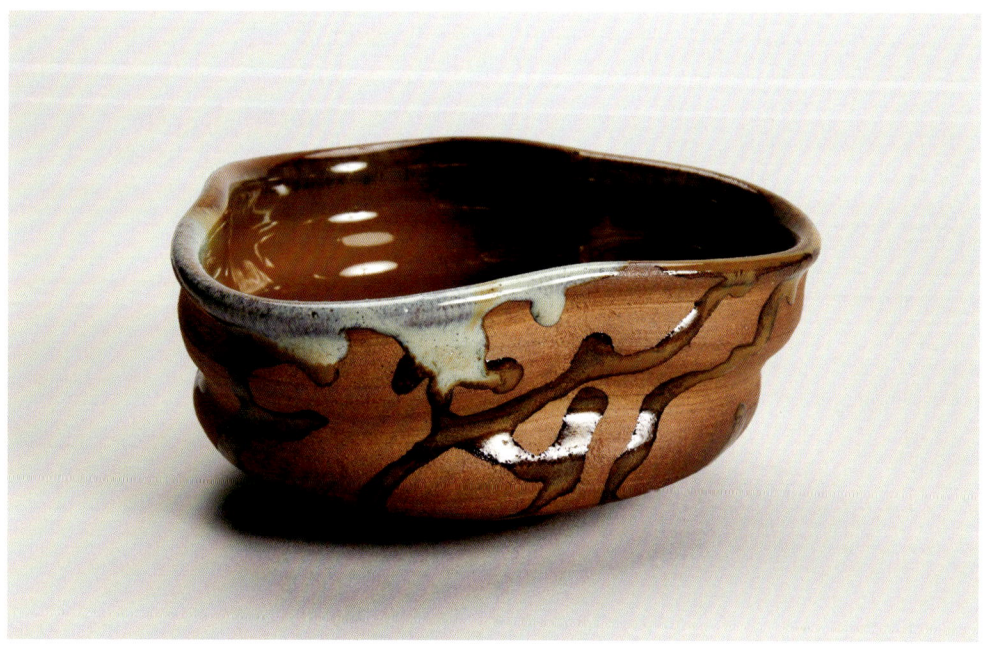

| HISAAKI KAMEI | 亀井久彰 |
| Tea Bowl with Icchin Decoration | 珍掛茶盌 |
| 2022 | 2022年 |
| Kakewake glaze | 掛分 |
| HK45 | |

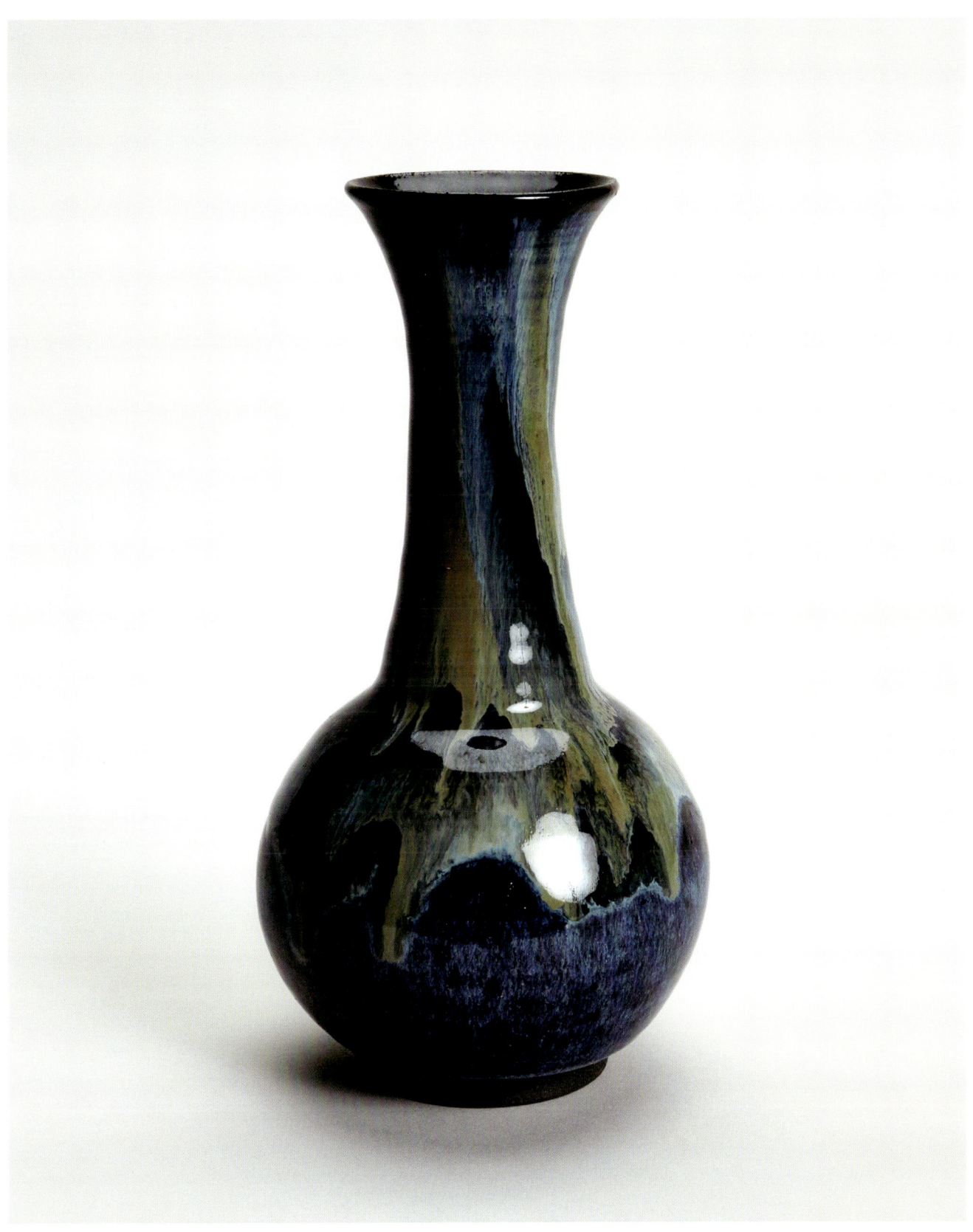

HISAAKI KAMEI
**Flower Vase with Wide Mouth**
2022
Aurora glaze
**HK48**

亀井久彰
広口花入
2022年
極光釉

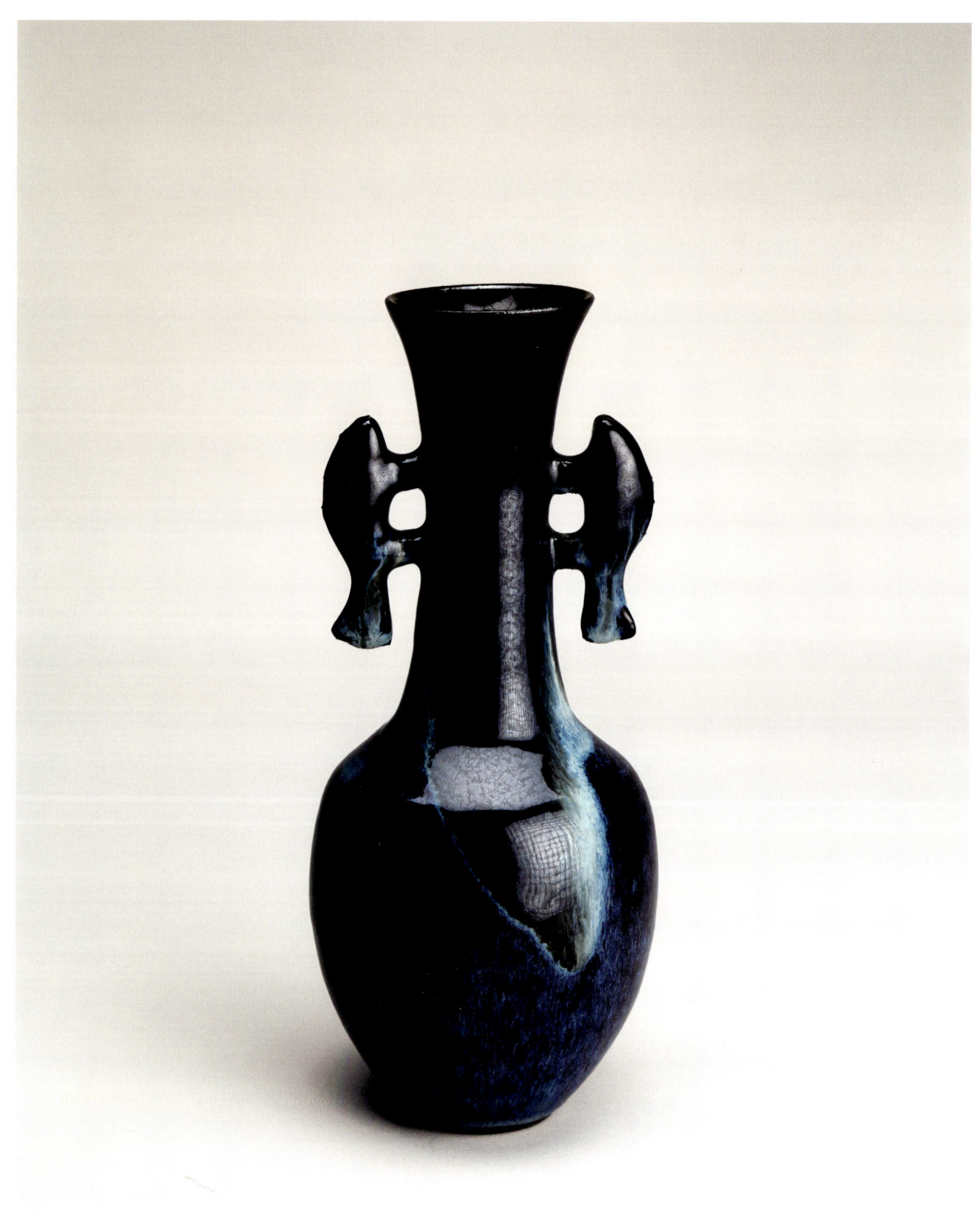

HISAAKI KAMEI
**Flower Vase with Carp-shaped Handles**
2020
Aurora glaze
HK30

亀井久彰
鯉形耳付花入
2020年
極光釉

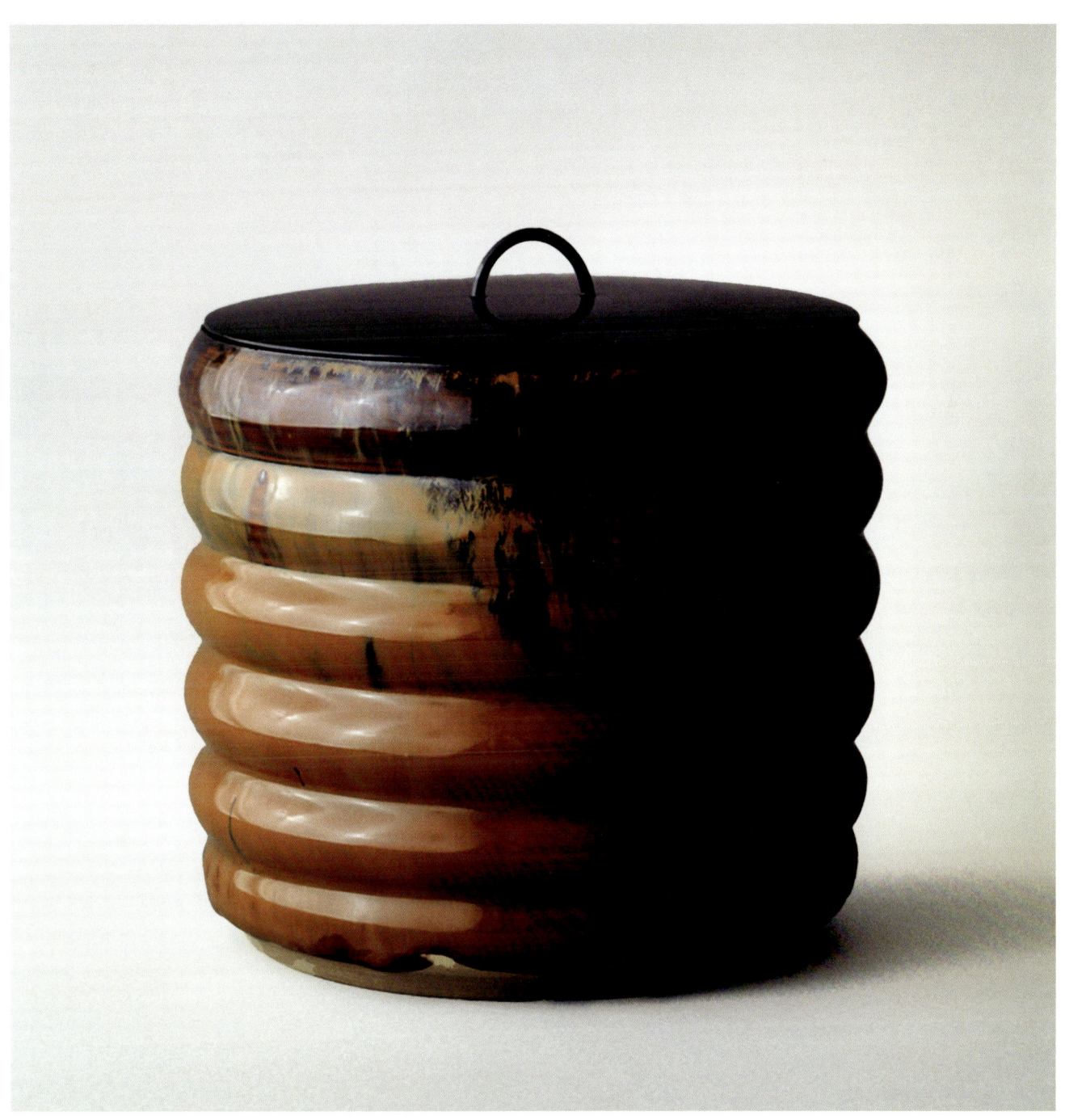

HISAAKI KAMEI · 亀井久彰
Water Container with Lacquer Lid and Coil Design · うるし蓋付千段巻水指
2020 · 2020年
Yellow glaze · 黄釉

Hisaaki Kamei adds iron to the traditional Takatori clay, which makes the clay body darker and gives the white glaze the blue finish he seeks.

亀井久彰氏は高取の土に鉄分を加えることにより、本体の黒および白と青の仕上がりを作り出す。

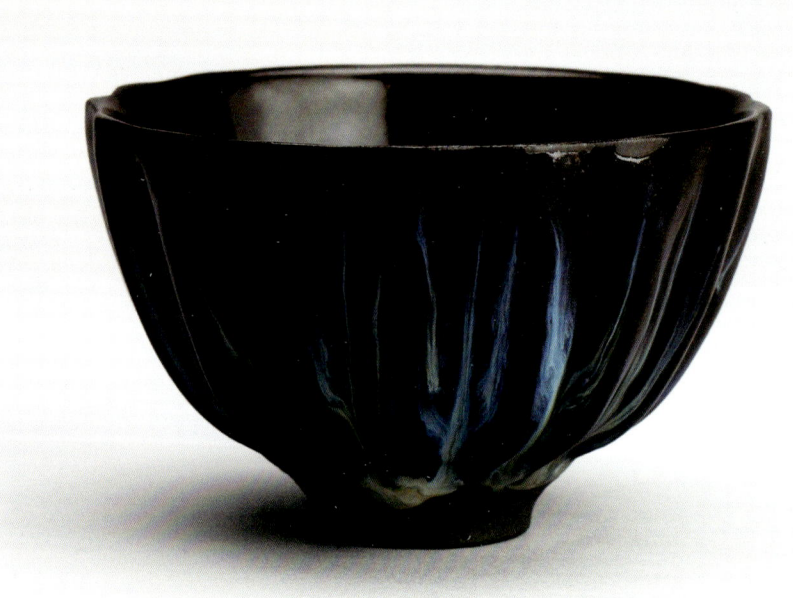

**HISAAKI KAMEI**　　亀井久彰
**Tea Bowl**　　茶盌
**2018**　　2018年
**Aurora glaze**　　極光釉
**HK20**

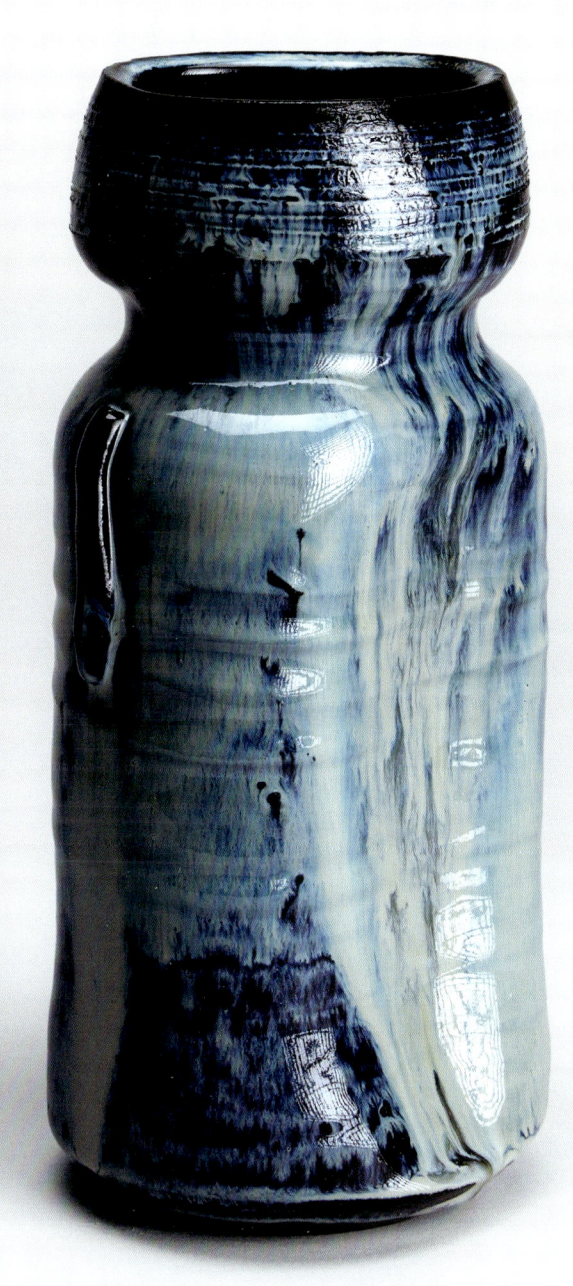

HISAAKI KAMEI    亀井久彰
Flower Vase      花入
2024             2024年
Aurora glaze     極光釉
HK58

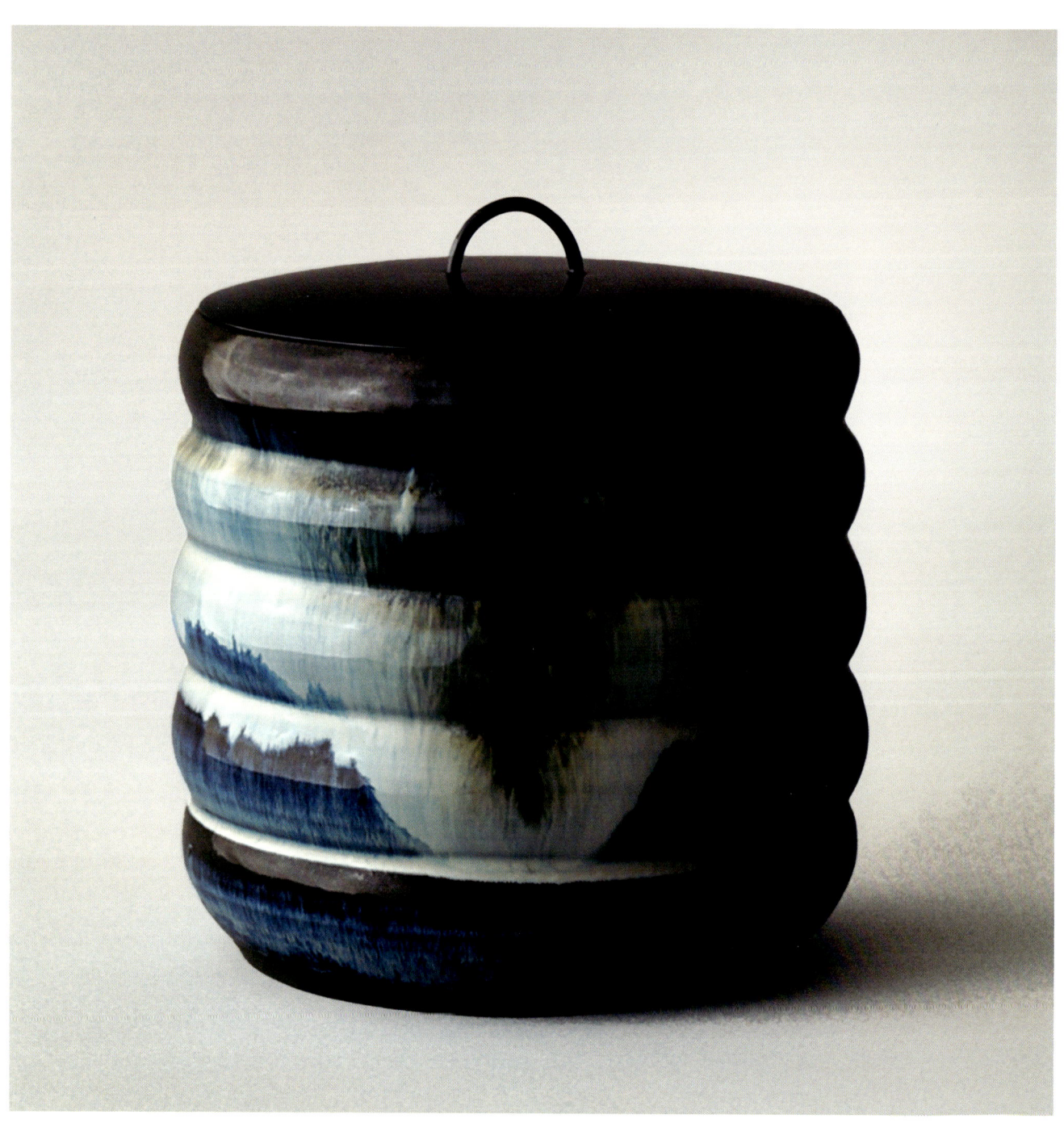

HISAAKI KAMEI
Water Container with Lacquer Lid and Coil Design
2020
Aurora glaze

亀井久彰
うるし蓋付千段巻水指
2020年
極光釉

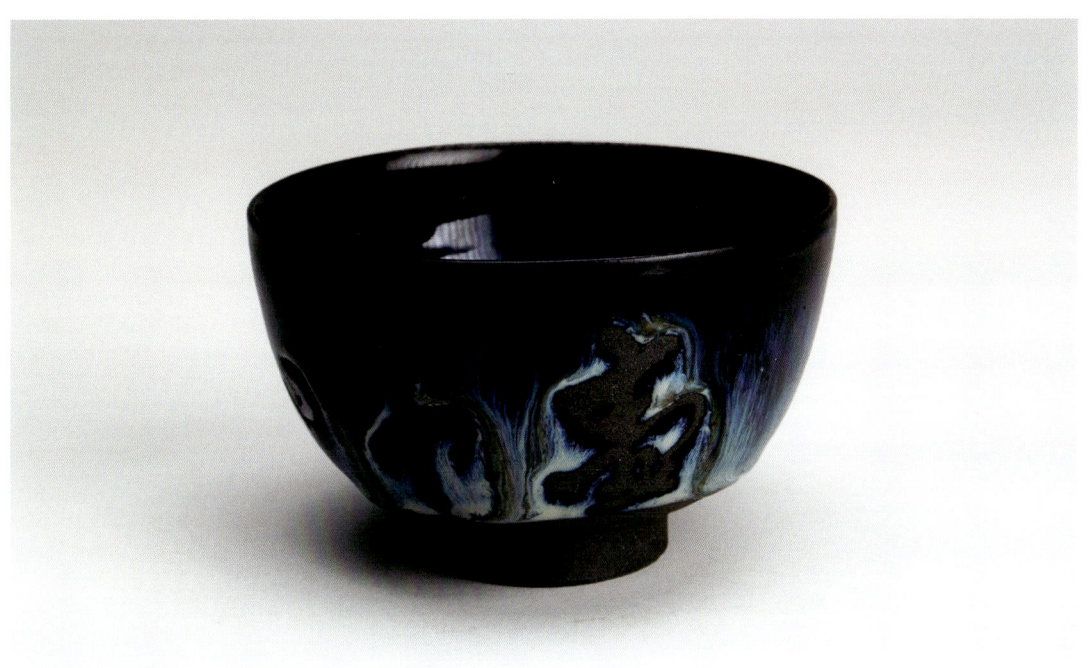

HISAAKI KAMEI
Tea Bowl
2020
Calligraphy of Shiramine Hosokawa, 133rd head
priest of the temple Shōfuku-ji, Fukuoka, Japan
Aurora glaze
HK34

亀井久彰
茶盌
2020年
福岡聖福寺133世 細川白峰老師による書
極光釉

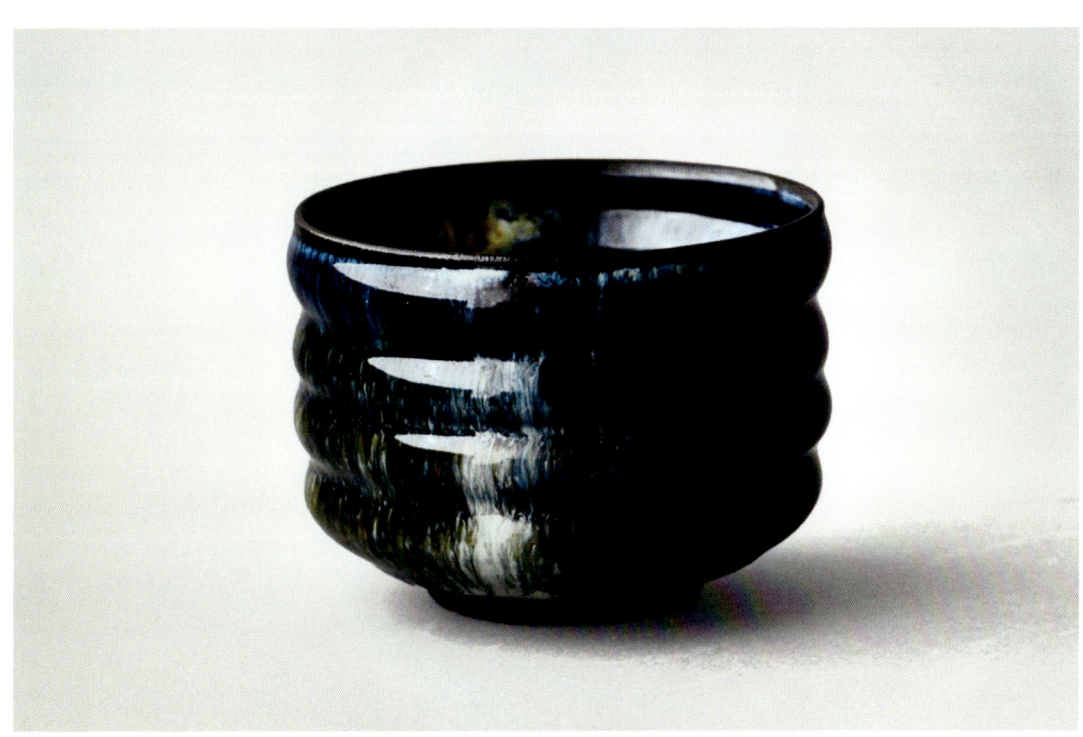

HISAAKI KAMEI
Tea Bowl with Coil Design
2018
Aurora glaze

亀井久彰
千段巻茶盌
2018年
極光釉

The gourd shape used by the Kamei family is a nod to their individuality, as tea utensils traditionally conform to a limited range of forms.

伝統的な茶具の形状は限定されているため、亀井家の瓢形は個性の証と言える。

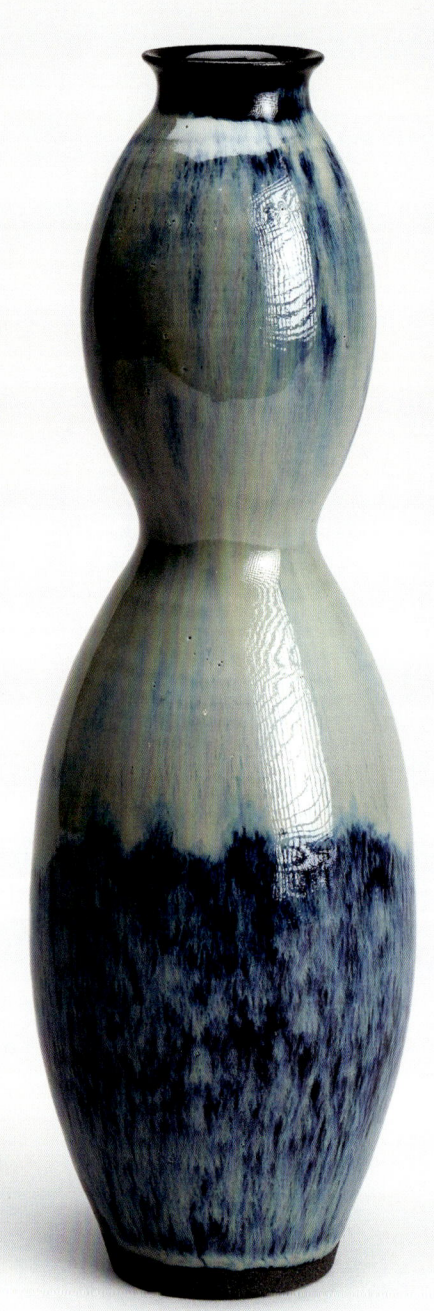

**HISAAKI KAMEI**
**Gourd-form Flower Vase**
**2024**
**Aurora glaze**
**HK59**

亀井久彰
瓢形花入
2024年
極光釉

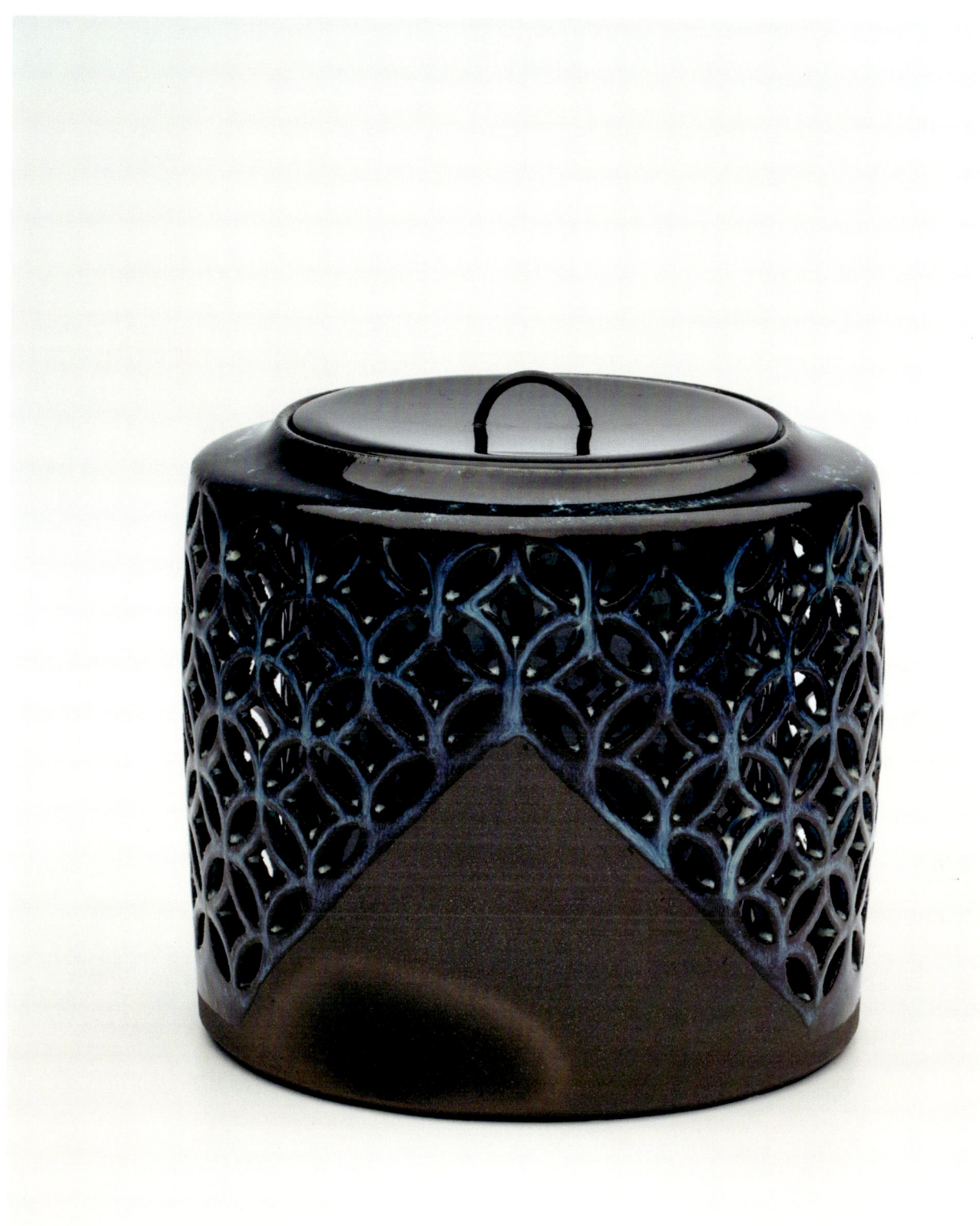

HISAAKI KAMEI
Water Container with Lacquer Lid and Shippō (openwork)
2020
Aurora glaze
HK24

亀井久彰
七宝透うるし蓋付水指
2020年
極光釉

# Afterword

## Bernard H. Pucker

"What is old and beautiful is always new and
what is beautiful and new, is always old."

– BROTHER THOMAS BEZANSON (1929-2007) –

IT IS OUR PRIVILEGE TO SHARE THE ART that has resulted from 16 generations of Takatori creativity. Our first meeting with the 14th generation Master, Miraku Kamei XIV, graciously arranged by Professor Andrew Maske, has at last led us to present this monograph. Their 400 years of commitment to the way of Tea, and the ceramic utensils that accompany the experience, has informed their practice and is now also recognized as fine art.

Working directly with Miraku Kamei XV, his wife Maki, and now their son, Hisaaki, has enriched our appreciation for the fine art of the Tea Ceremony and the accompanying ceramics.

This monograph is intended to provide access to centuries of beauty that has been created, and to show how respect for the strictures of the Ceremony has been enhanced by the individual talents of each generation.

Andrew Maske remains our guide, authority, colleague, and friend. Our sincere thanks.

Our thanks to the Kamei family for providing us, in addition to your art, with the past and present of your history.

To Jeanne Koles, our editor, for your quiet intelligence and vision, and for all you do to realize dreams and share beauty.

To John Davenport, our photographer, who has captured each work and made its best self available.

To Mugi Hanao, for communicating with the artists and translating the texts so both English and Japanese speaking audiences have access to this document.

A joint effort to add to the rich traditions of Tea and beauty.

# あとがき

バーナード・H・パッカー

## 「古くて美しいものは常に新しく、美しくて新しいものは常に古い」

トーマス・ブザンソン修道士

16世代にもわたる高取焼の創造性の結果である芸術作品をここにお見せできるのは、私たちの喜びとするところである。アンドルー・マスキ教授がご親切にも紹介してくださったおかげで、14代亀井味楽氏との最初の邂逅が実現したのであるが、その結果このモノグラフを世に送り出すことができたのである。亀井家の400年にもわたる茶道、そしてそこで使用される茶道具に対する献身はその作品群に反映されており、芸術作品として認められている。

15代亀井味楽氏、亀井真貴夫人、そして御子息である久彰氏との直接の関わりにより、茶道そして茶陶の芸術的価値に対する私たちの認識はより深く豊かなものになっている。

このモノグラフを通じて、何世紀にもわたって作り出されてきた美に触れ、茶道における様々な制約を尊重することで、各世代の個々の才能がより豊かになっていった過程を見ることができる。

このモノグラムの制作にあたって、以下の方々に心からの感謝の意を表したい。

常に私たちの導き手、師、同僚、そして友であるアンドルー・マスキ教授。

作品のみならず、過去から現在までの史実を提供してくださった亀井家の皆様。

静謐な知性と洞察力を兼ね備え、このモノグラムの出版と美の共有を実現するため、惜しみなく労力を費やした当ギャラリーの編集者であるジーン・コール氏。

各作品の本質を捉え、最も素晴らしい写真を提供してくださった写真家であるジョン・デブンポート氏。

作家たちとの連絡および日英の読者のための翻訳に従事した花生 麦氏。

これは、茶道と美の豊かな伝統に新たな価値を付け加える共同の取り組みである。